Multicultural Issues In Counseling: New Approaches to Diversity

D1010354

Edited by:

Courtland C. Lee, PhD

Bernard L. Richardson, PhD

American Association for
Counseling and Development
5999 Stevenson Ave., Alexandria, VA 22304

American Association for Counseling and Development
5999 Stevenson Avenue
Alexandria, VA 22304

Cover design by Sarah Jane Valdez

Library of Congress Cataloging-in-Publication Data

Multicultural issues in counseling : new approaches to diversity / edited by
  Courtland C. Lee and Bernard L. Richardson.
      p.   cm.
    Includes bibliographical references.
    ISBN 1-55620-082-X
    1. Cross-cultural counseling—United States.   I. Lee, Courtland C.
II. Richardson, Bernard Lester.
BF637.C6M84   1991
158'.3—dc20   91-4372
                                                                   CIP

Pictured on cover, clockwise from upper left corner: Arabic for "country,"
Spanish for "name," Chinese for "world," Cheyenne for "spirit who told me
in sleep," Swahili for "freedom."

Printed in the United States of America

To our respected elders,
both historical and contemporary

CONTENTS

FOREWORD

Paul Pedersen

Multiculturalism provides a serious challenge to the profession of counseling. Is it possible for counseling professionals to apply counseling effectively to a culturally diverse population? If the profession fails this test, counselors will have a difficult time in the coming years.

The world is changing quickly. Multicultural issues have suddenly become critically important. Disparities that could long be overlooked are now urgently important. The flood of literature on multicultural issues has attempted to respond to this urgent need. Too often, that literature has not gone beyond a theoretical discussion. Too often, that discussion has lacked practical relevance for the practicing professional. Too often, there have been no program proposals for action.

Unless and until those of us writing about multiculturalism can persuade our skeptical colleagues that learning and applying multicultural counseling techniques will make their job easier, increase their accuracy and competence, and enhance the pleasure they find in their work, the skeptics are likely to remain unconvinced. Too often multiculturalism has been used as a stick to beat on the "bad guys," without offering any alternatives.

This book emphasizes practical approaches. Case studies are provided in most of the chapters. Outlines for courses and training programs are presented for replication. New and creative ideas about how to work with people from different cultures are discussed.

Like the Chinese character for "crisis" that combines the character for "danger" and the character for "opportunity," multiculturalism also entails promises and pitfalls. Some of the promises presented include (a) a diverse and inclusive perspective, (b) a culturally appropriate approach to social responsibility, (c) a viewpoint that includes internationalism, and (d) the promise of a "new" kind of counselor. Some of the problems that multiculturalism presents as well include: (a) that multiculturalism may be defined so inclusively that it will lack definition, (b) that cultural groups will be fossilized into rigid categories, (c) that overemphasis on culture will result in a new kind of racism, (d) that the enormity of multiculturalism will intimidate counselors, and (e) that counseling has a long way to go to overcome its bad reputation for protecting the status quo.

This book addresses the tension in the field between the positive and the negative aspects of multiculturalism. This tension describes a controversy in which every counselor will be forced to participate, to have an opinion, and ultimately to make a decision. This book provides a starting point in that process.

The authors take a perspective that culture should be limited to categories of race or ethnicity, although they also emphasize the importance of within-group differences such as gender, age, and socioeconomic status. Although my own perspective tends to favor a broad definition of culture, everyone certainly agrees that race and ethnicity are extremely important cultural categories. In this case, limiting the focus of the book to differences of race and ethnicity provides a focus that is helpful to the reader.

Many important multicultural issues are raised in several chapters in reference to different racial/ethnic groups. The importance of the history of a group, for example, cannot be overlooked. The process by which a group is "named" is another important vehicle for deliberate or accidental cultural bias. The reality of being excluded from power changes a group's perspective. The lack of fit of developmental theories to many ethnic/racial groups becomes an issue. The importance of defining nontraditional counseling roles becomes apparent. The importance of religion as a mediating force for counselors in various ethnic/racial settings becomes obvious. The possibility of "nonassertiveness" as a valued perspective is raised. The impact of internment and the undeserved shame it brings with it are discussed. The controversy of "adjustment" (to which norm?) is outlined. The values of collectivism as an alternative to individualism are presented. The importance of "balance" as a culturally defined goal is explained. The friendliness of complexity is discussed. The central role of the family is emphasized. The importance of ethnic identity development is explained. The role of language in counseling and communication is defined. These and many other issues will provoke a discussion between you and the authors as you read this very interesting volume. The authors hope that this discussion will result in *practical* changes in how you do counseling.

This book will contribute to the ongoing development of multiculturalism in the field of counseling. It will help us adapt theories and techniques. It will help us identify and define learnable/teachable skills. It will help us find ways to experience, rather than just talk about, other cultures. It will help us go beyond our own monocultural perspective toward a world characterized by diversity.

Paul Pedersen, PhD, is professor of education in the Department of Counselor Education at Syracuse University.

PREFACE

Multicultural issues have become critically important in counseling and related human development professions. Every sector of the profession seems to be searching for new ways to intervene successfully in the lives of people from increasingly diverse cultural backgrounds. This would seem natural because American society in the last several decades has become more pluralistic, and projections suggest that cultural diversity will have an even greater impact on population demographics as we approach the 21st century.

In the wake of the reverberations of cultural diversity on the profession, there have been a spate of books and scholarly articles on multicultural counseling. Although this body of work represents landmark thinking in the field of counseling and human development, the bulk of it has primarily presented **theoretical** ideas and concepts on the impact of culture on mental health intervention. It has tended to stop short of providing programmatic direction for counseling practitioners who face the challenges of cultural diversity. Even though scholars and practitioners alike have called for the development of counseling interventions to meet the needs of culturally diverse client groups, to date, little has been done to examine the development of such approaches in any systematic fashion. The editors have done extensive consulting with educational institutions and community agencies in the area of multicultural counseling. It is evident to us that there is a pressing need for practical ideas on intervention strategies and skills development for multicultural counseling among practicing helping professionals.

This book is an attempt to bring together, in one volume, new directions for counseling **practice** with culturally diverse groups. Its purpose is to present direction for culturally responsive counseling in a variety of settings. Although the book offers guidance for multicultural counseling practice, it is not intended to be a "cookbook" or a "how-to" manual. It is designed to help counselors apply their awareness of and knowledge about cultural diversity to appropriate interventions with specific client groups. It provides practicing counseling professionals, as well as those preparing to enter the field, with direction for optimal mental health intervention with clients from a variety of cultural backgrounds.

The Focus of the Book

This book deals with multicultural counseling, defined as a relationship between a counselor and a client that takes both personal **and** cultural experiences into consideration in the helping process. The focus of the book is on cultural experiences related to racial or ethnic factors in counseling. It deals with the counseling and human development needs of selected groups of people, commonly referred to as racial or ethnic minorities in American society.

Each chapter includes a review of the cultural dynamics of these selected groups and their role in shaping mental health, as well as the social challenges that affect development. The contributors introduce and explore strategies or techniques for addressing these challenges. These strategies and techniques are derived from both the professional and personal experiences of the contributors, who are scholars from the specific cultural group in question, or have an intimate working knowledge of a particular group.

Overview of Contents

The book is divided into three major parts: **part 1, Introduction, part 2, Direction for Culturally Responsive Counseling, and part 3, Conclusion.** Courtland C. Lee and Bernard L. Richardson in chapter 1, **"Promise and Pitfalls of Multicultural Counseling,"** discuss how the evolution of multicultural counseling as a specialty area has spawned much promise for the profession. They caution, however, that counselors must be aware of pitfalls inherent in counseling across cultures.

In chapter 2, **"Cultural Dynamics: Their Importance in Multicultural Counseling,"** Courtland C. Lee provides a context for the concept of culture in multicultural counseling. He also explores some dynamics that may need to be considered in culturally responsive counseling practice.

In the second part of the book, ideas and concepts for culturally responsive counseling interventions with selected racial and ethnic groups are presented. Each chapter in this section offers direction for incorporating the cultural dynamics of a particular group into individual or group counseling interventions.

The first section of part 2 focuses on the American Indian/Native American experience. In chapter 3, **"Counseling American Indian**

Adults," Grace Powless Sage examines the unique relationship that American Indians have had with the United States government and how that relationship has affected adult development among these people. She examines the therapeutic aspects of an Indian women's group that incorporates traditional and contemporary practices.

Roger D. Herring in chapter 4, **"Counseling Native American Youth,"** examines sociocultural challenges to the development of Native American children and adolescents. Stressing that counselors need to become familiar with both content and process concerns when counseling Native American youth, he provides direction for counseling practice that incorporates traditional Native American cultural attitudes, beliefs, and values.

The second section of part 2 deals with aspects of the African American experience. Janice M. Jordan examines important issues related to the development of African American women. These include myths and stereotypes that affect them. She presents a developmental counseling model for promoting pride and dignity among African American women in chapter 5, **"Counseling African American Women: 'Sister-Friends.' "**

The role of the African American church in promoting mental health is explored by Bernard L. Richardson in chapter 6, **"Utilizing the Resources of the African American Church: Strategies for Counseling Professionals."** He offers intervention strategies that employ the resources of this important African American institution. In addition, he provides counselors with specific guidelines for working within a church context.

The Asian American experience is explored in the third section of part 2. In chapter 7, **"Counseling Strategies for Chinese Americans,"** David Sue and Derald Wing Sue examine some important Chinese cultural values and their impact on Chinese American development. They present a case study that illustrates the importance of these values and their influence on the counseling process. An assertiveness training group for Chinese Americans is also described in this chapter.

Satsuki Ina Tomine explores an important, but unfortunately relatively unknown, aspect of Japanese American culture in chapter 8, **"Counseling Japanese Americans: From Internment to Reparation."** She examines the internment experience of many Japanese Americans during World War II and the resulting psychological ramifications for both internees and members of their families. An intensive group counseling experience for former internees is presented that highlights the social, political, and cultural issues affecting the development of Japanese Americans.

Chapter 9 explores the cultural dynamics of Americans from Southeast Asian backgrounds. In their chapter, **"Counseling Americans of Southeast Asian Descent: The Impact of the Refugee Experience,"** Rita

Chi-Ying Chung and Sumie Okazaki examine the cultures of Southeast Asia and the refugee experience of many Americans from that part of the world. They discuss how the refugee experience presents mental health. challenges to these people. Specific approaches to counseling Americans of Southeast Asian descent that employ important aspects of Asian culture are provided.

Julie C. Lee and Virginia E. H. Cynn in chapter 10, **"Issues in Counseling 1.5 Generation Korean Americans,"** examine the important issues that confront the generation of Korean Americans who are foreign-born, but have spent the majority of their developmental years in the United States. They offer direction for culturally responsive counseling with members of the 1.5 generation by presenting a case study that illustrates the stresses and challenges confronting them.

The fourth section of part 2 examines the Latino American experience. In chapter 11, **"Counseling Latinas,"** Patricia Arredondo examines the cultural dynamics of women from Latino backgrounds as well as differences among these women. She discusses Latino culture in terms of values, sex roles, and mental health. She also offers a group approach for working with immigrant Latinas that provides a means for them to network and to build support systems.

Gerardo M. Gonzalez in chapter 12, **"Cuban Americans: Counseling and Human Development Issues, Problems, and Approaches,"** reviews the effects of immigration and acculturation on this group of Latino Americans. He offers examples of counseling approaches developed to respond to the most pressing needs of Cuban Americans related to acculturation issues, family adjustment, and career development.

Augustine Barón, Jr., in chapter 13, **"Counseling Chicano College Students,"** examines ways to modify and apply specific counseling skills in working with this client population. He explores some key Chicano cultural concepts that are useful to consider when developing counseling interventions for this group of college students. He captures these cultural concepts in an individual case study and a group counseling intervention for male Chicano students.

In chapter 14, **"Puerto Ricans in the Counseling Process: The Dynamics of Ethnicity and Its Societal Context,"** Jesse M. Vázquez presents a historical and political overview of the Puerto Rican experience. He also discusses the impact of socioeconomic status on Puerto Rican development in the United States. Through a case study, he explores the challenges of racial/ethnic identity and the problems of racism that confront Puerto Ricans, along with implications for counselors.

The fifth section of part 2 focuses on the growing Arab American experience. In chapter 15, **"Counseling Arab Americans,"** Morris L. Jackson examines this cultural group, which has not received a great deal of attention in the counseling literature. He provides a comprehensive examination of Arab culture, particularly religion and family dynamics and their influence on Arab American mental health. The diversity of Arab American culture is explored, and the traditional providers of guidance and counseling for Americans of Arab ancestry are identified. The author offers specific intervention strategies and techniques that counselors can use to increase their effectiveness with Arab American clients. In particular, he provides some linguistic suggestions for developing rapport with clients of Arab ancestry.

Courtland C. Lee concludes the book with chapter 16, **"New Approaches to Diversity: Implications for Multicultural Counselor Training and Research."** In this chapter he examines some important implications of cultural diversity for future counselor training. He also provides an agenda for future research in the area of multicultural counseling.

Acknowledgments

The editors are indebted to a number of individuals for their contributions to and assistance with the development of this book. First and foremost are the contributors. Without their scholarly output, this book would not have been possible.

We are also indebted to the AACD Media Committee for entrusting the development of this project to us. Their support is greatly appreciated. Special appreciation is expressed to Elaine Pirrone, AACD Acquisitions and Development Editor, who shepherded us through the publication process from concept formation to the final product. We are extremely grateful for her patient oversight and unabashed enthusiasm for the project.

We are also indebted to Maria Oh, our editorial assistant, who kept the files and maintained the flow of correspondence necessary to develop the book. Without her assistance the book, no doubt, would not have become a reality.

Special thanks also go to Theresa Jones, Anne Mountcastle, and Robyn Nelson Jackson, who assisted in the typing, proofreading, and preparation of the manuscript. Your many efforts on this project are greatly appreciated.

Finally, we must acknowledge our families, who endured some neglect while the book was in preparation. Thank you for your love, support, and understanding.

CONTRIBUTORS

Editors

Courtland C. Lee received his BA from Hofstra University, his MS from Hunter College of the City University of New York, and his PhD from Michigan State University. He is the director of Counselor Education and an associate professor at the University of Virginia. His areas of research specialization include multicultural counseling and adolescent development. He has published numerous articles and book chapters on adolescent development and counseling across cultures. He is the former editor of the *Journal of Multicultural Counseling and Development* and serves on the Advisory Board of the *International Journal for the Advancement of Counselling*.

Bernard L. Richardson received his BA from Howard University, his Master's of Divinity from Yale University, and his PhD from Michigan State University. He is an associate professor of counseling in the graduate school at Southern Connecticut State University. He has worked with multicultural concerns in a variety of counseling settings, including community mental health centers and a university counseling center. Dr. Richardson is also an ordained minister with extensive pastoral counseling experience.

Contributors

Patricia Arredondo received her BS from Kent State University, her MEd from Boston College, and her EdD in counseling psychology from Boston University. A licensed psychologist and former professor, she is the founder and director of Empowerment Workshops. She designs personal growth workshops for the workplace and consults on interracial concerns. She has held leadership roles with the ACES & AACD human rights committees.

Augustine Barón, Jr., received his BA, magna cum laude, from Loyola University, New Orleans, and his MA and PsyD in clinical psychology from the University of Illinois at Urbana-Champaign, where he was a Ford Foundation fellow. He presently serves as assistant director of the Counseling and Mental Health Center at the University of Texas in Austin. Dr. Barón is a Diplomate in Clinical Psychology of the American Board of Professional Psychology. His interests include cross-cultural counseling and the psychology of shame. He is the editor of *Explorations in Chicano Psychology* (Praeger, 1981).

Rita Chi-Ying Chung received her PhD from Victoria University of Wellington, New Zealand. As a result of her experiences in working with Southeast Asian refugees, she was awarded the Medical Research Council of New Zealand Fellowship. She is currently a postdoctoral fellow at the National Research Center on Asian American Mental Health-UCLA, were she is involved in various research projects on Southeast Asian refugees.

Virginia E. H. Cynn received her PhD in clinical psychology from the University of Hawaii at Manoa. She is a licensed psychologist and a past postdoctoral fellow at the National Research Center on Asian American Mental Health-UCLA. She is currently finishing a postdoctoral fellowship in pediatric neuropsychology at the Neuropsychiatric Institute-UCLA. She will be joining Kapiolani Counseling Center at the Kapiolani Medical Center in Honolulu, Hawaii.

Gerardo M. Gonzalez received his BA in psychology from the University of Florida and his PhD in counselor education from the same university. He is active in Hispanic educational issues and is the founding president of the Association of Hispanic Faculty at the University of Florida, where he serves as professor and chair of the Counselor Education Department.

Roger D. Herring received his BS from Pembroke State University, his MA in history and his MA in psychology from Appalachian State University, his EdS from Appalachian State University, and his EdD from North Carolina State University. He is currently an assistant professor of counselor education at the University of Arkansas-Little Rock.

Morris L. Jackson received his BS and MEd from the University of Hartford and his EdD from the George Washington University. He has contributed insights for cross-cultural counseling during the last 19 years. He has been adjunct professor at the Virginia Polytechnic and State University, American University, and the George Washington University. He studied Arabic language and culture at the King Saud University in Saudi Arabia. Currently, he is the University Academic Advisor at the Royal Embassy of Saudi Arabia Cultural Mission in Washington, DC.

Janice M. Jordan received her BA from Antioch College, her MEd from the University of Delaware, and her PhD from the University of Maryland. She is the associate director of the Center for Counseling and Student Development and assistant professor of education at the University of Delaware. She is a past president of the Association for Multicultural Counseling and Development.

Julie C. Lee received her BA in psychology from the University of California, Berkeley. She is a research associate at the National Research Center on Asian American Mental Health-UCLA. She is currently involved in the Asian Pacific Youth Project (substance abuse prevention) and the California State Asian/Pacific American Drug Service Needs Assessment. Her current research interests are in the fields of developmental psychopathology and Asian American mental health.

Sumie Okazaki received her BS from the University of Michigan and her MA from the University of California, Los Angeles. She is currently a graduate student in the doctoral program for clinical psychology at UCLA and conducts research at the National Research Center on Asian American Mental Health.

Grace Powless Sage received her BA, MA, and PhD from the University of Montana. She works at the Multicultural Center for Counseling and Community Development at the University of Colorado, Boulder. She is a research associate at the National Center for American Indian and Alaska Native Mental Health Research at the University of Colorado Health Sciences Center. She has interests in cross-cultural training, with specific emphasis on American Indian issues.

David Sue received his PhD from Washington State University. He is a professor and director of the Clinical/Counseling Program at Western Washington University. He is a licensed psychologist and an associate of the Center for Cross-Cultural Research at Western Washington University.

Derald Wing Sue received his PhD from the University of Oregon. He is professor of counseling psychology at California State University, Hayward. He is a licensed psychologist and works as a consultant to various campuses, public health agencies, and private industry.

Satsuki Ina Tomine received her BS from the University of California, Berkeley, and her EdM and PhD from Oregon State University. She is on the faculty at California State University, Sacramento, as Director of Clinical Training and is in private practice as a licensed marriage, family, and child counselor. As a founding member of the Consortium for Change in Sacramento, she has provided consultation on cross-cultural issues in Europe, Japan, and throughout the United States.

Jesse M. Vázquez received his BA from Long Island University, and his MA and PhD from New York University. He is an associate professor in counselor education in the School of Education, Queens College of the City University of New York. In addition, since 1975, he has been the director of the college's Puerto Rican Studies Program. He has worked as a counselor and consultant in a variety of social service agencies and educational settings.

PART I

INTRODUCTION

Chapter 1
PROMISE AND PITFALLS OF MULTICULTURAL COUNSELING

Courtland C. Lee and Bernard L. Richardson

American society has experienced tremendous change over the past three decades. The turmoil of the civil rights movement of the 1960s, for example, gave rise to a recognition that the United States is a pluralistic society. This recognition ushered in a period in our national history that may be referred to as the era of cultural pluralism (Axelson, 1985). The concept of cultural pluralism has received its impetus not only from the great economic, legislative, and social gains made during the civil rights struggles of the 1960s, but, more recently, from changing population demographics. Projections of the U.S. population into the 21st century indicate that people of color will experience a substantial rate of growth while the White population will decline significantly. In addition, over the next 20 years the American population will swell with large numbers of immigrants who began entering the country after 1986 (Spencer, 1989). This new immigration phenomenon will bring people with new hues and worldviews into the United States (Lee, 1989a).

The rise of cultural pluralism has had an important impact on the counseling profession. Major changes in population demographics have been the impetus for the evolution of multicultural counseling as a significant discipline within the helping professions. Broadly defined, multicultural counseling is a helping process that places the emphasis for counseling theory and practice equally on the cultural impressions of both the counselor and the client (Axelson, 1985). Within this context, counseling professionals must consider differences in language, social class, and, most importantly, culture between helper and client. These factors may be potential impediments to effective intervention, and counselors need to work to overcome the barriers such variables might produce in the helping process (Sue & Sue, 1990).

Promise and Pitfalls of Multicultural Counseling

The evolution of multicultural counseling as a concept has generated much promise for the mental health profession. However, counseling across cultures can be fraught with potential pitfalls.

Promise

The promise of multicultural counseling has been manifested in several significant ways. First, it is evident that traditional counseling theory has been enriched by the diverse notions of optimal mental health and normal development inherent in multicultural thought. The ideas proposed by scholars from diverse cultural backgrounds that have emerged in the counseling profession in recent years have generated an important new knowledge base. This base includes the fundamental concept that cultural differences are real and must be actively considered in mental health interventions. The awareness growing out of this new area of thought has generated a realization that counseling as a profession must be inclusive: It can no longer concern itself with clients from just one cultural group.

Second, multicultural notions of counseling have fostered a new sense of social responsibility and activism within the profession. Working with culturally diverse clients, counselors have often been forced to consider the negative effects of phenomena such as racism and oppression on the development of culturally diverse client groups (Bryson & Bardo, 1975; Vontress, 1976). This has led to an awareness that the etiology of problems often lies not with clients, but rather with restrictive environmental forces. The only way that many client groups will be able to maximize abilities and interests is by the eradication of these systemic impediments to their development.

Multicultural counselors, therefore, have been called on to become systemic change agents (Gunnings & Simpkins, 1972), channeling energy and skill into helping clients from diverse backgrounds break down institutional and social barriers to full development. When necessary, a counselor must be willing to act on behalf of disenfranchised clients in an advocacy role, actively challenging long-standing traditions and preconceived notions that may stand in the way of optimal mental health and development (Lee, 1982, 1989b). Such challenges may need to take the form of social and political activism to help empower clients in the fight against negative societal forces (Davis & Sanderson, 1974; Banks & Martens, 1973). With the evolution of multicultural counseling, mental health professionals are beginning to understand that if they are not a part of the solution, they are a part of the problem.

Third, the thought and practice associated with multicultural mental health intervention have fostered the emergence of an international perspective on counseling as a potential force in human development. This perspective has been bolstered by universal improvements in communication and travel that have made the world, in many respects, a "global village." Due in large measure to the growing acceptance of diversity in the United States, there has been increased awareness within the American counseling profession about indigenous models of helping that exist among cultural groups throughout the world. Those models are found primarily in areas of the world with cultures that predate that of Western Europe. Multicultural counseling also has stimulated major efforts on the part of American professionals to establish links with their mental health colleagues in other parts of the world. These links have been forged through international forums for the exchange of ideas concerning mental health and human development. There has been greater understanding among helping professionals, in response to the stimulation provided by the multicultural counseling knowledge base, that **multicultural** implies **international**.

Finally, the promise of multicultural counseling is evident in the gradual emergence of a new type of helping professional—**the culturally skilled counselor**. Such an individual has the **awareness**, **knowledge**, and **skills** to intervene successfully in the lives of clients from culturally diverse backgrounds (Sue, Bernier, Durran, Feinberg, Pedersen, Smith, & Vasquez-Nuttall, 1982). A culturally skilled counselor uses strategies and techniques that are consistent with the life experiences and cultural values of clients. In order to implement these strategies and techniques, such a professional must have awareness and knowledge related to issues of cultural diversity.

A culturally skilled counseling professional is able to view each client as a unique individual while, at the same time, taking into consideration his or her common experiences as a human being (i.e., the developmental challenges that face all people), as well as the specific experiences that come from the client's particular cultural background. Furthermore, the counselor must constantly be in touch with his or her own personal and cultural experiences as a unique human being who happens to be a helping professional (Lee, 1989a).

The growing demand for this type of individual has brought about a renaissance in the professional development of counselors. The need to be culturally skilled has put the responsibility on counselors to examine their own cultural heritage, values, and biases and how these might affect clients from diverse backgrounds. In addition, counselors have been required to gain knowledge about the history, experiences, and cultural values of diverse client groups. The acquisition of such cultural knowledge has been found to be important in developing empathy toward culturally diverse clients (Lee, 1989a).

Pitfalls

Although multicultural counseling holds much promise as an emerging specialty within the profession, some potential pitfalls to its practice must be considered. First, as the theory and practice of multicultural counseling continue to gain greater acceptance, the term as well as the specialty itself are at risk for losing their definitional focus. **What is multicultural counseling?** The term is in imminent danger of becoming so inclusive as to be almost meaningless. This is due, in large measure, to the fact that **culture** as a concept has been so broadly defined within the profession as to include ever-expanding constituent groups who perceive themselves as being disenfranchised in some fashion. In many respects, multicultural counseling has lost a coherent conceptual framework, which has made training and research in the discipline, at times, extremely difficult. As the term has been increasingly stretched to include virtually any group of people who consider themselves **different**, the intent of multicultural counseling theory and practice has become unclear.

Second, in discussing the concept of multicultural counseling, there is the danger of assuming that all people from a specific group are the same and that one methodological approach is universally applicable in any counseling intervention with them. Indeed, when reviewing much of the psychological or counseling literature related to multicultural issues, one might be left with the impression that there is an all-encompassing reality for a particular cultural group and that all people from that group act, feel, and think in a homogenous fashion. Such an impression often leads to a monolithic perspective on the experiences of a specific group of people as well as to stereotypical thinking in which individuals are considered indistinguishable from one another in terms of attitudes, behaviors, and values. Counseling professionals with such a perspective run the risk of approaching clients not as distinct human beings with individual experiences, but rather merely as cultural stereotypes.

Third, in a similar vein, it has been suggested that the focus on cultural dissimilarities in multicultural counseling theory and practice serves to accentuate human differences and has the potential for fostering renewed forms of racism (Margolis & Rungta, 1986; Pedersen, 1983). This is a distinct possibility if counselors reduce cultural realities to a stereotypical level.

Fourth, as multicultural counseling thought continues to question the validity of traditional counseling practice with particular groups of people, there is a danger of helping professionals becoming self-conscious about their level of competence to work with diverse clients. A question counselors often ask in a frustrated tone is: **"How can I really be effective with a client whose cultural background is different from mine?"** Groping for an answer to this crucial question has the potential of driving many talented professionals away from multicultural counseling practice.

Fifth, although much promise is inherent in modalities that are culturally sensitive, it must be understood that counseling, as a formal profession, has often not been highly valued among many groups of people. Traditional counseling theory and practice often run counter to important developmental aspects of indigenous helping models found among various cultural groups. In addition, traditional counseling practice has often failed to meet the needs of people from diverse cultural backgrounds. This has generally been borne out, for example, by research findings that indicate that people of color are inappropriately served by mental health services (Special Populations Task Force of the President's Commission on Mental Health, 1978) and are likely to terminate a relationship after one session with a counseling professional in significantly greater numbers than their White counterparts (Sue, McKinney, Allen, & Hall, 1974; Sue & McKinney, 1974; Sue, 1977; Ivey & Authier, 1978).

It must be understood that when traditional counseling is considered in a multicultural context, it often becomes a sociopolitical process (Sue & Sue, 1990). Specifically, many people of color have perceived counseling as a tool of oppression and social control (Katz, 1985; Pine, 1972). This is due, to a large extent, to the fact that the only counseling many of these people have received has been a forced, rather than a voluntary, experience with a culturally insensitive agent of some social welfare agency. In addition, counseling has often followed the commission of an offense against the social order. Generally, in both situations the goal of counseling is not development, but either remediation or punishment. Many people from diverse cultural backgrounds, therefore, perceive counseling as a process that the dominant society employs to forcibly control their lives and well-being.

The final pitfall of multicultural counseling involves the challenge of moving beyond awareness and knowledge to actual practice. Although the renaissance in the professional development of counselors has advanced the notion of culturally skilled helpers, the concept of multicultural counseling **skills** is actually still rather tenuous. In many instances, pre- and in-service training provide opportunities for counselors to develop a new level of awareness and an updated knowledge base to address the concerns of culturally diverse clients. However, such training tends to stop short of actual comprehensive skill acquisition. There is generally little exposure to counseling and therapeutic modalities that incorporate cultural dynamics or indigenous aspects of helping. Counselors on the front lines of mutlicultural service delivery often express the need for less theory and more practical direction for addressing client concerns in a culturally sensitive manner.

It must be pointed out that there are probably no "cookbooks" or "how-to manuals" that can realistically be developed for working with culturally diverse clients. If multicultural counseling is to continue evolving as a discipline, however, comprehensive approaches to service delivery must be developed, implemented, and evaluated. Personal awareness and cultural knowledge must be translated into effective multicultural counseling practice.

Conclusion

The approach of the 21st century portends an American culture in which diversity and pluralism will be hallmarks of the society. People who represent diverse cultural backgrounds characteristic of this pluralism will be attempting to develop their abilities and interests within this new social order. Multiculturalism as a social force, therefore, represents a significant challenge to the counseling profession. It brings with it great potential, as well as potential pitfalls. If counselors are to have an impact on the development of increasingly diverse client groups, counseling practice must be grounded in sensitivity to cultural diversity. Developing such sensitivity should be an integral part of the personal growth process of all counselors. This process involves acquiring not only the awareness and knowledge, but also the skills for effective multicultural intervention. Moreover, it entails appreciating the great promise and avoiding the precarious pitfalls of multicultural counseling practice.

References

Axelson, J. A. (1985). *Counseling and development in a multicultural society.* Monterey, CA: Brooks/Cole.

Banks, W., & Martens, K. (1973). Counseling: The reactionary profession. *Personnel and Guidance Journal, 5,* 457–462.

Bryson, S., & Bardo, H. (1975). Race and the counseling process: An overview. *Journal of Non-White Concerns in Personnel and Guidance, 4,* 5–15.

Davis, T., & Sanderson, F. (1974). Community counselors and the counseling process. *Journal of American Indian Education, 14,* 26–29.

Gunnings, T. S., & Simpkins, G. (1972). A systemic approach to counseling disadvantaged youth. *Journal of Non-White Concerns in Personnel and Guidance, 1*, 4–8.

Ivey, A., & Authier, J. (1978). *Microcounseling: Innovations in interview training.* Springfield, IL: Charles C Thomas.

Katz, J. H. (1985). The sociopolitical nature of counseling. *Counseling Psychologist, 13*, 615–624.

Lee, C. C. (1982). Helping professionals as student advocates: An in-service training model. *The Humanist Educator, 20*, 161–166.

Lee, C. C. (1989a). Multicultural counseling: New directions for counseling professionals. *Virginia Counselors Journal, 17*, 3–8.

Lee, C. C. (1989b). Needed: A career development advocate. *Career Development Quarterly, 37*, 218–220.

Margolis, R. L., & Rungta, S. A. (1986). Training counselors for work with special populations: A second look. *Journal of Counseling and Development, 64*, 642–644.

Pedersen, P. B. (1983). The cultural complexity of counseling. *International Journal for the Advancement of Counselling, 6*, 177–192.

Pine, G. J. (1972). Counseling minority groups: A review of the literature. *Counseling and Values, 17*, 35–44.

Special Populations Task Force of the President's Commission on Mental Health. (1978). *Task panel reports submitted to the President's Commission on Mental Health: Vol. 3.* Washington, DC: U.S. Government Printing Office.

Spencer, G. (1989). *Projections of the population of the United States by age, sex, and race: 1988 to 2080.* Washington, DC: Current Population Reports. Population Estimates and Projections. Series P-25, No. 1018. Bureau of the Census.

Sue, D. W., Bernier, J. E., Durran, A., Feinberg, L., Pedersen, P., Smith, E. J., & Vasquez-Nuttall, E. (1982). Position paper: Cross-cultural counseling competencies. *The Counseling Psychologist, 10*, 45–52.

Sue, D. W., & Sue, D. (1990). *Counseling the culturally different: Theory and practice* (2nd ed.). New York: Wiley.

Sue, S. (1977). Community mental health services to minority groups: Some optimism, some pessimism. *American Psychologist, 32*, 616–624.

Sue, S., & McKinney, H. (1974). Asian Americans in the community mental health care system. *American Journal of Orthopsychiatry, 45*, 111–118.

Sue, S., Mckinney, H., Allen, D., & Hall, J. (1974). Delivery of community mental health services to black and white clients. *Journal of Consulting and Clinical Psychology, 42*, 594–601.

Vontress, C. E. (1976). Racial and ethnic barriers in counseling. In P. Pedersen, W. J. Lonner, & J. G. Draguns (Eds.), *Counseling across cultures* (pp. 42–64). Honolulu: The University Press of Hawaii.

Chapter 2
CULTURAL DYNAMICS: THEIR IMPORTANCE IN MULTICULTURAL COUNSELING

Courtland C. Lee

A major challenge confronting counseling professionals is understanding the complex role of culture in practice. A knowledge of cultural realities has become a professional imperative as counselors encounter increasingly diverse client groups. When culture is considered as a variable in the counseling process, however, it has the potential of becoming a source of conflict and misunderstanding. This may create barriers between helper and client who differ in terms of cultural background. The purpose of this chapter is twofold: first, to provide a conceptual framework for understanding the context of **culture** in multicultural counseling, and second, to examine some important dynamics that should be considered in culturally responsive counseling practice.

Webster's dictionary (1989) defines culture as "the customary beliefs, social forms and material traits of a racial, religious, or social group" (p. 314). This broad definition implies that culture is a multidimensional concept that encompasses the collective reality of a group of people. As Axelson (1985) indicated, it is from this collective reality that attitudes, behaviors, and values are formed and become reinforced among a group of people over time.

It has been suggested that **all** counseling interventions, to some extent, are multicultural or cross-cultural in nature (Pedersen, 1988). Both counselor and client bring to the counseling relationship a set of attitudes, behaviors, and values that have been reinforced through long-term association with a specific group. Although it is possible that counselor and client can be members of the same group, in most cases their individual differences presume the presence of subtle cultural differences.

The breadth of Webster's definition lends credence to the notion that *all* counseling is a multicultural process, but this broad conceptual-

11

ization tends to cloud some important issues that must be considered when obvious cultural differences exist between client and counselor. Such differences make a broad definition of the concept of culture somewhat tenuous in actual multicultural counseling practice.

Culture in Context

If the discipline of multicultural counseling is to have any relevance in addressing differences between helper and client, a context must be developed for understanding the concept of culture. The present realities of, and demographic projections for, American society suggest that the counseling profession may need to move from a broad conceptualization of culture to a more refined view of this construct as it relates to practice.

The aspect of Webster's definition dealing with the beliefs, forms, and traits of a **racial group** may provide the most important context for understanding the concept of culture in contemporary counseling practice. Webster's dictionary (1989) defines a racial group as "a family, tribe, people or nation belonging to the same stock" (p. 969). The notion of race may be extended to include the concept of **ethnic group**. This concept has developed much credibility as a multicultural counseling construct. According to Webster's dictionary, an ethnic group relates to "large groups of people classed according to common racial, national, tribal, lingusitic, or cultural origin or background" (p. 427). Although race is primarily a biological term and ethnicity is a sociological one, they are often used synonymously to refer to groups of people who share similar physiological traits and personality characteristics. These traits and characteristics are either genetically transferred or have become reinforced through group association over long periods of time. Scholars in the field have suggested a need to clarify the concept of culture within the context of multicultural counseling (Johnson, 1990; Ponterotto & Benesch, 1988; Sue & Zane, 1987). Implied in these suggestions is the idea that **culture** as a construct be clarified in terms of **race** or **ethnicity**.

Such contextual suggestions seem logical for two important reasons. First, as American society approaches the 21st century, issues of race and ethnicity are assuming new dimensions. Groups that have traditionally held racial or ethnic minority status within the society are beginning to outnumber that portion of the population that traces its cultural origins to Europe (Spencer, 1989; Henry, 1990). Second, it must be understood that counseling has traditionally been a professional activity that represents White, European, European-American culture. Counseling practice has generally been most effective with those people whose cultural traditions and social background have mirrored that culture (Lee, 1989).

Given the changing face of America, it is evident that the counseling profession is confronted with some new realities. Therefore, in terms of present and future practice, **culture** as it is used within the context of multicultural counseling may need to be understood primarily in terms of the mental health issues and developmental needs of those racial or ethnic groups in American society that do not trace their origins to Europe. This would include Native Americans/American Indians and people with African, Asian, or Middle Eastern backgrounds. Likewise, it would include those people whose culture represents an amalgam of Spanish, Indian, or African influences from the Caribbean Basin or Mexico. The needs of people with these cultural backgrounds have generally been misunderstood and inadequately addressed within the European, European-American cultural context that forms the framework of the counseling profession (Atkinson, Morten, & Sue, 1979; Sue & Sue, 1990).

The Dynamics of Culture as Race or Ethnicity: Themes for Culturally Responsive Counseling

Any discipline that would seek to affect the development of a group of people must take into account the dynamics that shape that development. Culturally responsive counseling strategies and techniques must be predicated on an understanding of cultural dynamics and their crucial role in fostering optimal mental health. Given this, counseling professionals need to find ways to incorporate cultural dynamics into the helping process.

When culture is considered in terms of either race or ethnicity, a number of dynamics may need to be considered in counseling interactions with clients from non-European cultural backgrounds. Implicit in these dynamics are the beliefs, social forms, and material traits that constitute distinct cultural realities. Dynamics that might be considered in culturally responsive counseling include: level of ethnic identity and acculturation, family influences, sex-role socialization, religious and spiritual influences, and immigration experience.

Although this list of dynamics is by no means exhaustive, given the new realities of American society, a cursory review of many groups with non-European cultural backgrounds would indicate that these are some of the more important influences on individual development. These dynamics may not be important variables in the lives of *all* clients, but if culturally responsive counseling is to take place, they may need to be considered in the helping process.

Level of Ethnic Identity and Acculturation

Counseling effectiveness with members of racial or ethnic groups with non-European cultural origins may ultimately hinge on an understanding of the concepts of ethnic identity and acculturation. An appreciation of these dynamics, and their influence on human development, is fundamental to culturally responsive counseling.

In broad terms, ethnic identity refers to an individual's sense of belonging to an ethnic group and the part of his or her personality that is attributable to ethnic group membership (Rotherman & Phinney, 1987). Acculturation, within the context of American society, refers to the degree to which an individual identifies with the attitudes, life-styles, and values of the predominant macroculture. For groups with non-European cultural origins, the development of ethnic identity has been conceptualized as an evolutionary stage process (Atkinson, Morten, & Sue, 1979; Cross, 1971; Jackson, 1975; Sue & Sue, 1971). Generally, these stages can range from little or no identification with the macroculture (and complete identification with the racial/ethnic group of origin) to complete identification with the macroculture (and little identification with the group of origin). An individual's level of ethnic identity or acculturation may be influenced by a variety of factors such as age, length of residence in the United States, level of education, extent of experience with racism, and socioeconomic status.

Individual development is greatly influenced by the level of ethnic identity and acculturation among groups of people with non-European cultural origins. The manner in which members of these groups view themselves in relation to others in American society can shape attitudes, behaviors, and values. The dynamics of ethnic identity and acculturation, therefore, are important considerations for multicultural counseling. Counseling professionals need to be sensitive to issues of ethnic identity and carefully explore the degree of cultural similarity or dissimilarity between themselves and their clients. Analysis of ethnic identity or acculturation levels should guide the focus of counseling intervention. Understanding a client's level of ethnic identity and degree of acculturation should provide direction for the cultural appropriateness of specific counseling interventions.

Family Influences

Immediate and extended family networks must be considered as primary sources for promoting mental health and normal development among many racial or ethnic groups. Within these networks can be found hierarchical structures and carefully defined age or gender roles that provide traditional methods for help in decision making and formulating new ways of thinking, feeling, and behaving.

Family support networks are crucial in providing resolution to both situational and developmental problems related to educational, career, or personal-social matters. In many instances, the supportive dynamics of these networks keep an individual from having to seek assistance outside the family. Culturally responsive counseling practice, therefore, must include an understanding of and appreciation for the role of family dynamics in mental health and well-being.

Sex-Role Socialization

Sex-role socialization is an important dynamic to consider when counseling across cultures. Many racial or ethnic groups with non-European cultural origins have different perceptions of the role of men and women. These differential gender perceptions can influence the expectations considered normal for development. Such expectations, therefore, can account for fundamental differences in personality development for men and women.

When necessary, sex-role socialization and its effects on development should be considered in culturally responsive counseling. Counselors may need to be aware of how gender-based differences in developmental expectations are manifested in decision making and problem resolution among the men and women of a particular racial or ethnic group.

Religious and Spiritual Influences

Although religion is universally accepted as a major influence on human development, it is not always considered an important or appropriate aspect for the counseling process. However, multicultural counseling practice may be enhanced if the influence of religion or spirituality is considered a crucial dynamic in the helping process. Many racial or ethnic groups often ascribe little distinction between religious and secular life. The philosophical tenets inherent in religious or spiritual beliefs influence all aspects of human development and interaction.

Within the cultural traditions of many groups, religious institutions are important sources of psychological support. Concomitantly, religious or spiritual leaders have been expected not only to provide for spiritual needs, but also to offer guidance for physical and emotional concerns. These institutions and their leaders have been an important indigenous source of counseling for decision making and problem resolution.

Immigration Experience

Many members of racial or ethnic groups are relatively recent arrivals to the United States. For these people, the immigration experience
may be an important dynamic to consider in the counseling process.

Immigration, in some instances, has been prompted by political
upheaval in other parts of the world. Many recent immigrants arrive
here as refugees who have escaped repressive governments. In addition
to cultural beliefs and practices, these people bring with them the trauma
associated with forced separation from family and homeland. In other
cases, recent immigrants have been lured here by the age-old promise
of economic and social opportunity. Often, a major challenge for these
people is reconciling the desire to maintain cultural customs from back
home with the pressure to adopt major aspects of American culture.

Whatever the reason for immigration, the experience of suddenly
finding oneself a stranger in a new land can affect human development
in ways that need to be considered in culturally responsive counseling.
Counseling professionals, therefore, should be aware of the possible
influence of immigration experiences on the attitudinal orientations,
behavioral repertoires, and value systems of clients from specific racial
or ethnic groups.

Conclusion

Although all counseling contains an element of cultural diversity,
the demographic realities of present and future American society clearly
suggest that multicultural counseling must focus primarily on racial and
ethnic differences and their influence on the helping process. Culturally
responsive counseling strategies must be based on an understanding of
culture in a racial or ethnic context. In addition, the cultural dynamics
of racial and ethnic groups, particularly those groups with non-European
origins, that foster mental health and promote human development must
become important themes in multicultural counseling practice.

References

Atkinson, D. R., Morten, G., & Sue, D. W. (1979). *Counseling American minorities:
A cross-cultural perspective.* Dubuque, IA: Wm. C. Brown.
Axelson, J. A. (1985). *Counseling and development in a multicultural society.* Mon-
terey, CA: Brooks/Cole.
Cross, W. E. (1971). The Negro-to-Black conversion experience. *Black World,
20,* 12–27.

Henry, W. A. (1990, April). Beyond the melting pot. *Time*, pp. 28–31.

Jackson, B. (1975). Black identity development. MEFORM. *Journal of Educational Diversity and Innovation, 2*, 19–25.

Johnson, S. D. (1990). Toward clarifying **culture, race, and ethnicity** in the context of multicultural counseling. *Journal of Multicultural Counseling and Development, 18*, 41, 50.

Lee, C. C. (1989). Multicultural counseling: New directions for counseling professionals. *Virginia Counselors Journal, 17*, 3–8.

Pedersen, P. (1988). *A handbook for developing multicultural awareness*. Alexandria, VA: American Association for Counseling and Development.

Ponterotto, J. G., & Benesch, K. F. (1988). An organizational framework for understanding the role of culture in counseling. *Journal of Counseling and Development, 66*, 237–241.

Rotherman, M. J., & Phinney, J. S. (1987). Introduction: Definitions and perspectives in the study of children's ethnic socialization. In J. S. Phinney & M. J. Rotherman (Eds.), *Children's ethnic socialization* (pp. 10–28). Beverly Hills, CA: Sage.

Spencer, G. (1989). *Projections of the population of the United States by age, sex, and race: 1988 to 2080*. Washington, DC: Current Population Reports. Population Estimates and Projections. Series P-25, No. 1018. Bureau of the Census.

Sue, D. W., & Sue, D. (1990). *Counseling the culturally different: Theory and practice* (2nd ed.). New York: Wiley.

Sue, S., & Sue, D. W. (1971). Chinese-American personality and mental health. *Amerasia Journal, 1*, 36–49.

Sue, S., & Zane, N. (1987). The role of culture and cultural techniques in psychotherapy. *American Psychologist, 42*, 37–45.

Webster's ninth new collegiate dictionary. (1989). Springfield, MA: Merriam-Webster.

PART II

Direction for Culturally Responsive Counseling

THE AMERICAN INDIAN/NATIVE AMERICAN EXPERIENCE

Contemporary American Indians or Native Americans are the descendants of the original inhabitants of the North American continent. As a cultural group they have had both a long and a troubled history. The basis of their trouble has been the relationship they have experienced with the United States government—a relationship often marked by conflict and oppression. There is a great deal of diversity among this cultural group, but culturally responsive counselors need to be aware of some common elements that contribute to American Indian mental health. These include a strong reverence for nature and a deep respect for their people.

Chapter 3
COUNSELING AMERICAN INDIAN ADULTS

Grace Powless Sage

History

Although much has been written on the history of the American Indian, I would be remiss if I did not attempt to share the wholly unique relationship that this group has had with the United States government. It cannot be overstated that tribal relationships with the U.S. government have affected each tribal group immeasurably (Deloria, 1969, 1970). Three important issues must be highlighted to strengthen the reader's understanding of the dynamics of the tribal relationships with the federal government. Awareness and sensitivity to the impact of the government on tribes and the consequent relationship to mental health and mental health services is one issue. In tandem with that is the role of traditional healers and traditional health care and the circumstances that prevail that lead to choosing one system over another (Guilmet & Whited, 1988). Finally, one must explore how the historical relationship between the American Indian tribes and the U.S. government created a dependency perspective that invariably results in tribal problems being perceived as the responsibility of federal agencies (Trimble, Manson, Dinges, & Medicine, 1984).

The most obvious area in which the federal government affected and continues to affect American Indians is their need and demand for land. Indeed, there are few tribal groups that have not been the victims of relocation on one or more occasions. Furthermore, no tribe has escaped the severe loss of population through starvation, disease, and warfare, often at the hands of the federal government.

The government is ambivalent toward the American Indian—love versus hate, reservation versus romanticization, colonialization versus

This chapter is dedicated to my family—Tom, Chad, Den, and Max and my friends—Carol, Elease, Karen, and Liz. My special thanks to Joe Trimble.

extermination, self-determination versus subjugation, treatment versus neglect. On one hand, the federal government signed treaties with tribes that were recognized, at the time, as sovereign nations, while on the other hand, the same tribes were exterminated or forced into dependent relationships with the United States vis-à-vis reservation status (Deloria, 1983; Trimble, 1988). The dominant view was that the only way to manage the Indian situation was for Indians to give up their distinctive and unique way of life and adopt the dominant culture (Deloria, 1983; Witt, 1980; Trimble, 1988). At the same time, the "guardians and stewards" of the American Indian made available to Indians services that would engage and increase the Indians' adaptiveness and acculturation to the dominant society (Trimble, 1988). But the confusing sentiments and policies had already been established, and the difficulty in making the Indians understand what was "good for them" continued (Deloria, 1983). The American Indians were left to cast about trying to identify who they were and what their needs were while being influenced directly by the roller-coaster relationship with the U.S. government. Is it any wonder that American Indians believe the only way to independence is through continued dependence on the U.S. government? The long history of confusing messages from the federal government to the tribes has created a double bind from which there is no escape. For example, the government has given American Indian people no reason to trust it, yet the contemporary mental health services are provided by a government agency, the Indian Health Service. To utilize these services, the agency must be trusted.

Sociocultural Development

The following case study illustrates some of the aforementioned dilemmas. One woman tells the story of her son and her father. Her father was the medicine man of the tribe, and because his own sons were killed or had died, he looked forward to teaching and leaving to his grandson the ways of the medicine man. He would say to his grandson that one day, when he died, the grandson would be able to heal the people of the tribe and be held in great respect and esteem. The grandson had been raised in a missionary boarding school and felt that his grandfather was out of step with the 20th century. He would argue with his grandfather about the practical usefulness of his medicine and would look with disdain at the people who sought his grandfather's help, advice, and healing. The grandson would often feel disgusted and angry with his mother for making him visit his grandfather. His mother could not validate the grandfather's way of life because she, too, had gone away to school. Although she had not completed school, she had learned enough to know that some things were simply not discussed, like her father being a medicine man. She, herself, had some difficulty "fitting in" when she returned to the reservation. Even though it pained the mother greatly to see the widening gap between her father and her son, she felt powerless to do anything about it. She didn't understand her father's ways and could not really understand her son either. She became more and more depressed and began to drink heavily in response to the growing distance between the two men. She blamed herself for not understanding her father's beliefs and for having sent her son to a missionary school. She felt totally disenfranchised by her family and her community, and wrestled constantly with trying to discover her own identity.

Let us look briefly at the case study and see how the sociocultural developmental process affects the individuals involved. For one thing, we have a reservation-born and raised American Indian medicine man. It is likely that when he was little, his family lived on original tribal lands. Additionally, because of his status as a medicine man, his family must have had political influence and power in his community. His daughter was not born on the original tribal lands. In fact, she was born on the reservation where her father currently lives. She was sent away to school when she was 12 and did not return to the reservation until she was 20. By the time she returned her mother had died from pneumonia. She didn't remember her father very well and barely knew her brothers, two of whom had been born after she left. Shortly after she returned, she became pregnant by a non-Indian man she had met in a bar. When her son was old enough, he went to the mission school on the reservation, but because he was a bright child, the priest encouraged the mother to move to an urban area about 1,000 miles from the reservation. She moved when her son was 6 years old. Although she made occasional visits to the reservation when she could afford to, the son never lived on or near the reservation.

It becomes abundantly clear that by the time people are referred for treatment or seek counseling services, their relational and historical identities will play a major role in what course treatment should take. By the time that intervention and treatment could begin, the mother's drinking and depression had become quite disabling. While at the Indian Center she heard about an Indian Women's Group that was forming. A woman who was currently a member of the Women's Group encouraged her to join. Although she was initially hesitant about the Women's Group and not quite sure what it meant, she decided to join. It would give her a chance to get away from the tension in her home and to enjoy her favorite pastime—beading. While attending the Women's Group, she found other women, who, like herself, were busy working on crafts they enjoyed and talking about how things were going in their lives. She began to feel that there wasn't anything terribly wrong with her and that other women had questions and concerns about their families similar to her own. While there, the woman learned that others in her group were experiencing the same ambivalence and feelings of disenfranchisement that she often felt. Many felt dislocated upon their return to the reservation after they had attended boarding school. She learned that many women felt sad and depressed like she did. She also discovered that the reasons for their depression were basically the same as her own. She was amazed that other women in her tribe were experiencing the same family difficulties. Although she was aware that many of them drank, she had never connected their drinking with their depression. In fact, she had never connected her own drinking with her own depression.

There are two important considerations that run parallel to the importance of the historical perspective. The first involves the differences between urban and rural-reservation American Indians as well as tribal differences among American Indians. Second, intergenerational differences must be taken into consideration to understand experiential information and the sociocultural developmental process and context.

Urban American Indians are more than likely extremely migratory. The migratory pattern might be from urban setting to urban setting or from reservation to urban setting and back. Some are in search of the "American dream," some look for economic opportunity and adequate housing, and others seek educational opportunity (Witt, 1980). Many are of mixed blood and have limited, if any, relationship to the reservation of their parent or parents. They experience quite different Indian and non-Indian relationships than their parents do. For example, close identification with the non-Indian world increases the American Indians' sense of invisibility, which decreases their sense of identity and self-esteem (Ablon, 1964, 1971). This results in individuals' rarely identifying themselves as American Indians when they access or utilize services, or participate in cultural events or ceremonies. They accept any identification that is given to them by service professionals or others, resulting in a sense of isolation and a feeling of being removed from the non-Indian world as well as from the American Indian world (Ablon, 1964, 1971).

Conversely, not identifying with the dominant culture (non-Indian world) leads to isolation, passivity, increased stress, anxiety, and depression (Trimble, Manson, & Dinges, 1983). The most pervasive and eroding of these is isolation. When they migrate to urban settings, many Indians lose their traditional role models and images, which may exacerbate their feelings of psychological vulnerability. Returning to the reservation can be a "booster shot" to help regain balance, self-esteem, and self-concept and to steady a fragile self and tribal identity as American Indians (Guilmet & Whited, 1988).

It is important to note that those American Indians who are born and raised either on a reservation or in an urban setting and haven't engaged in migratory behavior have a different permutation of the aforementioned problems. The sense of being invisible simply does not exist on a reservation because everyone knows their genealogy. That fact, in and of itself, provides a strong sense of community and tribal identity. For instance, on a reservation when a person of mixed blood participates in traditional tribal ceremonies or seeks the services of a medicine man or woman, the reservation community perceives this as an assertion of one's Indianness. On the other hand, seeking services from an Indian Health Service counselor might reinforce the reservation community's perception that the individual is not really Indian. Alternatively, the test for some urban Indians' identification is less strained because their perceptions and understandings of traditional Indian ceremonies are similar to those their dominant culture counterparts hold. Thus, they would be unlikely to seek services other than those considered appropriate by the majority culture, such as counseling and psychotherapy.

Finally, it is important to understand regional differences among American Indians. The significance of making such a distinction may seem unnecessary unless one has had the occasion to work or live with an Eastern woodlands tribal member, a Northern Plains tribal member or, perhaps, a Southern Plains tribal member. Regional differences affect worldviews, traditional ceremonial practices, cultural beliefs, language, eating habits, and clothing habits (Trimble, 1986). Successful functioning, being "in balance," as well as underlying pathology can be highly influenced by tribal and regional differences (Trimble et al., 1983; Neligh, 1988). These regional variables do not exist in isolation but rather are defined and develop in tandem with tribal, urban, reservation, and intergenerational differences. It is difficult to try to discern the level of impact from each of these differences while keeping in mind the impact of the majority culture and its sociodevelopmental processes. Understandably, this difficulty often leads to neglect and omission by practitioners.

Intergenerational differences are often magnified, depending on where a child was raised. Difficulties between generations exist because of the child's having to relate 20th-century living, school, music, technology, and other areas to more than one generation. Additional problems are created when there is alcohol or substance abuse in the family. Often the pressures, stress, and depression can be devastating; communication is neglected because the individual expends all energy in meeting basic survival needs. Thus, tribal identity is affected by history, distinct tribal differences, urban, reservation, and regional differences, and intergenerational differences. All of these affect the rates of mental/ emotional/physical illness and well-being, alcoholism, substance abuse, and suicide (Beiser, 1981; Beiser & Attneave, 1982). It would be redundant and it is not the purpose of this chapter to yet again survey the statistics that capture the identity of a people. Although the statistics are revealing, they fail to encompass the variety of, or to foster an appreciation for, the unique group called American Indians (Trimble, 1988).

Other influences have affected the whole issue of this group's mental health and well-being. There is an enormous amount of cultural difference and heterogeneity within the group called American Indians or Native Americans (Deloria, 1983). Each tribe has its own understanding of equilibrium and balance within its oral history and religion. People's behavior is talked about in terms of where it lies on that continuum of balance (Trimble et al., 1984). For example, virtually all American Indian tribes have some understanding of and explanation for the diseases of the body and the mind. Although they may make the discrimination between the two, the underpinning of their understanding comes from the interwoven healing that must take place if there is to be a "cure." Hence, one might be plagued by diabetes, gall bladder problems, or infections; however, that does not mitigate the healing benefits of seeking services vis-à-vis ceremonies or medicine men or women in addition to contemporary medical treatment. The balance, therefore, may lie in using the total healing system.

Of course, missionaries from other organized religious groups have influenced American Indians' thinking and definition of what is appropriate behavior. This has served to create yet another dilemma for American Indians from different tribes. For example, if one were a good "Christian," how could one partake of "pagan" ceremonies? And, alternatively, if one were a good Indian, then how could one disown his or her own culture and tradition and adopt other beliefs? So, if you were feeling "out of balance" with your world, would you choose to see a traditional healer, would you go to "talk" with someone about your difficulties, or would you pray? And, after all, would you have problems of mental illness, alcoholism, and substance abuse if the U.S. government hadn't treated Indians the way it did? So, therefore, isn't it the government's responsibility to "take care of the problem"?

In speaking with my elders, it becomes clear that an understanding of mental health and "appropriate" mental health care can be viewed as a system that is given significance and develops only within a sociocultural context. For example, many elders do not understand the role or the responsibilities of conventional counselors. They are caught in a maze of misunderstanding where medical technology develops quickly and assumes superiority. What they do understand is their experience: American Indian people go to the hospital and die or their "spirit" is transformed into something unrecognizable such as mental illness or a coma.

Historically, the mental health model has followed a medical model because of dominant Eurocentric beliefs, financial power, prejudices, and stereotypical attitudes toward the traditional healers of most American Indian tribes (Guilmet & Whited, 1988). Only recently have different perspectives been supported and the need for holistic health care advocated by many health care professionals (Guilmet & Whited). But the neglect or outright obliteration of the traditional healer and healing has had its own set of consequences. Today some elders and many American Indian adults, who have had a history of isolation from their culture and experienced domination from the U.S. government, lack the understanding of the role of traditional healers in their own tribes. Furthermore, they are almost totally uninvolved with non-Indian alternative healing practices that have been flourishing for some years (Guilmet & Whited). At this point, for some tribes and many American Indian adults, the isolation seems total and creates a culture of its own.

Strategies and Techniques to Facilitate Treatment

Given conventional counseling and psychotherapy training and techniques plus the assumption that they have something to offer American Indians, which American Indians might benefit from what interventions? "Cross-cultural therapy implies a situation in which the participants are most likely to evidence discrepancies in their shared assumptions, experiences, beliefs, values, expectations, and goals" (Manson & Trimble, 1982). In casting and molding a model that would be most beneficial to the largest number of individuals, the focus shifts to two specific questions, and to the identification of appropriate client factors. First, what competencies and lessons does a counselor/psychotherapist need in working with adult Indians? Second, how does one engage and empower American Indians as a group by combining what sometimes are, and what sometimes appear to be, two contrasting systems of healing? Perhaps the best place to start is to give the reader an understanding of what might be defined as a "healthy" individual according to an individual's community, whether that be a reservation or an urban setting. (Although these definitions are generally appropriate, keep in mind the diversity between tribal groups, their history in relation to the U.S. government, and the urban, reservation, and regional differences.)

First, practitioners are more likely to be successful in the treatment of individuals who seek their services if they are cognizant of the prac-

tices, travel, and activities of the American Indian client. That is, practitioners must understand the meaning and intent of the migratory
practices for American Indians and acknowledge the necessity of developing a supportive network to maintain a sense of balance in their
world. Furthermore, professionals must recognize the conflict inherent
in American Indians' trying to operate in differing cultural milieux. That
recognition by practitioners is sometimes more therapeutic and supportive than any contemporary counseling intervention. The community
(reservation or urban) sees the migratory practices as necessary and
supports the pattern vis-à-vis money, information dissemination (who is
traveling where and when), and considerable pressure to remain connected with the family. Many American Indians believe that to be poor
in the Indian world means being without family and relatives (Primeaux,
1977). It is clear that aspects of contemporary counseling and therapy
techniques conflict with migratory practices in a multitude of ways, such
as in set appointment times, or utilizing a linear process leading to specific
goals.

Implicit in the identification of the reference group's "healthy" individual is the American Indian who designs a life that maintains a
connection to family. A second powerful component of that connect-
edness is provided through the ceremonial practices that give expression
to the restoration and preservation of one's identity. To alleviate the
feeling of being caught between two cultures, counselors can provide
support for preserving what is strong and enduring from the history,
tribe, and family in one culture, while continuing to adapt to the technology and progress of the dominant culture. Practitioners and programs that confront these complicated processes of integration without
trying to suppress cultural patterns are much more likely to engender
success with American Indian clients.

These processes also involve the identification of value conflicts for
both the counselor/psychotherapist and the client (i.e., individual vs.
group accomplishment; goal-oriented therapy vs. ceremonies as therapeutic agents, etc.). Additionally, conflicts surrounding issues such as
education need to be explored. The expectations and values the non-
Indian places on members of the American Indian community to con-
form to the dominant culture's beliefs about achievement and compe-
tition often lead to feelings of inadequacy, frustration, and a poor self-
image for the American Indian (Jilek-Aall, 1976).

One last area that is often in conflict with non-Indian culture because
of different values and definitions includes communication styles and a
sense of self-worth, self-concept, and understanding. Communication
styles are often in conflict with those of the non-Indian culture. Because
the history of American Indian identity is maintained through oral tradition, an individual is likely to define words as powerful and value-
laden. The tendency to use words casually, as in small talk, or frivolously,

as in anger, might be avoided at any cost. The fact that the main entry into the counseling or therapeutic setting is with words increases the potential for a problemmatic situation. American Indians accept periods of silence, especially in unfamiliar circumstances such as counseling or psychotherapy. Speaking and silence should be allowed to come naturally and as part of a process.

An issue related to communication is the sense of self-worth as well as self-identification. It becomes clear that those individuals valued in the non-Indian society are often more verbal and demonstrative, have an advanced educational degree and steady employment, define and promote their individualism and individual identity, and are competitive on an individual level. It is often into this context that American Indians are cast and left to make their own identity, but within these dominant-culture guidelines. Thus, it often means alienating oneself from one's own culture to adopt another culture, even though by adopting the dominant culture the American Indian almost never finds membership, acceptance, understanding, success, or power in the non-Indian culture. Ironically, this is usually true despite the strengths American Indians possess or the contributions they make. Of course, the criteria of acceptance, success, or power are all defined/achieved/seen differently based on each system (e.g., the dominant culture, the American Indian culture, or the individual American Indian's own criteria). This state of affairs has been the history and remains the status quo.

Although these issues are important and vital to the success of any intervention, it would be worthwhile to focus on one specific and practical area of treatment that proved beneficial to the family in the case example. Many interventions are possible; the Indian Women's Group illuminates the therapeutic aspects of combining traditional and contemporary practices. The goal of the group was not complex but really rather simple and achievable. The purpose for the women in gathering together was to encourage support for each other and to serve as an alternative to their drinking. It was clear, though, that one did not have to be drinking to be involved in the Indian Women's Group. This was also a time for socializing and reestablishing relationships within the community. The group leader was a woman who had left the reservation to complete a degree in postsecondary education. Some of her feelings were similar to those of the other group members in terms of disenfranchisement, but she felt that this was one way that she could assist in her own healing as well as the group's. In addition, she was influenced strongly by an elderly medicine woman who was willing to serve as her mentor in the group process. Thus, the two women agreed to start this Indian Women's Group.

Initially, the women in the community were solicited to join the group and, despite hesitation and numerous questions, the younger woman encouraged while the older medicine woman patiently waited.

After the initial group was established, it became clear that other women wanted to join and some needed to leave. Eventually, the rhythm of the group stabilized, so that a steady number of women always participated and there were a few "new" members and a stable group of "older" members.

The group was unique because of the blend and integration of traditional and contemporary therapeutic practices. For example, bead-work was commonplace, as well as sewing ribbon shirts, and, sometimes, making favorite foods. Tanning hides and cutting dancing outfits were also tasks performed to help in the healing process. At the same time, the women exchanged ideas and their worldviews with one another. No one was diagnosed or labeled. Although everyone in the group "knew" who was having drinking problems or relationship issues, the group would somehow focus on a story or "recipe" for how they had handled a similar situation in their life, most often without direct confrontation. Occasionally, the young woman whose brainstorm it had been to start this group would make a comment or offer an "interpretation," but always in the context of what the other group members had said. The older medicine woman would end the group with a prayer that would tie together the learning and relationship building that had been part of the group members' experience that night. Everyone would remark on the enjoyable experience and, almost always, suggest someone else in the community who might benefit from the Indian Women's Group.

The woman in our case study tells this story to explain a number of important points. First, she was able to identify what she was feeling and give it a name: depression. She felt that this enabled her to deal more effectively with it and it gave her a sense of control over her own life. She also felt that identifying the circumstances for her drinking was empowering. She saw the role of the group of women as healing and as helping to continue part of her own tribal history, which had been ne-glected. She was not stigmatized nor labeled for her membership in the group and, in fact, was sought out by other women in the tribe as some-one they could turn to for support. Furthermore, she was able to identify the conflict that resulted in her father's and son's relationship as well as her own conflict with her American Indian identity and beliefs. Although no answer resulted from the experience, she relates that she achieved balance by identifying what she had control over and what she could not control. The power she began to feel within herself came from the integration of both her worlds.

Each member of this family, although all contributing to this process and communication breakdown, must be recognized as unique and dif-ferent if intervention or treatment is to be effective. For example, the woman's son did initially seek treatment from the Indian Health Service on the reservation. This did not present an overwhelming conflict for him, but it should be noted that he later sought the assistance of another younger medicine man on the reservation. (Interestingly enough, the boy's grandfather was the spiritual and medicine leader for the young medicine man from whom he sought assistance.) The woman's father continued to use and offer his medicinal and spiritual leadership to those who requested and sought it, and no longer pressured his grandson to partake of the ceremonies.

Generally speaking, the competencies and lessons necessary for the counselor/psychotherapist in treating American Indians result from a mixture of different elements. Although some of these can be gleaned from an advanced educational background, it is worthwhile to attribute the success of the aforementioned Indian Women's Group in part to the combination of worldviews. For example, the theoretical underpinnings for the group process may have come from an educational setting, but the relationships, bonding, reinforcement, and sense of community came from the sharing of values and cultural understanding group members had for one another. In fact, there is no quick or easy "cookbook" recipe on how to achieve either the competencies, the lessons, or the ability to combine different healing systems. Some suggestions for the practitioner might include gathering information about different cultures and cultural views, learning about cross-cultural psychotherapy/counseling techniques, diagnostic issues, and pathology, and beginning to explore the racism that exists in mental health systems. Additionally, practitioners should have some experiential training that includes an exploration of their own biases and prejudices.

Conclusion

It is important to recall the risk of generalizations, especially when applied to American Indian or Native American populations. However, a few recommendations merit summarizing. First, it is important to have a cross-cultural curriculum for training potential counselors or psychotherapists. Finding a cross-cultural curriculum in counseling/psychotherapy training programs can be time-consuming, frustrating, and, far too often, unsuccessful. Even so, all practitioners should be familiar with the work of Pinderhughes et al. (1990). Second, practitioners will contribute to the sense of invisibility if they are not aware of and sensitive to the diversity between and within the group of people called American Indians or Native Americans. The warning 20 years ago from Vine Deloria, Jr., in *We Talk, You Listen*, is still appropriate today:

> Further generalizations about how we are all alike—all people—
> are useless today. Definite points of view, new logic, and dif-

ferent goals define us. All we can do is try to communicate what we feel our group means to itself and how we relate to other groups. Understanding each other as distinct peoples is the most important thing. (1970, pp. 15–16)

Third, helping professionals must have a thorough understanding of the American Indians' history, their relationship to the U.S. government, and their unique sociodevelopmental experiences. Finally, practitioners must understand and be able to integrate the variety of, and acknowledge the viability of, traditional and contemporary treatment practices.

References

Ablon, J. (1964). Relocated American Indians in the San Francisco Bay area: Social interactions and Indian identity. *Human Organization, 23*, 296–304.

Ablon, J. (1971). Cultural conflict in urban Indians. *Mental Hygiene, 55*, 199–205.

Beiser, M. (1981). Mental health of American Indian and Alaska Native children: Some epidemiological perspectives. *White Cloud Journal, 2*(2), 37–47.

Beiser, M., & Attneave, C. L. (1982). Mental disorders among Native American children: Rates and risk periods for entering treatment. *American Journal of Psychiatry, 139*, 193–198.

Deloria, V., Jr. (1969). *Custer died for your sins.* New York: Avon.

Deloria, V., Jr. (1970). *We talk, you listen.* New York: Dell.

Deloria, V., Jr. (1983). Indians today, the real and the unreal. In D. R. Atkinson, G. Morten, & D. W. Sue (Eds.), *Counseling American minorities: A cross-cultural perspective* (2nd ed.). Dubuque, IA: Wm. C. Brown.

Guilmet, G., & Whited, D. (1988). Mental health care in a general health care system: The experience of the Puyallup. In S. M. Manson & N. Dinges (Eds.), *Behavioral health issues among American Indians and Alaska Natives: Explorations on the frontiers of the biobehavioral sciences* (Monograph 1, pp. 290–324). Denver, CO: The Journal of the National Center Monograph Series.

Jilek-Aall, L. (1976). The western psychiatrist and his non-western clientele. *Canadian Psychiatric Association Journal, 21*(6), 353–359.

Manson, S. M., & Trimble, J. E. (1982). American Indian and Alaska Native communities: Past efforts, future inquiries. In L. R. Snowden (Ed.), *Reaching the underserved: Mental health needs of neglected populations* (Volume 3, pp. 143–163). SAGE Annual Reviews of Community Mental Health.

Neligh, G. (1988). Major mental disorders and behavior among American Indians and Alaska Natives. In S. M. Manson & N. Dinges (Eds.), *Behavioral health issues among American Indians and Alaska Natives: Explorations on the frontiers of the biobehavioral sciences.* (Monograph 1, pp. 116–159). Denver, CO: The Journal of the National Center Monograph Series.

Pinderhughes E., McGoldrick, M., Sue, D., Sue, S., Katz, J., & Ward, K. (1990). *A curriculum integration workbook.* Carbondale: Southern Illinois University.

Primeaux, M. (1977). Caring for the American Indian patient. *American Journal of Nursing, 77*, 91–94.

Trimble, J. E. (1986). American Indians and interethnic conflict: A theoretical and historical overview. In J. Boucher, D. Landis, & K. Arnold (Eds.), *Interethnic conflict: Myth and reality* (pp. 127–144). Beverly Hills, CA: Sage.

Trimble, J. E. (1988). Stereotypical images, American Indians, and prejudice. In P. Katz & D. Taylor (Eds.), *Eliminating racism: Profiles in controversy* (pp. 199–220). New York: Plenum Press.

Trimble, J. E., Manson, S. M., & Dinges, N. (1983). Toward an understanding of American Indian concepts of mental health: Some reflections and directions. In A. Marsella & P. Pedersen (Eds.), *Intercultural applications of counseling therapies* (pp. 177–204). Beverly Hills, CA: Sage.

Trimble, J. E., Manson, S. M., Dinges, N., & Medicine, B. (1984). American Indian concepts of mental health. In P. Pedersen, N. Sartorius, & A. Marsella (Eds.), *Mental health services: The cross-cultural context* (pp. 181–202). Beverly Hills, CA: Sage.

Witt, S. H. (1980, Spring). Pressure points in growing up Indian. *Perspectives*, pp. 24–31.

Chapter 4
COUNSELING NATIVE AMERICAN YOUTH

Roger D. Herring

Even though between 1.5 and 1.8 million Native Americans live in the United States, most non-Native Americans lack an adequate awareness of this ethnic group and its diversity. This ignorance implies the idea that Native Americans are one people—a serious insult to 517 federally recognized native entities (196 in Alaska and 321 in the lower 48 states) and 365 state-recognized Indian tribes (U.S. Senate Select Committee on Indian Affairs, 1985). Each of these entities maintains unique customs, traditions, and social organizations.

The purpose of this chapter is to assist counselors and other mental health professionals in developing basic skills for proactive counseling interventions with Native American youth.

Social and Cultural Challenges to the Development of Native American Youth

Current social and cultural challenges to the development of Native American youth can be attributed, in large measure, to the history their people have experienced at the hands of the federal government. This history has been characterized by military defeat, ethnic demoralization, and forced displacement. The historical conflict of cultures and worldviews between Native and non-Native Americans continues to create negative influences on the development of Native American youth. Many challenges associated with this conflict can be summarized in four important areas: (1) ambiguous terminology; (2) poverty and unemployment; (3) family dissolution; and (4) educational underattainment.

Ambiguous Terminology

A generic term for Native Americans does not exist. Statistically, Native Americans have either been ignored or placed in the "other" category of racial identification. This designation has served to foster a lack of recognition. Native Americans can be described as the "invisible" or "faceless" ethnic minority due to this statistical designation. Concurrently, the use of varied designations compounds the identification problems for Native Americans. The more commonly used designations include: **American Indian, Native American, First or Original American,** and **Amerindian or Amerind**. It is important to note, however, that there are resented aspects to each of these terms. For example, although the term **American Indian** is preferred by most tribes and national organizations, there is a valid objection to its use. Early European explorers, believing they had reached India when they landed in the Americas, called the native people "Indians." For many contemporary native people, use of that term perpetuates this misconception. The term Native American is used in this chapter because of its inclusive nature and omission of reference to the term "Indian." Ideally, the name of Native tribes or groups should be used rather than a generic name. Native American people tend to identify first as members of a tribe, then as Native Americans or American Indians. It is important to note that although some tribal names are based on beautiful images, some might be considered unflattering. For example, Navajo means "stealer of crops," Apache implies "enemy," and Mohawk refers to "man-eater." Other terms present similar difficulties. Such labels as tribe, band, reservation, rancheria, nation, and clan may produce resentment and cause insult to many. Likewise, labels such as "savage," "noble warrior," and "squaw" also infer discriminatory stereotypes. Using appropriate tribal designations recognizes the diversity of native people and may enhance Native American youth's pride in self and community.

Adding to the problem of terminology is a definitional problem related to the question—**Who is a native person?** The Indian Law Center at the University of New Mexico has researched 52 different definitions or sets of criteria used in law to define an "Indian" (American Indian Education Handbook Committee, 1982). The choice of definitions ultimately depends on the legal application of the term.

Ambiguous terminology can have a profound impact on Native American youth. Already confused about their ethnic identity due to the historical legacy of Native Americans, the additional burden of being mislabeled serves to hinder further the development of a positive self-concept among many Native American children and adolescents.

Such ambiguity affects not only how Native American young people view themselves, but the perceptions non-Native Americans hold of them as well. One of the most significant perceptions non-Native Americans hold is that Native American young people represent one people with one set of needs. Such narrow perceptions on both the part of Native and non-Native Americans may serve to limit Native American youth's vision of themselves, their potentialities, and their future (Schafer, 1990).

Poverty and Unemployment

Poverty and unemployment are constant challenges to Native Americans. The Bureau of Indian Affairs (BIA) estimated in 1987 that 48% of the potential Native American labor force aged 16 and older and living on or adjacent to reservations were unemployed, and of those 38% were seeking work. Twenty-six percent were employed and earning over $7,000 per year. Of the adults over 25 years old, 57% had not finished high school and 16% had completed less than 5 years of school (BIA, 1987, p. 1). Total unemployment, depending on the reservation, ranged from 20% to 70%. The median income for Native Americans was reported to be $13,680, compared to the U.S. median of $19,920 (U.S. Senate Select Committee on Indian Affairs, 1985).

Native American youth are negatively affected by issues related to poverty and unemployment. For example, Native American juvenile alcoholism and drug abuse are at critical levels. The U.S. Senate Select Committee on Indian Affairs (1985) reported that 52% of urban and 80% of reservational Native Americans are experiencing either alcohol or other drug abuse, compared to 23% of urban non-Native American citizens. Similarly, the annual suicide rate in some tribes has increased by about 200% in the past two decades to a rate of 18 per 100,000 (Harras, 1987). Twenty one percent of reservational Native Americans have homes without piped water, and 16% are without electricity (*American Indians*, 1985).

Chronic poverty and unemployment may also contribute to the persistence of career myths among Native American youth (Herring, 1990a); these myths are manifested frequently in low career aspirations. Having few positive career role models places limitations on the career choices of Native American youth. Such limitations continue the cycle of unemployment and underemployment and stifle the natural potential of Native American youth.

Family Dissolution

The breakup of the traditional Native American family structure has had a major effect on the development of young people. Family dissolution can be attributed, in large measure, to coercive efforts on the part of the U.S. government (Herring, 1989). Between 25% and 55% of all Native American children are separated and placed in non-Native

American foster homes, adoption homes, boarding homes, or other institutions. This is often done with little justification (Unger, 1977). The
effects of separating youth from their natural families and placing them
in alien home environments are well documented (Adler, 1985; Fuller,
1986). With respect to Native Americans, such practices have greatly
influenced the number of dysfunctional Native American families (Herring, 1989; Herring & Erchul, 1988).

The dissolution of Native American families has had a significant
psychological impact on Native American youth. Many are being reared
in non-Native American families. Because of this, they may experience
child-rearing styles that contrast with those of their native culture. In
addition, many Native American youth in such family situations are
receiving little traditional education in areas such as language, customs,
and ethnic culture—historically provided by tribal elders and parents.

Educational Underattainment

The current social and cultural plight of Native American youth is
evidenced in their educational underattainment. Over the past 200 years,
these young people have experienced various forms of education in on-
and off-reservation federal boarding schools, on-reservation federal
schools, mission schools, and public and private schools. The degree and
quality of education offered within each of these educational settings
has varied. Many non-Native educators generally have viewed Native
American culture as detrimental to the learning and assimilation processes of young people. Native American parents and students, therefore, could not help but be influenced by such views. Consequently, they
have held alternating attitudes toward education, seeing it as a threat,
an opportunity, or a combination of the two (American Indian Education
Handbook Committee, 1982).

It is significant to note that Native Americans have the highest school
dropout rate of any ethnic group. The National Center for Educational
Statistics reported a Native American dropout rate of 35.5%, compared
to 22.2% for Blacks and 27.9% for Hispanics. More revealing is that
Native Americans account for 3.1% of all dropouts despite the fact that
they constitute only 0.9% of all elementary and secondary students (National Center for Educational Statistics, 1989). These statistics are reflected in the educational attainment level of Native Americans, which
is the lowest of all ethnic minority groups. Fifty-six percent of Native
Americans 25 years or older are high school graduates, compared to
67% of the overall population. Native Americans (25 years or older)
have an average of 9.6 years of formal education, compared with the
national mean of 10.9 years; this average is the lowest of any major

ethnic group in the United States (Brod & McQuiston, 1983). Only 16% enter universities and complete an undergraduate degree, compared to 34% of Anglo Americans (Astin, 1982). Statistics such as these seem to result, in large measure, from the impact of continual miseducation and misunderstanding of Native American culture and people. In addition, poverty and prolonged unemployment have combined with substandard housing, malnutrition, inadequate health care, shortened life expectancy, and high suicide rates to affect and limit opportunities for educational attainment (LaFromboise, 1988).

Facilitating Change in the Lives of Native American Youth: Counseling for Optimal Development

Given these social and cultural challenges, counselors in schools and other settings are confronted with some major tasks in promoting the academic, career, and social development of Native American young people. Before examining counseling practice for Native American youth, however, three important issues need to be considered: Native American culture and its relationship to optimal mental health, the barriers to effective counseling with Native American youth, and the importance of adopting a proactive approach to counseling Native American children and adolescents.

Native American Culture: The Key to Counseling Practice

To intervene effectively in the lives of Native American youth, counselors and other helping professionals must have knowledge about the dynamics of Native American culture. Although there are variations across groups, in general, Native American values encompass a cosmic identity, a harmony of the individual with the tribe, the tribe with the land, and the land with the Great Spirit. Central to this harmony is constancy—the timelessness and predictability of nature as the foundation of existence. This cycle symbolizes eternity—one reality—and it transcends everything and gives respect to everything.

Within this context, counselors and other mental health professionals should explore ways to incorporate Native American cultural dimensions into the helping process. Culturally relevant approaches to counseling intervention transform basic aspects of Native American culture into positive developmental experiences.

Barriers to Effective Counseling With Native American Youth

Many potential barriers may prevent effective counseling with Native American children and adolescents. For example, many Native

American youth live as both Native Americans and as Americans. Most are attempting to retain their traditional values but are seeking as well to live in the dominant culture. This dualistic life places much stress and strain on these young people. Also, to further complicate counseling efforts, cultural and familial diversity among Native Americans negates the possibility of treating young people as a homogeneous group.

The social, cultural, and political influences discussed previously may produce a high degree of alienation among many Native American youth by the time they reach adolescence, the normally tumultuous period of psychological identity striving. These young people not only experience the very personal identity crisis of adolescence, but also the additional burden of the identity crisis of their culture. The psychological helplessness and increasing sense of hopelessness these circumstances create may serve to further alienate the youth from counseling professionals.

Another barrier to effective counseling with Native American youth reflects an important cultural dimension. Research indicates that Native Americans seldom look to traditional counseling processes as a means of improving their chosen way of life (LaFromboise, 1988). Many Native Americans recognize the need for professional aid only when community-based helping networks are unavailable or undesirable (Weinbach & Kuehner, 1985). Such reluctance to use professional counseling may also be attributable to Native Americans' historical memory of the often tragic interactions they have experienced with non-Native people. Additionally, many Native Americans believe that mental illness is a justifiable outcome of human weakness or the result of avoiding the discipline necessary to maintain cultural values and community respect (Harras, 1987).

Native Americans who enter counseling often express concern about how conventional Western psychology superimposes biases onto Native American problems and shapes the behavior of the client in a direction that conflicts with Native American cultural life-style orientations (LaFromboise, 1988). This incompatibility between conventional counseling approaches and indigenous approaches constitutes another possible barrier to effective counseling with Native American youth.

The Promise of a Proactive Perspective

Effective counseling with Native American children and adolescents is predicated on adopting a proactive developmental perspective. This would include gaining a thorough knowledge of past and contemporary Native American culture and history. It would also entail having an expanded understanding of the social and cultural challenges to the development of Native American young people.

Counseling professionals need to develop strategies to modify the effects of political, social, and economic forces on Native American youth. They may need to become systemic change agents, intervening in environments that impede the development of Native American youth (Eberhard, 1989). In the school setting, for example, they can encourage the revision of curricula to include the impact of cultural environment on Native American youth's behavior (Trimble, LaFromboise, Mackey, & France, 1982). They can also encourage Native American tribes and groups to assume a more active role in providing mental health services.

Direction for Counseling Practice

Counselors can be successful in their interactions with Native American youth. However, success often hinges on understanding traditional Native American cultural attitudes, beliefs, and values and being able to incorporate them into counseling interventions. Counselors also may need to become familiar with both content and process concerns when working with Native American youth (Herring, 1990b). Content concerns might include worldview differences between counselor and counselee or the special needs and unique problems of Native American youth, whereas process concerns might include varied levels of acculturation or differences in socioeconomic status.

The role of social influences in the counseling process as perceived by Native Americans may need to be considered. For example, the underuse of mental health services by Native Americans is associated with the tension surrounding power differentials in counseling relationships and perceived conflicting goals for acculturation between counselors and Native American clients (LaFromboise, Trimble, & Mohatt, 1990).

Given these concerns, the following are important ideas to consider for counseling practice with Native American youth in educational and related settings. From the beginning of the counseling encounter, Native American young people may be evaluating the total presentation of the counselor (e.g., manner of greeting, physical appearance, ethnicity, nonverbal behavior and communication, and other subtle characteristics). The first few minutes of the session are very important to its success or failure. The counselor has to demonstrate content knowledge of the culture to gain the respect of the young counselee. For example, awareness of the tribal identity and familial pattern of the counselee may need to be acknowledged immediately. Such an acknowledgment will convey to the young person the attitude and concern of the counselor relative to his or her understanding of Native American culture.

Counselors may also need to be aware of three distinct family patterns among Native Americans: (1) the *traditional* family, which overtly attempts to adhere to culturally defined styles of living; (2) the *nontraditional* family, which retains only rudimentary elements of historical Native American family life, preferring to live within the majority culture; and (3) the *pantraditional* family, which desires to return to an ancestral culture of nomadism and isolation from non-Native Americans (Herring & Erchul, 1988). Knowledge of these three distinct familial patterns is essential if appropriate counseling is to take place with Native American children and adolescents. Counselors need to be able to match their counseling strategies with the appropriate family pattern. A young person's family pattern may be recognized generally by choice of attire, manner of self-presentation, and location of residence (e.g., reservation, urban setting, rural location).

Given these family patterns, several ideas can be suggested to enhance effective counseling interventions with Native American children and adolescents. First, most Native American history and culture is characterized by an oral tradition of communication. In counseling activities, this oral tradition can easily be integrated with the Native American respect for elders. Community and tribal leaders can be effective resources in sharing customs and the "old way" through oral histories. Such oral communication can be an important adjunct to school guidance activities.

Second, counselors might consider using various media resources in their interventions. Media resources that are authentic and free from stereotypes and cultural bias are available. Easy-to-read books can assist elementary counselors in areas such as decision making, respect, cultural awareness, and learning. Examples of such readings include the Navajo story *Annie and the Old One* (Miles, 1971) or *Hokahey* (Dorian, 1957). More recent novels by Louise Erdrich and Mike Dorris as well as works by James Welch, Paula Gunn Allen, and Leslie Silko also provide stereotype-free readings.

More advanced students can benefit from the accurate portrayal of Native Americans and their culture in appropriate films. For example, movies such as "Cheyenne Autumn," "Windwalker," and "Soldier Blue" present graphic accounts of Cheyenne tribalism, as well as Native American interactions with non-Native Americans. "A Man Called Horse" and "Return of Horse" render graphic portrayals of Native American initiation rituals into warriorhood. "Sacred Ground" recounts the story of a mountain man and his Paiute wife unknowingly settling on a sacred Paiute burial ground. "Isaac Littlefeathers" describes how members of the Jewish faith help a Native American boy cope with contemporary racial prejudice. Films such as "The Last Warrior," "Thunder Warrior," and "Powwow Highway" also depict contemporary Native Americans' struggles with modern non-Native American society. "A Girl Called Hatter Fox" poignantly chronicles the plight of a Navajo girl's ordeals after being psychologically misdiagnosed as a drug-addicted juvenile delinquent.

Videos and films are also available depicting Native American art, crafts, and music. Such media examples can augment non-Native American perspectives, as well as expand Native American views about different tribal and clan characteristics. The counselor, however, must always remember not to generalize a particular media presentation to all Native Americans.

Conclusion

Native Americans have endured constant threats to their existence. These threats have taken their toll on the positive development of Native American young people. Consequently, counselors attempting to provide services to Native American children and adolescents face significant challenges. However, counseling professionals can be successful in promoting the development of these young people. Counseling success is contingent upon accepting and using traditional Native American attitudes, beliefs, and values in the helping process. Counselors who use this knowledge can expect more successful encounters with Native American youth.

References

Adler, P. M. (1985). Ethnic placement of refugee/entrant unaccompanied minors. *Child Welfare, 64*, 491–509.

American Indian Education Handbook Committee. (1982). *American Indian education handbook*. Sacramento: California State Department of Education.

American Indians, Eskimos and Aleuts on identified reservations and in the historic areas of Oklahoma (excluding urbanized areas): 1980 census of population. (1985, November). Washington, DC: U.S. Department of Commerce, Bureau of the Census. (Subject Report PC80–2–1D, Part 1).

Astin, A. W. (1982). *Minorities in American higher education*. San Francisco: Jossey-Bass.

Brod, R. L., & McQuiston, J. M. (1983). American Indian adult education and literacy: The first national survey. *Journal of American Indian Education, 1*(1), 1–16.

Bureau of Indian Affairs, U.S. Department of the Interior. (1987, January). *Indian service population and labor force estimates*. Washington, DC: Author.

Dorian, E. (1957). *Hokahey*. New York: McGraw-Hill.

Eberhard, D. R. (1989). American Indian education: A study of dropouts, 1980–1987. *Journal of American Indian Education, 29*(1), 32–40.

Fuller, M. L. (1986). Teachers' perceptions of children from intact and single-parent families. *The School Counselor, 33*, 365–374.

Harras, A. (1987). *Issues in adolescent Indian health: Suicide* (Division of Medical Systems Research and Development Monograph Series). Washington, DC: U.S. Department of Health and Human Services.

Herring, R. D. (1989). The American Native family: Dissolution by coercion. *Journal of Multicultural Counseling and Development, 17*, 4–13.

Herring, R. D. (1990a). Attacking career myths among Native Americans: Implications for counseling. *The School Counselor, 38*, 13–18.

Herring, R. D. (1990b). Understanding Native American values: Process and content concerns for counselors. *Counseling and Values, 34*, 134–137.

Herring, R. D., & Erchul, W. P. (1988). *The applicability of Olson's Circumplex Model to Native American families* (RC 017 116). Ann Arbor, MI: University of Michigan. (ERIC/CRESS AEL Document Service No. ED 308 050).

Miles, M. (1971). *Annie and the Old One*. Boston: Little-Brown.

LaFromboise, T. D. (1988). American Indian mental health policy. *American Psychologist, 43*, 388–397.

LaFromboise, T. D., Trimble, J. E., & Mohatt, G. V. (1990). Counseling intervention and American Indian tradition: An integrative approach. *The Counseling Psychologist, 48*, 628–654.

National Center for Educational Statistics. (1989). *Dropout rates in the U.S.: 1988*. Washington, DC: Author.

Schafer, C. (1990). Natividad cautions counselors to guard against stereotypes. *Guidepost, 32*(14), 4, 22.

Trimble, J. E., LaFromboise, T., Mackey, D., & France, G. (1982). American Indians, psychology and curriculum development: A proposal reform with reservations. In J. Chunn & F. Ross-Sheriff (Eds.), *Mental health and people of color* (pp. 43–64). Washington, DC: Howard University Press.

Unger, S. (Ed.). (1977). *The destruction of American Indian families*. New York: The Association of American Indian Affairs.

U.S. Senate Select Committee on Indian Affairs. (1985). *Indian juvenile alcoholism and eligibility for BIA schools* (Senate Hearing 99–286). Washington, DC: U.S. Government Printing Office.

Weinbach, R. W., & Kuehner, K. M. (1985). Selecting the provider of continuing education for child welfare agencies. *Child Welfare, 64*, 477–488.

Additional Resources

Boyd, D. (1974). *Rolling Thunder*. New York: Random House.

Boyer, L. R. (1981). *United States Indians: A brief history*. Reynoldsburg, OH: Advocate Publishing.

Bryde, J. F. (1971). *Indian students and guidance*. Boston: Houghton Mifflin.

Burland, C. (1965). *North American Indian mythology*. London: Hamlyn Publishing Group.

Carlin, G. (1989). *North American Indians*. New York: Penguin.

Marriott, A., & Rachlin, C. K. (1968). *American Indian mythology*. New York: Mentor.

Neihardt, J. G. (Flaming Rainbow). (1961). *Black Elk speaks: Being the life story of a Holy Man of the Oglala Sioux*. Lincoln, NB: University of Nebraska Press.

Turner, F. W., III. (Ed.). (1977). *The portable North American Indian reader*. New York: Penguin.

Walters, F. (1977). *Book of the Hopi*. New York: Penguin.

Washburn, W. E. (Ed.). (1964). *The Indian and the white man*. New York: Anchor Books.

Weatherford, J. (1988). *Indian givers: How the Indians of the Americas transformed the world*. New York: Crown.

Zychowicz, M. J. (1975). *American Indian teachings as a philosophical base for counseling and psychotherapy*. Unpublished doctoral dissertation, Northern Illinois University, De Kalb.

THE AFRICAN
AMERICAN EXPERIENCE

Counseling interventions with African Americans should be predicated on an understanding of their culture and its crucial role in fostering optimal mental health. An examination of this culture will reveal that Americans of African descent have developed a worldview that is grounded in African-oriented philosophical assumptions. These assumptions constitute a cultural tradition that places a high premium on harmony among people and fosters development through cognitive, affective, and behavioral expressiveness.

Counseling professionals need to find ways to incorporate African American cultural dimensions into the helping process. For example, kinship or collective unity is an important consideration for African American mental health intervention. Group approaches to counseling, therefore, constitute important culturally responsive strategies with African American client populations.

Likewise, within African American communities, institutions that provide a network of indigenous social support can be incorporated into the counseling process. The African American church is one of these traditional institutions that has been instrumental in promoting psychological well-being. A culturally skilled counseling professional will explore ways to incorporate the resources of indigenous sources of support, such as the African American church, into the counseling process.

Chapter 5
COUNSELING AFRICAN AMERICAN WOMEN: "SISTER-FRIENDS"

Janice M. Jordan

African American women have historically been one of the most oppressed groups in U.S. history. They have been oppressed as African Americans, as women, and often as members of the lower socioeconomic group (Collier, 1982). Often in statistical reports, the African American woman is reported as a woman or as a minority, making it difficult to distinguish her from White women or all minorities. Because she is represented in labor force statistics in two categories, she is often sought for employment by organizations needing to increase their numbers of minorities or women. However, little is known about her, nor does it seem that many care to know more.

Stereotypes and myths, many originating in slavery, are still a part of the perception that many people have of African American women. They have been referred to as domineering, emasculating, promiscuous, and as superwomen (Helms, 1979). These stereotypes developed from the failure of society to place the behaviors of the African American woman in context. Historically, African American men have been denied the privileges thought to be inherent in manhood (Lee, 1987), especially the right to support and protect their families. As a consequence, the African American woman has had to accept the challenge of working hard, most often in menial positions, to take care of the family. During slavery the men were sold, and later they were denied access to a job that paid enough to support a family. Out of necessity the woman often seemed to be dominating, controlling. It was this behavior that was also seen to be emasculating. She was forced into sexual relationships with the more powerful White men, but bore the shame in the form of children and the promiscuous label. Perhaps the most unfortunate consequence of the stereotypes and myths is that many African American women have internalized them as truth (Helms, 1979).

The contemporary women's movement has done little to address the plight of the African American woman. Initially those rights for which the movement pushed, particularly the right to work outside the home, were foreign to a group that had always had to work outside the home, even when considered middle class, and would have loved to have the option. The women's movement was perceived as a movement of and for White middle-class women. Also, African American women tended to perceive their condition primarily as a result of racism rather than sexism (Collier, 1982). Many felt that it was racism that kept the women's movement silent on issues of concern to Black women. Although the women's movement encouraged research on women and better strategies for meeting women's needs, it seemed that the research and the strategies were conspicuously geared to the White middle-class woman.

The counseling profession has been equally remiss in attending to African American women (Helms, 1979). The underlying humanism of the counseling profession, which advocates that all individuals be treated equally in counseling encounters, has worked against helping the African American woman develop her fullest potentials (Jackson, 1980). Counselors must possess more than the knowledge of accepted practices for women in general. They must acquire an appreciation for the African American culture, the importance of women in that culture, and the manner in which the culture has helped to define the role of women. In doing so, counselors will begin to understand the effects of the oppression against which African American women have historically struggled.

The purpose of this chapter is to present the practicing counselor with some knowledge and skills for counseling African American women from a developmental, proactive perspective. A brief discussion of developmental issues will be followed by a section on issues to consider in counseling African American women. A developmental counseling intervention model is then presented.

Sociocultural Challenges to African American Female Development

Traditional theories of human development cannot easily be applied to the development of the African American woman. The interplay and presses of two cultures, often in conflict, play a major role in the development of her womanhood. Traditional theories, built mostly on research with members of the dominant culture, postulate that the development of trust is an essential first task. The experiences of African Americans with the dominant culture, however, have taught them that trust, especially of Whites, must be limited. Instead, African American women have learned what Grier and Cobbs (1968) termed a "healthy paranoia."

Independence is another major developmental task. Jeffries (1976) observed that Black girls of lower socioeconomic status tend to take on the adult responsibility of caring for the house and siblings at an early age. A shortened period of carefree childhood results. This physical independence may result in a false sense of womanhood, leading African American girls into adult behaviors for which they are neither economically nor emotionally ready.

The most important, most complex, and most difficult developmental task is identity formation. Adolescence has been widely accepted as the period of time most crucial for this task. An integral component of identity formation for women is physical beauty. No matter how much a young girl or adolescent hears the parental message that internal beauty is paramount, the strong impact of the media takes its toll. This is a particularly unfortunate situation for the African American woman. They do not see themselves in the pictures of beauty and womanhood presented by the media. However, Black women have made Herculean attempts to make themselves more like the pictures, more like the oppressor (Memmi, 1967). They have suffered the blotches of bleaching creams and the harshness of hair straighteners, all in futile efforts to be accepted as attractive, as women.

All these presses have been stressors in the development of the African American woman. She has had to face developmental challenges without concomitant support. As a result she has developed a self-reliance, independence, and sense of responsibility that are positive, not negative, traits (Collier, 1982). It is only when these traits are taken to the extreme, or are not perceived as positive by the woman herself, that they create problems for the African American woman.

African American Culture and Mental Health

Theories that explain the development of the self in the context of African American awareness emphasize that a positive sense of self and mental health are determined by how accepting and proud a woman is of her blackness (Kirk, 1975). The ultimate stage of development in these theories is the integration of a woman's pride and dignity as a Black with the acceptance of her part in society. This leads to confidence about the self as part of the external world (Kirk, 1975). Denial or rejection of her blackness, an integral part of self, results in an unhealthy state. Therefore, counseling programs for African American women must help them move toward the ultimate stage of self-development. Anything less can only be antidevelopmental.

Consideration must also be given to the delivery of services from an African American worldview. This entails an emphasis on the development of the group as well as the self and on the importance of the harmony among all things—humans and nature, internal and external (Nobles, 1980). African American women must feel free to express themselves in their own language and rhythms. "When many ethnic subjects are asked to perceive or describe themselves . . . they may attain greater specificity and finer discrimination when they do so in a familiar idiom, and conversely, may lose subtlety and complexity if they are required to do so in standard English" (Jones & Korchin, 1982, p. 24).

Barriers to Effective Counseling

As American society as a whole has become more mobile, many African American families no longer live in close geographical proximity. The immediate and extended families, as well as the church, have traditionally been therapeutic forces for the African American woman. The loss of these traditional forces has led to an increased incidence of psychological distress. However, the African American woman, especially if she is from the core community (Pasteur & Toldson, 1982), is often reluctant to seek help from professional sources. Her unwillingness to "tell her business" and her belief that she should be able to handle her own life feed this reluctance.

Another barrier to effective counseling with African American women is the very real issue of what to do with children while the mother is in a counseling session. If forced to choose between giving time to self for counseling and staying home with her children, most African American women will choose to stay home. A counseling program wishing to serve women with small children will also provide for concurrent child-care. Women of lower socioeconomic status will also have difficulty with transportation unless counseling is made available within their communities.

The Developmental Approach

The developmental approach to counseling African American women focuses on assisting them in working toward their fullest potential. This approach will also help women to dispel myths and stereotypes in order to allow counseling for identity formation to be as proactive as possible. However, the African American woman will already have felt some of the stresses of being Black in White society. She will come to the counseling encounters having experienced the pulls from family, work, and society. The professional will have already faced the loneliness and isolation of being a Black professional woman. The developmental approach to counseling acknowledges and accepts that stresses exist, that they are a natural part of being in society, but that with help from peers they can be minimized, thus preventing dysfunction.

One caveat to counselors is that all African American women are not alike. Common threads are their blackness and their womanhood, and society's response to them because of their membership in these two groups. Economically, socially, and politically they run the gamut from rich and powerful to poor and powerless (Jeffries, 1976). Therefore, the counselor must attend to individual differences as well as to group characteristics and environmental presses that affect the African American woman.

Group Counseling Experience for African American Women: "Sister-Friends"

The group counseling experience described here is entitled "Sister-Friends." It is a proactive approach designed to assist African American women develop pride and dignity as Black women. "Sister-Friends" is a title borrowed from author-poet Maya Angelou. Randolph (1990) stated that having sister-friends can often be "the difference between holding on or letting go, going on or giving in" (p. 38). Sister-friends have always played an important role in the lives and development of African American women. Sister-friends are honest, protective, nurturing, and powerful (Randolph). They understand and share the stresses of being a Black woman in the United States. As quoted in Randolph (1990), Angelou stated:

> The relationship between Black women who are chosen sisters provides a climate where each can revel in the other's triumph without the crippling factor of jealousy entering into the revelry. And with sister-friends, one sister can inform the other of unacceptable behavior and make the sister laugh at herself. . . . Having a sister means I can cry and my sister-friend will know the difference between being sad and being sorry. A sister-friend—another Black woman—will know that life will make you cry. (p. 42)

This group experience is a multisession, developmental opportunity for Black women to move toward fulfilling their fullest potential in a challenging, but supportive, atmosphere.

This model for counseling African American women is designed to be community-based. It can be conducted in churches, community centers, educational institutions, or any other venue within the community of the participants. It is imperative that this group be facilitated by an African American woman. If a counselor is not available, a competent, sensitive African American woman should be sought out and trained to facilitate. Postsession meetings can be held to process sessions and plan for future sessions. Participants in the experience presented here should be 18 years of age or older. The optimal group size is 8 to 10 participants. Heterogeneity of group participants in terms of age, education, family status, and socioeconomic status will provide the wealth of experiences necessary for developing "sister-friends."

The model presented is an eight-session model, with each session lasting approximately 2 hours. Longer sessions will tend to result in participant dropout due to family obligations at potentially crucial junctures in the sessions. This same concern makes the provision of on-site competent, concurrent child-care services an essential component of the group plan when participants have children. The presence of men will inhibit the women from forming the network intended by this group experience. Those interested in a similar experience for African American men are directed to the work of Lee (1990).

The Model

The model is intended to assist African American women to heighten their awareness and appreciation of the uniqueness and beauty of Black womanhood. In addition, this experience is designed to enable participants to widen their support network of women who share a common experience.

Session 1: Introductions

Goal: To have participants begin thinking about and sharing experiences of being an African American woman.

Process:

1. Facilitator introduces herself and explains the purpose of the group experience. Inform participants of the goal of this session.

2. Facilitator then should assure participants of the confidentiality of the sessions.

3. Have participants introduce themselves by name.

4. Initiate group input for other ground rules for the sessions. Facilitator will want to let participants know that they will get the most from the experience if they participate actively by sharing and listening carefully to others; by offering feedback that can be challenging, but not threatening; and by giving support to their sisters. Participants should

be encouraged to talk about any other group rules that will help them to feel comfortable in sharing their experiences.

5. When ground rules have been set, have the participants introduce themselves again. This time ask them to include the phrase, "To me, being an African American woman in the United States means. . ."

6. After all introductions have been made, allow participants to ask each other any questions related to their introductions.

7. Discuss statements participants make, asking them to create a group statement that would begin "To us, being African American women in the United States means. . ." Write this group statement on newsprint or chalkboard visible to all participants.

8. End the session by asking participants to share their feelings about being at this session.

9. Summarize the activities of the session and announce the topic for the next session.

10. Encourage participants to think about the group statement between sessions in order to refine it if necessary.

Session 2: Queens and Priestesses

Goal: To help participants increase dignity through knowledge and appreciation for the noble origins of Black women.

Process:

1. Elicit from participants any further thoughts or feelings about the last session. Process.

2. Introduce the focus for the present session.

3. Ask participants to share what they know about the roles and images of ancient Black women.

4. Read passage about priestesses from part 1 of Alice Walker's *The Temple of My Familiar* (1989). The passage begins: "Now the story of the priests is a sad one. . ." and ends at the conclusion of the chapter.

5. Initiate a discussion of the passage with questions such as: What does this particular passage mean to you? How does this make you feel as a Black woman? How does this passage relate to our group definition from last week?

6. Ask the group if anyone feels a need to change the group statement/definition of African American women in any way. If changes are suggested, make sure that they are consensus changes.

7. End the session by asking participants to express their feelings about the current session. Process.

8. Have participants read aloud in unison the current group definition of African American women. Encourage participants to continue to explore this definition.

9. Inform participants of the topic for the next session.

Note: Inform participants that session 8 will be a celebration.

Session 3: Recent Roots

Goal: To increase participants' awareness of their more recent origins as African American women.

Process:

1. Ask participants to share any reactions from last session. Process.

2. Introduce participants to the current session's topic by saying, "Last session we explored our beginnings as queens and priestesses in ancient times. Today let's move forward and look at our more immediate roots."

3. Have participants take a few moments to remember the oldest female family member they know or have known.

4. Have each participant take a few minutes to share with the group who the family member is and what she most remembers about her.

5. Initiate further discussion by asking: "What special traits, abilities, or talents have you learned or inherited from this woman? What other women in your family have special meaning for you and why? What spiritual connection do you feel with them?

6. Ask participants to share with the group the *one* bit of wisdom they consider most influential in their lives that they learned from a grandmother, great grandmother, great aunt, or another person.

7. Have participants reconsider the group definition in terms of the changes, if any, the identified influential woman would make.

8. Discuss the reasons for any changes.

9. Ask participants if the group wishes to make any changes in their definition. Changes must be consensus changes.

10. Inform the group of the topic for the next session. Encourage them to express their feelings about the group experience through their writings, drawings/paintings, songs, or dance in order to share them in session 8.

11. Have participants read aloud in unison the group definition of African American women.

Session 4: Self

Goal: To increase participants' awareness of their concept of self and the role that concept plays in their treatment of themselves.

Process:

1. Ask participants for any reactions to the last session. Process.

2. Introduce the focus for the current session by explaining the importance of self-concept in everyday living.

3. Ask participants to consider what they think about themselves and how they perceive themselves. Emphasize that they should do this as best they can without considering their relationships to others. Encourage them to avoid thinking about themselves in such roles as mother, wife, or daughter.

4. Have participants share their images.

5. Ask participants about the level of difficulty of thinking about themselves apart from others. Explore what makes that difficult.

6. Ask participants to share what time they take for themselves and how they spend that time. Ask how they feel when they do take time for themselves.

7. Encourage the group to help those participants who state they do not have time by suggesting ways they can create that time in their busy schedules.

8. Explain the importance of taking time for oneself and how we are more apt to create that time if our image of ourselves is more positive; how giving time to ourselves also benefits those around us.

9. Assign each participant the *pleasure* of taking at least one half hour of time for herself before the next session.

10. Ask participants to consider the group definition for any changes they would like to make.

11. Inform participants of the focus for the next session.

12. Have participants read aloud in unison the group definition of African American women.

Session 5: Physical and Spiritual Beauty

Goal: To assist participants to enhance the appreciation of their African beauty and to explore the role spirituality plays in their lives.

Process:

1. Ask participants for reactions from last session. Have participants share how they spent their assigned time and their feelings about it.

2. Introduce the topic for the session.

3. Lead participants in a discussion of what is beautiful and what is not. Ask participants to talk first only about physical beauty.

4. Have participants share any experiences they have had in doing things to look different than they naturally do.

5. Explore the role of spirituality in the lives of the participants. Emphasize that spirituality transcends organized religion and religious belief.

6. Ask participants for any changes they would like to make in their group definition.

7. Inform the group of the topic for the next session.

8. Have participants read aloud in unison the group definition of African American women.

Note: The topic of physical beauty always seems to lead to prolonged discussion, especially when Black women begin to talk about hair. The facilitator will need to pay particular attention to time. She will also need to confront any negativity about African features with scientific reasons for their existence as well with as information about African standards of beauty that differ from European standards.

Session 6: Paying Family Dues

Goal: To increase participants' awareness of the nature and origins of their role responsibilities in African American families.

Process:

1. Ask participants for any reactions to last session's topic.

2. Introduce the topic for the current session with an explanation about the importance of family and the responsibility the African American woman has usually had to assume in the family.

3. Ask participants to express their feelings about their role responsibilities in their families.

4. Engage participants in a discussion centering around the questions: Do your family responsibilities sometimes feel too burdensome? How did you get these responsibilities? Are they prescribed by family tradition or are they self-imposed? If they are self-imposed and they feel too burdensome, what can you do to relieve some of the burden?

5. Have participants generate one strategy for relieving any burden they have talked about and ask them to try that between sessions.

6. Ask participants for any changes in the group definition.

7. Have participants read aloud in unison the group definition.

Session 7: Female/Male Relationships

Goal: To provide a safe, supportive forum for participants to examine and share feelings about relationships between African American women and men.

Process:

1. Ask for any reactions from the previous session. Process.

2. Introduce the focus of the current session. Encourage participants not to get into men bashing.

3. Ask participants to share their concerns about the status of the relationship between African American women and men. Ask for feelings they have about the future of that relationship.

4. Have participants brainstorm solutions to any problems they may have identified.

5. Inform participants that the last session will be a celebration of African American women. Encourage them to bring in any of their writings, drawings, or music that celebrate their womanhood.

6. Ask for any changes to the group definition of African American women.

7. Have participants read aloud in unison the group definition.

Session 8: Celebration

Goal: To provide closure to the group experience by having participants celebrate their African American womanhood.

Process:

1. Ask participants for any final changes in the group definition of African American women. Make those changes. Have each participant write the final definition on an index card that she will take with her.

2. Start the celebration with the group reading aloud in unison the group definition.

3. Have participants who have brought in creations share them with the group in their respective forms. Allow ample time for this.

4. Have participants say goodbye to each other and the group experience in the manner most comfortable for them.

The model presented in this chapter is meant to be only a starting point for the group counseling of African American women. After experience with the present model, counselors may need or want to adapt it for use with a younger group. Several components of the model, however, should be retained to create the bonding for "sister-friends." The first is the group's definition of themselves as women and the group reaffirmation of this at the end of each session. Also, the opportunity for the participants to express themselves through their own media in their own rhythms should never be eliminated. Celebration is essential as well.

Counselors may want to increase their own knowledge about Black women, their lives, and their feelings by reading such novelists as Maya Angelou, Alice Walker, Toni Morrison, and Gloria Naylor, to name only a few modern ones. References and Additional Resources for this chapter will also serve as a valuable tool for counselors. In order to stay abreast of African American women today, it is recommended that counselors read current African American publications such as *Ebony*, *Essence*, and *American Visions*.

Conclusion

There is no one way in which African American women should be counseled. However, it is not enough to colorize participants in a traditional counseling model. African American women have suffered enough from inattention on the part of the profession. They deserve to have the profession begin to create specific interventions for them. The counselor who attempts to do so must have a heightened awareness of and appreciation for African American womanhood, at least a basic knowledge of the history and culture of African Americans, and the flexibility to flow with the current of the group.

References

Collier, H. (1982). *Counseling women: A guide for therapists*. New York: Free Press.

Helms, J. (1979). Black women. *The Counseling Psychologist, 8*, 40–41.

Jeffries, D. (1976). Counseling for the strengths of the black woman. *The Counseling Psychologist, 6*(2), 20–22.

Jones, E., & Korchin, S. (1982). Minority mental health: Perspectives. In E. Jones & S. Korchin (Eds.), *Minority mental health*. New York: Praeger.

Kirk, W. (1975). Where are you? Black mental health model. *Journal of Non-White Concerns in Personnel and Guidance, 3*, 177–188.

Lee, C. C. (1987). Black manhood training: Group counseling for male blacks in grades 7–12. *Journal for Specialists in Group Work, 12*, 18–25.

Lee, C. C. (1990). Black male development: Counseling the "Native Son." In D. Moore & F. Leafgren (Eds.), *Problem solving strategies and interventions for men in conflict*. Alexandria, VA: American Association for Counseling and Development.

Memmi, A. (1967). *The colonizer and the colonized*. Boston: Beacon Press.

Nobles, W. (1980). The psychology of Black Americans: An historical perspective. In R. Jones (Ed.), *Black psychology* (2nd ed.). New York: Harper & Row.

Pasteur, A., & Toldson, I. (1982). *Roots of Soul: The psychology of Black expressiveness*. New York: Anchor Press/Doubleday.

Randolph, L. (1990, July). Networks help celebrities deal with fame and pain. *Ebony*, pp. 36–42.

Walker, A. (1989). *The temple of my familiar*. New York: Harcourt Brace Jovanovich.

Additional Resources

American Visions: The Magazine of Afro-American Culture. Washington, DC: The Visions Foundation.

Angelou, M. (1974). *Gather together in my mame*. New York: Random House.

Angelou, M. (1977). *Singing and swinging and getting merry like Christmas*. New York: Bantam Books.

Angelou, M. (1981). *The heart of a woman*. New York: Random House.

Angelou, M. (1986). *All God's children need traveling shoes*. New York: Random House.

Bennett, L. (Ed.). *Ebony*. Chicago: Johnson Pub. Co.

Giddings, P. (1984). *When and where I enter: The impact of black women on race and sex in America*. New York: Morrow.

Grier, W. H., & Cobbs, P. M. (1968). *Black rage*. New York: Basic Books.

Hay, M. (1988). *Queens, prostitutes, and peasants*. Boston: African Studies Center.

Hull, G., Scott, P., & Smith, B. (Eds.). (1982). *All the women are white, all the blacks are men, but some of us are brave*. Old Westbury, NY: Feminist Press.

Jackson, G. G. (1980). The emergence of a black perspective in counseling. In R. L. Jones (Ed.), *Black psychology* (pp. 294–313). New York: Harper & Row.

Jones, J. (1985). *Labor of love, labor of sorrow*. New York: Basic Books.

Moore, E. K., Vassall, M. A., & Wilson, G. (1985). *Beyond the stereotypes: A guide to resources for Black girls and young women*. Washington, DC: National Black Child Development Institute.

Morrison, T. (1972). *The bluest eye*. New York: Washington Square Press.

Naylor, G. (1983). *The women of Brewster Place*. New York: Penguin.

Sterling, D. (1979). *Black foremothers*. Old Westbury, NY: Feminist Press.

Taylor, S. (Ed.). *Essence*. New York: Essence Communications.

Terborg-Penn, R., Harley, S., & Rushing, A. (1987). *Women in Africa and the African Diaspora*. Washington, DC: Howard University Press.

Chapter 6

UTILIZING THE RESOURCES OF THE AFRICAN AMERICAN CHURCH: STRATEGIES FOR COUNSELING PROFESSIONALS

Bernard L. Richardson

A growing awareness in the mental health profession is that counselors who want to be effective in African American communities must discover and use nontraditional methods of service delivery (June, 1986; Lee, 1990). June suggested an aggressive outreach strategy that utilizes indigenous helping resources in these communities. Smith (1982) argued that counselors cannot ignore the cultural or social and historical context in which they practice. Therefore, counseling practice with African Americans should incorporate those institutions, organizations, and strategies that are consistent with their cultural and life experiences.

The African American church is an indigenous institution that counseling professionals can turn to in providing counseling services to African Americans (Boyd-Franklin, 1989; June, 1986; Richardson, 1989). In this chapter the term **African American church** is used in a generic sense to describe the traditions of those religious institutions in African American communities represented by a variety of Christian denominations. Smith (1982) described the African American church as having been born in bondage. "It was, from its inception, a servant church embedded and engaged in the anguish and freedom of an oppressed people" (p. 15). Slavery and then segregation denied African Americans access to the rights and privileges accorded other Americans. The church was the only institution that African Americans had to meet their emotional, spiritual, and material needs. Today, the church remains at the center of community life, attending to the social, spiritual, and psychological needs of scores of African Americans. No other institution claims the loyalty and attention of African Americans as does the church. Boyd-Franklin (1989) described the church as a "multifunctional community institution," serving the needs of a disfranchised population. The sig-

65

nificance of the church among African Americans has important implications for providing mental health services. Setting assumes important
dimensions when counseling African Americans. Many associate traditional counseling settings with institutional or individual racism. Settings
perceived as oppressive or racist may promote a defensive posture among
many African Americans, which may hinder therapeutic progress (Katz,
1985; Sue, McKinney, Allen, & Hall, 1974). The African American church
offers a familiar and supportive environment for counseling. In this
environment, individuals may confront issues that affect their lives in
an open and honest way.

African American Religion and Spirituality: Their Role in Mental Health

There are many reasons why the African American church should
be considered as a vehicle for providing mental health services. One
important reason is related to the role of religion and spirituality in the
lives of African Americans (Mbiti, 1969; Frazier, 1963). "Some of the
most cogent historical and psychosocial experiences of Black Afro-Amer-
icans and their families are strongly rooted in religious and spiritual
background and experience" (Boyd-Franklin 1989, p. 91). The church
is, therefore, the key symbol and the vehicle of expression of religion
and spirituality for many African Americans. Ironically, it is this spiritual
and religious orientation that may be at the root of why the African
American church has not been utilized by many counseling professionals,
who may have a conscious or unconscious desire to stay clear of religious
or spiritual issues and symbols in the treatment process. Many counselors
are not trained to deal with such issues and thus often ignore religion
and spirituality as therapeutic concerns even when initiated by clients.
This failure to consider the issues of religion and spirituality in counseling, especially when they play such an important role in the lives of
many African Americans, will undoubtedly result in less than successful
outcomes. Therefore, counseling professionals who work with African
Americans should be sensitive to the possible roles religion and spirituality play clients' lives. This does not mean that a counselor must be
theologically trained to work with African Americans for whom religion
and spirituality are important. To be sensitive within this context means
a willingness to explore with clients the role that these issues play in their
lives.

Knox (1985) documented, in her work with African American alcoholics and their families, that spiritual beliefs have become a part of
the survival system of African Americans. She argued that these "coping

methods" should be explored just as any other psychosocial area in the assessment process. Accordingly, Lovinger's (1984) insight about the role of religion in the lives of clients is especially relevant for working with African Americans:

> . . . a patient's religious belief and experiences contain impor-
> tant meanings about past experiences and can characterize the
> quality of a patient's relationship with others. When these issues
> emerge in therapy, they can aid therapy if approached with
> interest and respect. None of this requires any change in the
> therapist's own attitudes toward religion, other than relinquish-
> ing (if held) that religion is silly or meaningless. No phenomena
> can be usefully approached this way. (Preface)

The proclivity toward religion and spirituality does not mean that African Americans are not amenable to psychological interpretations and insights. The author has observed in counseling African Americans in both pastoral and secular situations that many interpret the events of their lives theologically as well as psychologically. The following was related to the author at the close of an initial session in a pastoral context by an African American client who was himself a mental health worker:

> This session made me realize that I am now ready to deal with
> some of the issues that I have been resisting for some time. I
> wish the process didn't have to be so painful. I guess it is true
> that it sometimes hurts to grow. I wonder what God is trying
> to teach me by this trial?

Accordingly, this author agrees with Smith (1982) that many African Americans seek out certain counselors because of their religious and pastoral identification.

It must be acknowledged that many counseling professionals are reluctant to engage in any dialogue concerning religious or spiritual beliefs not because of a disregard of these beliefs but because they fear that they would not know how to integrate the information into their own understanding of the dynamics of human behavior. In counseling situations where a client's religious belief is counterproductive to positive mental health, such a fear on the part of the counselor can lead to unsuccessful therapeutic outcomes. In working through this type of im-passe, counseling professionals may consider enlisting the aid of the church. In counseling situations where a mental health professional feels that a client's belief is counterproductive to positive mental health, he or she should consult with a clergyperson. The counseling professional should not assume that the client's belief is supported by the client's pastor or church. After consulting with the client's pastor, the counselor might recommend that the client receive instruction from the church about particular beliefs. A counselor should be as comfortable consulting a member of the clergy about a client's religious belief and its possible effect on the helping process as consulting a physician about a physical condition that might affect medical treatment. This kind of collaborative relationship could enhance the quality of care counseling professionals provide.

The Role Of African American Clergy

At the center of the church is the African American clergy, who have traditionally been recognized as major leaders in their respective communities. In attending to spiritual needs, they have had a significant influence on mental health interventions. Often the pastoral counseling activity has represented the only resource available to address emotional and psychological crises (Washington, 1964). An important aspect of the clergyperson's role that has important implications for mental health practitioners is that of **pastoral initiative.** Historically, clergy are expected to go where the people are and intervene when necessary on their own initiative and without specific invitation (Switzer, 1986). Switzer, in discussing the idea of pastoral initiative, rightly noted that with their entree to homes, clergy are able to discover problems in their early stages.

Another important aspect of the counseling that clergy perform is that clergypersons usually have prior relationships with the people who seek them out for counseling. Clergy, therefore, often may have an understanding of the family dynamics and living conditions of their parishioners. The unique role of African American clergy also affords them the opportunity to provide counseling that is proactive and preventive. Through activities such as educational programs, sermons, and interaction in organizations and business meetings, the minister, unlike other professionals, has an ongoing opportunity to educate people about potentially harmful situations in the community and potentially harmful individual behaviors. Switzer (1986), in discussing the role of ministers in crisis intervention, suggested that the clergyperson is unique in that no other professional has the kind of "platform or organizational context" in which to engage in sound education for mental health and problem solving. With the support of pastors and church leaders, the resources of the church can be available to counseling professionals. Counseling professionals have tremendous opportunities to be an instrumental part of the proactive and preventive aspect of the African American church. For example, workshops on such topics as addiction, parenting, male/female relationships, education, racism, and sexism are greatly needed in many African American communities. With the assistance and the cooperation of the pastor, counseling professionals can provide preventive counseling services to these communities.

It is recognized that the clergy's role is unique and that the mental health practitioner may not be able to duplicate their strategies and techniques. Mental health practitioners in partnership with clergy, however, can use the unique resources of the African American church to offer a more comprehensive, aggressive, and indigenous outreach program in African American communities. Nowhere is this more evident than in the area of referral. The counseling professional who has developed a working relationship with an African American pastor has access to a referral system that can enhance the relationship between counselor and client. A person is more likely to participate in counseling and feel more comfortable with a counselor who has the respect and trust of his or her pastor.

Considering the importance of counseling services, it is a cause for concern that the majority of these services aimed at African American communities do not have working relationships with churches and clergy. Boyd-Franklin (1989), drawing from her work with African American families, noted with amazement that mental health practitioners will routinely contact clinics, hospitals, or counselors who have previously worked with clients but will not make contact with ministers. She further noted that when a family counselor recognizes the significance of religious values for a client and is aware of the resources of the African American church, four types of intervention are possible: (1) involving a minister as a consultant, cocounselor, or integral part of the treatment process; (2) mobilizing the resources of the Black church network to help a family in crisis; (3) utilizing church networks as support for a family during times of illness, death, or loss; and (4) helping isolated African American families who are cut off from their original networks to create new ones.

A popular notion exists that the reason for the absence of working relationships between African American clergy and mental health professionals is that members of this clergy are not supportive of mental health professionals. It is believed that African American clergy are threatened and fear the loss of parishioners who would seek only psychological solutions to their problems. Research evidence suggests, however, that African American clergy hold favorable attitudes toward mental health professionals (Richardson, 1989). An important implication of this research is that the possibility exists for African American clergy and mental health professionals to work together to foster the social, spiritual, and psychological well-being of people in African American communities.

Intervention Strategies Using the Resources of the African American Church

The African American church provides counselors with a setting that can facilitate various intervention strategies. Two modes of intervention that can be used in counseling with African Americans are: (1) intervention that focuses on the church as a support system and (2) intervention that addresses systemic problems that affect African Americans. These intervention strategies utilize the many resources within the African American church.

Intervention That Focuses on the Church as a Support System

The African American church is in a unique position to bolster the self-esteem of its members. This is critically important when self-esteem has been negatively affected by the forces of racism and oppression, which is often the case with African Americans. A historical role of the church has been to provide a primary source for the development of African American self-esteem. The African American church provides avenues of self-expression and efficacy via church offices, titles, and responsibilities. Individuals who find their level of self-efficacy diminished by limited opportunities and who have jobs that do little to enhance self-esteem, gain a strong sense of self-respect and community recognition as a result of positions they hold in African American churches.

The communal aspect of working within the church serves to strengthen individual and group identity. The heritage of African Americans lends credence to this cultural phenomenon. Mbiti (1969), in his research on West African civilization, maintained that for the African, group membership is the preeminent source of identification in the development of a sense of self. Nobles (1972) stressed the importance of the African philosophical notion of kinship or collective unity as an important foundation for African American mental health intervention. Within this context, counselors could use the African American church as a support system for individuals facing various life challenges. For example, the church could be an important helping resource for individuals recently released from prison or others needing assistance in adjusting to community life.

The African American church has always emphasized the need for strong families, and, as part of its religious tradition, provides teachings and programs that support family life. The African American church, therefore, can also be utilized as a support system in the treatment of African American families (Boyd-Franklin, 1989). She argued that it is important for counselors to understand the concept of the "church family" as it relates to African Americans. Boyd-Franklin noted that for many African Americans the church functions as an extended family and as a surrogate family for single mothers. Another important family function of the African American church Boyd-Franklin identified is that of providing role models for young people. Finally, the church serves a social function by providing families the opportunity to mingle. It is significant to note that many African American parents who live in all-White neighborhoods and whose children attend predominantly White schools seek out African American churches not only for spiritual edification, but for the positive African American identity they instill in their children.

Counselors can utilize these unique resources in working with African American families. One strategy Boyd-Franklin (1989) suggested is for counselors to identify the church as a social support resource for isolated families who have a religious orientation. She noted that some African American families who enter community mental health centers are "socially isolated and emotionally cut off from their extended families." She asserted that assisting isolated African American families in identifying and locating a new church network can be a significant intervention. Boyd-Franklin rightly cautioned that this intervention is not for everyone. "It should be made only if it appears syntonic with the family's belief systems and earlier experiences" (p. 91).

Although the church can be a potent supportive resource, it is important to note that mental health professionals traditionally have considered it to be an institution that is noncompromising and holds a narrow perspective on morals and values. They often fail to recognize that in certain cases, the identification with the church can appropriately reinforce an individual's moral and ethical belief system. As an example, clergy, working in concert with counseling professionals, can offer alternatives and support to people contemplating engaging in self-destructive and community-disruptive economic enterprises such as the illegal drug trade. Such alternatives and support might include church-sponsored community forums that offer testimonials by former addicts and drug dealers who can point out the long-term negative effects of selling drugs.

Intervention That Addresses Systemic Problems That Affect African Americans

Historically the African American church has played a key role in fostering social change at the community and societal levels (Smith, 1982). The civil rights movement of the 1960s and the leadership of Dr. Martin

Luther King, Jr., attest to the role of the African American church and its clergy in social change. Thus, the counselor who works within the context of the African American church can educate clients about how systemic problems affect their lives and can also be part of the process that seeks to change these conditions. Counselors working in African American communities should seek to empower their clients to change racist and oppressive structures and policies that affect their lives negatively. Counselors should also be willing to be advocates on behalf of clients. The church is a vehicle that counselors can use to help them become effective advocates and to assist them in empowering clients. As examples, counselors can identify clients who have been victimized by unfair hiring practices, discrimination in housing, inadequate educational facilities, or inadequate health care. They can then refer these clients to pastors and church leaders who will in turn help them to organize and collectively confront oppressive systems and practices using the church as a base of operations. The use of the church, the support of pastors, and the identification with other victims of systemic injustice can give clients a sense of control over their lives.

Guidelines for Working Within a Church Context

It has been proposed by the author that counseling professionals should enlist the resources of the African American church in providing mental health services to African American communities. However, for most counseling professionals this is a new concept and direction is therefore needed for establishing working relationships with African American churches. The following guidelines can facilitate the development of such relationships.

Earn Acceptance

Some well-meaning counseling professionals come into the church believing that they will be immediately accepted because of their education or their professional accomplishments. However, they soon find that it takes more than credentials to be accepted as a helping professional within the African American church. To earn acceptance, counseling professionals must be perceived as sincere, trustworthy, not flaunting professional status, and having a genuine interest in the betterment of African Americans. Hunt (1988) rightly stated that "it is not what you know but who you are and how you use the information about a person's cultural characteristics that eventually allows the client to trust" (p. 116). With other conditions being right, if these attributes are perceived, the "word" will quickly spread among church members that you are a professional who is "down to earth and easy to talk to"—a description that is a sign of acceptance within the African American church community.

Explore Personal Beliefs

If the counselor is to be sensitive to the role spirituality and religion play in the lives of clients, the counselor must examine his or her own beliefs. Counselors should determine what aspects of their belief or nonbelief would interfere with being effective in working with certain presenting problems. This is especially important in dealing with religious matters such as spiritual healing or secular issues such as abortion and homosexuality. The counselor should not attempt to undertake this process alone but should explore his or her attitudes toward religion and spirituality with a clergyperson or religious professional.

Develop a Relationship With Pastors

In the African American church tradition there is a great deal of respect for the office and the authority of the pastor. Therefore, regardless of how skillful the counselor is, all efforts to use the African American church as a therapeutic ally will fail unless positive relationships are developed with pastors. An excellent way to meet and establish contact with clergy is through ministerial alliances. Most communities have such alliances where clergy meet once a week to discuss clergy and community concerns. These meetings can provide counseling professionals with an opportunity to meet African American clergy from various denominations. Rather than merely talking about skills and concerns, however, counseling professionals should use this opportunity to demonstrate them. Presenting a workshop on a relevant problem confronting African Americans, such as the problems facing youth, would be an excellent way to showcase counseling expertise.

Establish a Relationship With Local Churches

After you have developed a relationship with the pastor of a local church, the next step is to be introduced to a local congregation. Again, the workshop format is the best way to present yourself and your skills to the African American church community. Workshops on topics such as addiction, parenting, peer pressure, male/female relationships, racism, and prejudice are usually well received in church settings. If the workshop is successful, you will find that individual counseling referrals will follow.

Become Acquainted With the Religious Tradition of the Local Church or Denomination

The religious traditions of the African American church are represented by various denominations. These include African Methodist Episcopal Zion, African Methodist Episcopal, Baptist, Congregational, Church of God in Christ, Church of God, Seventh Day Adventist, Apostolic, Lutheran, Episcopal, and Roman Catholic. It is important for counseling professionals to have some knowledge concerning the beliefs of these denominations, especially because they can become therapeutic issues. Counseling professionals can become familiar with the religious beliefs and practices of these denominations by requesting denominational handbooks from pastors. *The Black Church in the African American Experience* (Lincoln & Mamiya, 1990) is an excellent resource that can provide counselors with essential background information on the African American church. In becoming familiar with the various traditions, counselors should play close attention to local church and denominational laws and attitudes toward the role of women in the church and society, attitudes toward divorce and remarriage, prohibitions against drugs and alcohol, abortion, homosexuality, and healing. There is the likelihood that these issues could become therapeutic issues.

Conclusion

The emergence of counseling professionals who recognize cultural diversity has initiated a search for innovative strategies and techniques for providing and delivering mental health services to African American communities. The African American church, with its rich history and significance in African American communities, can be a valuable resource for counseling professionals. The strategies put forth in this chapter will necessitate that counselors serve as advocates of social change, as consultants, and as mediators. Counselors also are encouraged to develop alliances with African American religious professionals. Finally, counselors need to become more aware of personal biases and fears that could prevent them from embracing indigenous helping resources such as the African American church. Counselors who are willing to meet the challenge will build a foundation that could ultimately lead to the discovery of new strategies and techniques for counseling in African American communities.

References

Boyd-Franklin, N. (1989). *Black families in counseling*. New York: Guilford Press.

Frazier, E. F. (1963). *The Negro church in America*. New York: Schocken.

Hunt, P. (1988). Black clients: Implications for supervision of trainees. *Psychocounseling, 24*(1), 114–119.

June, L. N. (1986). Enhancing the delivery of mental health and counseling services to Black males: Critical agency and provider responsibilities. *Journal of Multicultural Counseling and Development, 14*, 39–45.

Katz, J. H. (1985). The sociopolitical nature of counseling. *Counseling Psychologist, 13*, 615–624.

Knox, D. H. (1985). Spirituality: A tool in the assessment and treatment of Black alcoholics and their families. *Alcoholism Treatment Quarterly, 2*(3/4), 31–44.

Lee, C. C. (1990). Black male development: Counseling the "native son." In D. Moore & F. Leafgren (Eds.), *Problem solving strategies for men in conflict*. Alexandria, VA: American Association for Counseling and Development.

Lincoln, C. E., & Mamiya, L. H. (1990). *The Black church in the African American experience*. Durham, NC: Duke University Press.

Lovinger, R. J. (1984). *Working with religious issues in therapy*. New York: Aronson.

Mbiti, J. S. (1969). *African religions and philosophies*. Garden City, NY: Anchor Books.

Nobles, W. (1972). African philosophy: Foundations for a Black psychology. In R. L. Jones (Ed.), *Black psychology* (pp. 23–36). New York: Harper & Row.

Richardson, B. L. (1989). Attitudes of Black clergy toward mental health professionals: Implications for pastoral care. *Journal of Pastoral Care, 43*(1), 33–39.

Smith, A. (1982). *The relational self*. Nashville: Abingdon Press.

Sue, S., McKinney, H., Allen, D., & Hall, J. (1974). Delivery of community mental health services to black and white clients. *Journal of Consulting and Clinical Psychology, 42*, 594–601.

Switzer, D. K. (1986). *The minister as crisis counselor*. Nashville: Abingdon Press.

Washington, J. R. (1964). *Black religion: The Negro and Christianity in the United States*. Boston: Beacon Press.

THE ASIAN AMERICAN EXPERIENCE

Americans of Asian descent trace their cultural origins to countries such as China, Japan, Korea, Vietnam, and Cambodia. Each Asian American group has its own unique cultural history and traditions. However, some dynamics are rooted in centuries-old Asian religious traditions and play a major role in shaping the cultural values of Asian Americans, regardless of ethnic background. These dynamics must be appreciated if culturally responsive counseling is to take place with Asian American clients, and include factors such as moderation in behavior, self-discipline, patience, and humility. Many of these behaviors and values are dictated by family relationships that emphasize honor and respect for elders.

The Asian American Experience

Chapter 7
COUNSELING STRATEGIES FOR CHINESE AMERICANS

David Sue and Derald Wing Sue

About one million Chinese Americans live in the United States, nearly two thirds of whom are either foreign born or recent immigrants (Lorenzo & Adler, 1984). Because of the relaxation of immigration quotas, the number of Chinese Americans will continue to increase. The continuing influx of immigrants and refugees indicates the importance of gaining a knowledge of Chinese culture. The Chinese in America are a heterogeneous group. There are people from mainland China, Hong Kong, and Taiwan. In addition, many refugees and immigrants from Southeast Asia are of Chinese origin. Because of this, Chinese Americans may differ in terms of language and socioeconomic status. Differences in acculturation also exist among foreign-born and American-born Chinese Americans. Despite these differences, this chapter will focus on the commonalities in their experiences and traditions.

There is a pervasive view that Chinese Americans are a highly successful group with few problems. This is reflected in articles such as "To America With Skills" (1985), and "Asian Americans: Are They Making the Grade?" (1984). It is true that the percentage of college educated Chinese Americans and their household income are higher than those of White Americans (U.S. Department of Commerce, Bureau of the Census, 1980). Although some Chinese Americans are well educated, others have very low educational levels. A close examination of the statistics reveals a bimodal distribution: One group is highly educated, successful, and acculturated and the other is poor, living in poverty, and traditional in orientation (Kitano & Daniels, 1988; Sue & Sue, 1990). Compared to White Americans, nearly four times as many Chinese Americans have less than 4 years of schooling (Nishi, 1982).

Even among college-educated Chinese Americans, academic success has not led to commensurate rewards. Salaries are less than would be predicted according to educational levels, and Chinese Americans are underrepresented in managerial and supervisory positions (Sue & Okazaki, 1990; Sue, Sue, Zane, & Wong, 1985). In addition, the careers of

Chinese Americans are constricted; most are engineers or work in other technical occupations (McLeod, 1986). Studies of Chinese American men and women at several universities also show few entering into the social science fields (Sue, Ino, & Sue, 1983; Sue, Sue, & Ino, 1990).

Chinese Americans also face other problems. For example, China-towns are ghettos. The vast majority of the residents dislike the crowded conditions and believe that they are harmful to their health. A large percentage stay because of language and financial difficulties and not because of choice (Loo & Ong, 1984). Many who live in Chinatown are impoverished. Perhaps because of their loss of both status and extended families, elder Chinese American men and women have higher suicide rates than do White men and women (Liu & Yu, 1987).

Chinese American Cultural Values and Their Impact

Values have a tremendous impact in terms of how we view the world, what we consider to be right, the standards we uphold, and the way we assess and evaluate situations. However, it must be remembered that these values are influenced by acculturation. Leong and Tata (1990) found that highly acculturated Chinese American children were more likely to value self-actualization than those with low acculturation. Values and traditions often change at different rates. Chen and Yang (1986) found that Chinese American adolescents' attitudes toward dating and sex became more similar to those of White adolescents with acculturation, but that the Confucian values of loyalty, conformity, and respect for elders remained. The continuing arrival of additional Chinese to this country ensures the survival of cultural traditions. In this section, we will present some traditional Chinese values, contrast them with Western values, and discuss the implications of these differences for individual counseling. Later, we will present the format for an assertive training program for Chinese Americans.

Filial Piety

Filial piety is a very strong value in Chinese American families. It refers to the obligations, respect, and duty that a person has to his or her parents. This value is demonstrated through obeying the parents and holding them in high esteem. Allegiance to the parents is expected from the male offspring even after they have married and begun a family of their own. Many Chinese tales for children reflect the themes of filial piety. One such story, for example, tells of a destitute couple living with the husband's parents. Because there was not enough food for everyone, the couple decided to bury their youngest child. In doing so, they discovered gold (Tseng & Hsu, 1972). Their choice of sacrificing their child for the parents reaped a reward for the value of filial piety.

In Western culture, although parents are honored, there is also the emphasis on the nuclear family and independence, which reduces the importance of the family of origin. In fact, obligation to children is often stressed. Their feelings and desires are often seen as paramount. As Hsu (1953) indicated, "The most important thing to Americans is what parents should do for their children; to Chinese, what children should do for their parents" (p. 75).

In Chinese families, the parents often choose their childrens' career. For example, Taiwanese college students, as opposed to White American college students, were more likely to report being influenced by the parents for a particular field of study. In contrast, White college students indicated being influenced in career choice by peers and friends (Kuo & Spees, 1983). Obeying parents is emphasized in Chinese American families as an indication of filial piety, leaving little room for self-determination.

Such situations may lead to conflict, especially among Chinese Americans who have become more acculturated and exposed to the notion of personal choice. In one sample of 24 Chinese students (both foreign and American-born) seeking counseling, nearly all of them indicated stress associated with filial piety. Pressure to meet parental obligations and expectations clashed with individual goals and desires (Bourne, 1975).

In working with individuals who experience conflict between filial piety and individual goals, the counselor could help the clients identify the reasons for their stress. Chinese clients often will not know clearly the source of their conflict other than being aware that it involves their parents. Being able to understand that this conflict is connected with differences in cultural expectations may lead the way to resolution. The parents define love for the family in terms of having their offspring follow their direction. Exposure to Western values of self-determination and independence often produces conflicts in family relationships.

Stress on Family Bonds and Unity

Among Chinese Americans, child-rearing practices are focused on emphasizing the importance of family ties and obligations, not on helping individuals separate and become independent. Individual growth is not the accepted norm (Jung, 1984). Praise is given for actions that are seen as benefiting the family, and guilt-inducing techniques are used to maintain discipline. Children are expected to retain emotional ties with the mother and a respectful attitude toward the father even when they become adults. An individual who agonizes over career choice because of concern of upsetting the parents might be seen as overly dependent according to the Western perspective. Expecting and assisting the client to become more independent without considering the cultural implications, however, may lead to even greater conflict.

Roles and Status

Communication patterns among Chinese Americans are based on cultural tradition and flow down from those of higher status. Men and elders are accorded greater importance than women or younger individuals. In a family, the father makes the major decisions with little input from others. A well-functioning family is one that adheres to prescribed communication rules. Negotiations and democratic discussions to arrive at decisions, which are typical of White families, may be foreign to many Chinese American families (Jung, 1984; Saner-Yiu & Saner-Yiu, 1985). Indeed, such discussions may be seen as challenges to the authority figure, the father.

These role prescriptions make it necessary to alter traditional forms of therapy. For example, family counseling might seem to be an ideal modality for Chinese families. However, this approach rests on several assumptions: (a) The "identified client" is not the real problem. Instead, it involves dysfunctional family relationships, and (b) Communication patterns have to be altered. These assumptions may not be appropriate for Chinese American families. Bowen (1978) believes that dysfunctional families are the result of fused identities and overemotional dependence. In his approach, he assists family members to develop greater independence and differentiation. This would conflict with the Chinese American practice of maintaining strong family ties. Family therapy also employs confrontation, role playing, and the expression of strong feelings. Such an approach would threaten the traditional roles and practices of the Chinese American culture.

Does this mean that family counseling should not be used in working with Chinese American families? With some modifications, family therapy can be helpful. Shon and Ja (1982) indicated that it is first important to identify possible family issues. The father may feel threatened about his status in this country. He may have to depend on his children to translate for him. His wife may have assumed the role of the breadwinner, which encroaches on his primary role. As a reaction, he might demand more compliance to his wishes. The mother is responsible for socializing the children. If they become rebellious or overly acculturated, it is seen as reflecting poor parenting on her part. She also has to mediate between the dictates of her husband and the demands of her children.

If the mother has done her job well, the children will be respectful and provide for her in her old age. The greatest responsibility is placed on the eldest son. He is expected to help raise his younger siblings and to be a role model for them. He inherits the family leadership upon the death of the father and is expected to provide financial and emotional support for his mother. Daughters are expected to help in the household. Generally fewer demands are placed upon them because they become members of the husband's family when they marry.

Ho (1987) made the following suggestions when dealing with a Chinese American family in a counseling situation: Promote differences in roles by addressing the father and mother first. Reframe or relabel statements family members make. If a child becomes angry, restate the issue in terms of parental expectations. Do not encourage the child to communicate strong negative feelings to the parents. Promote filial piety also by gently reminding parents of the necessity of being positive role models for their children. Focus on the use of positive and respectful feelings between family members.

Somatization Versus Psychologization

In general, Chinese Americans perceive problems as difficulties with health. Discomfort and disturbance are expressed in terms of somatic complaints, such as headaches. In fact, symptoms of physical illnesses are believed to cause psychological problems. For example, having a headache may result in feelings of depression. White Americans, on the other hand, have a psychologization perspective. Physical symptoms and illnesses are often thought to be the result of psychological states.

In working with Chinese Americans, it would be a mistake to discount physical complaints. They are real problems. Both physical and psychological or family concerns have to be dealt with. One approach might be to inquire about the impact of the illness on the family or social functioning. Physical or medical treatment can be used with suggestions for improvements in other aspects of the client's life. The effectiveness of the intervention is based on the alleviation of both physical and psychological symptoms.

Control Over Strong Emotions

In traditional Chinese culture, emotional expression was restrained to prevent challenges to tradition and order. This is not to say that Chinese Americans do not show a variety of emotional reactions. Just like other human beings, they can be angry, sad, happy, jealous, confident, or anxious. However, these displays do not typically occur outside of the family. Feelings are not openly expressed except in the case of young children. Parents rarely show signs of physical affection, such as holding hands or saying, "I love you" (Shon & Ja, 1982). Instead, love is acknowledged through behaviors that benefit the family and its members. Children are rarely praised directly for their contributions. Parents express pride indirectly by telling friends or other siblings about the achievements or work of a particular offspring.

White Americans, however, believe that the expression of feelings is healthy and leads to better adjustment. In counseling, the Western focus on the importance of expressing emotions will present difficulties for the Chinese American client, especially when negative emotions are aired. The Chinese American client may lack the experience to identify, acknowledge, or communicate emotional states.

Forcing Chinese clients to express emotions directly will meet with resistance and be counterproductive. Instead, the emphasis should be on the indirect expression of positive and respectful feelings. Because love, respect, and affection are shown through behaviors, one approach might be to make the following statement, "We do different things to show that we care for our family. I would like to learn from you the ways you have of caring for your family" (Ho, 1987). Such an approach focuses on behavior, is respectful, and is indirect.

Academic and Career Orientation

In most Chinese American families, there is great stress on academic achievement. This might exist even if the parents received few years of formal education. It is not individual achievement that is desired, however. The work is for the enhancement of the family. The emphasis on academics is reflected in the statistic that the percentage of Chinese men who complete a college education is nearly double that of the average for the United States (Sue, Sue, & Sue, 1983).

Achievement comes at a price, however. Sue and Zane (1985) found that foreign-born Chinese American university students achieved higher grade point averages by taking reduced course loads, studying more hours per week, and limiting their career choices. Partly because of this, the students reported greater anxiety, loneliness, and feelings of isolation than did other college students. In addition, there is increasing evidence that universities are beginning to set quotas for the number of Asian students admitted (Sue, 1985).

The amount of parental pressure for their children to succeed academically can be great. Anything less than an "A" may be considered inferior and an indication that the student no longer cares for the family. There is also pressure to choose a career of which the parents approve.

Chinese American students continue to go predominantly into the scientific fields and not into the social sciences. Counselors must be careful to expose Chinese American students to a wide range of career options.

To aid readers in understanding the importance of Chinese American cultural values and their influence in the counseling process, we will present the following case study.

The Case of David Chan

David Chan is a 21-year-old student majoring in electrical engineering. He first sought counseling because he was having increasing study problems and was receiving failing grades. These academic difficulties became apparent during the first quarter of his senior year and were accompanied by headaches, indigestion, and insomnia. Since he had been an excellent student in the past, Dave felt that his lowered academic performance was caused by illness. However, a medical examination failed to reveal any organic disorder.

During the initial interview, Dave seemed depressed and anxious. He was difficult to counsel because he would respond to inquiries with short, but polite statements and would seldom volunteer information about himself. He avoided any statements that involved feelings and presented his problem as a strictly educational one. Although he never expressed it directly, Dave seemed to doubt the value of counseling and needed much reassurance and feedback about his performance in the interview.

After several sessions, the counselor was able to discern one of Dave's major concerns. Dave did not like engineering and felt pressured by his parents to go into this field. The counselor felt that Dave was unable to take responsibility for any of his actions, was excessively dependent on his parents, and was afraid to express the anger he feels towards them.

Using the Gestalt "empty chair technique," the counselor had Dave pretend that his parents are seated opposite him. The counselor had Dave express his true feelings toward them. Although ventilating true feelings was initially very difficult, Dave was able to eventually do so under constant encouragement by the counselor. Unfortunately, the following sessions with Dave proved nonproductive in that he seemed more withdrawn and guilt ridden than ever. (Sue, 1981, p. 266)

In analyzing the above case, a culturally aware counselor might entertain the following thoughts and hypotheses about Dave and the counseling process.

The counselor in the case values openness and elaboration of personal feelings. This is a White value, perhaps not shared by David. Instead he might be more comfortable with the Chinese American cultural values of restraint of feelings; his "short and polite statements" might reflect respect for elders and authority. David's cultural background might hinder the discussion of personal problems with outsiders.

The techniques the counselor used may be culturally inappropriate. "Talking back to parents" in the empty chair technique may ask the client to violate a basic cultural value of "honor thy parents." Dave's withdrawal and apparent depression may have been the result of guilt he experienced after the therapeutic intervention. Indirect and subtle strategies may be more effective with this client.

The counselor needs to understand that restraint of strong feelings, the stigma of personal problems, and the possible reflection on the family may be the basis for Dave's headaches, insomnia, and indigestion. It might be wise to address the physical complaints first and design treatment strategies for them before proceeding to the inter- and intrapersonal conflicts.

White culture values taking responsibility for one's life (individual responsibility and decisions). Chinese American culture values a family decision; the family is harmonious, and one is part of the family, not separate from it. To infer that David is avoiding responsibility and is "excessively dependent upon his parents" is a serious distortion of cultural values. From this case, one can see how Chinese American values such as filial piety, definition of family roles and status, somatization, control of feelings, and pressures to excel may strongly influence the counseling process.

Personality Studies and Assertiveness

On paper-and-pencil tests, Chinese Americans score high in deference, self-restraint, abasement, external locus of control, and need for structure. They also show a lower tolerance for ambiguity, lower dominance, and aggression (Fenz & Arkoff, 1962; Sue & Kirk, 1972; Abbott, 1976). A recent study of Chinese American boys found that they were more cooperative and had a more external locus of control than did White children (Cook & Chi, 1984). These characteristics would seem to make sense in terms of the cultural values and traditions just presented. Chinese Americans also consider themselves to be quiet and nonassertive. They report being uncomfortable in situations in which an evaluative component is present (Sue, Ino, & Sue, 1983; Sue, Sue, & Ino, 1990). Interestingly enough, during a presentation of research on Asian Americans, the Chinese Americans students attending voiced many questions and were quite responsive. However, when asked if they participated in classroom discussions at the university, few indicated that they did. Most indicated that they needed assertiveness training.

There is some controversy over whether or not these personality characteristics reflect cultural values or are responses to racism (Sue & Morishima, 1982). Tong (1971) contended that many findings result from situational factors rather than personality traits. In other words, Chinese Americans may display assertiveness in some situations. In fact, Sue et al. (1983) did find some evidence for the influence of situations on the assertiveness of Chinese American men.

Assertiveness Training for Chinese Americans

As we indicated earlier, Chinese American men and women often feel uncomfortable in social situations and believe that they lack assertiveness. Many have voiced an interest in assertiveness training. The following are guidelines that we have used in these groups:

1. Pregroup screening. We conduct a short 15-minute individual meeting with prospective group members. During this time, we explain the procedures and approach we will use. Client needs and the assessment of whether or not the group is appropriate for particular clients are also determined at this time. Some group leaders feel that having homogeneous members (same sex, same generational status, etc.) is important in the smooth operation of the groups. We have found this not to be necessary, although individuals who actively reject their own cultural identity are screened out.

2. First group meeting. We repeat information about the purpose of the group, the material that will be covered, and the techniques that will be employed. The importance of confidentiality is discussed and stressed. We next start out with personal introductions, beginning with ourselves to serve as models and to indicate what might be expected. We then designate who is to follow. This provides structure and reduces anxiety.

3. Culture and racism. During subsequent sessions, we discuss the roots of nonassertiveness of Chinese Americans. Child rearing patterns and family experiences are shared. For example, the use of shame and guilt in members' own families is discussed. Alternative ways of viewing nonassertiveness are presented. It is pointed out that in traditional Chinese culture nonassertiveness has often been viewed positively. Being quiet and respectful indicates filial piety. In addition, feelings of being a "person of color" in American society are discussed. An understanding of how our behaviors and expectations are molded by early experience is developed. The leader should ensure active participation by all members by directing specific questions to individuals. The idea of assertiveness is brought up, defined, and its advantages and disadvantages are discussed with respect to traditional Chinese and Western values. In gen-

eral, group members have agreed that assertiveness is useful in American society.

4. Situational assertiveness is discussed next. It is pointed out that an individual may be assertive in some situations but not in others. Experiences where assertive behaviors have been exhibited, such as with friends or siblings, are shared. It is pointed out that individuals can decide to be assertive with professors, classmates, and employers, but remain deferential to parents and relatives if they so desire.

5. Group members are asked to write down on paper some situations where they have difficulty being assertive. Suggestions can be gained from the assertion questionnaire completed earlier. The distinction between nonassertiveness, aggression, and assertiveness is made. Demonstrations of these behaviors are provided for different situations. Feelings are elicited after each performance. The group leader models the procedure first and then structures an easy situation for each participant.

6. From his or her list, each group member chooses a simple assertive response to practice outside of the group setting. The situation is first practiced in the group. Cognitions and affect about the situation are discussed. Possible consequences, both positive and negative, are acknowledged. Cognitive approaches that reframe or focus on task performance and realistic appraisal are employed. Use of the minimal effective response to achieve the desired goal is practiced, and alternative responses are also discussed. The members are asked to try out their assertive responses outside of the group. The easiest tasks are assigned first. The members are to note their feelings and thoughts during the assertion.

7. Group meetings involve discussion of homework assignments and cognitive coping strategies used. Members share what has worked for them. More complex assignments are given, and progress is assessed.

8. Final group sessions involve a summary by group members in terms of understanding the factors associated with nonassertiveness, their evaluation of their own success, and suggestions for improvement in the program.

With some modifications, the basic format of the group training can be used to discuss issues such as filial piety, conflicts over acculturation, sex-role conflicts and expectations, and career options.

Conclusion

Chinese Americans represent a growing and heterogeneous population. Because of this, counselors and other mental health professionals need to become aware of the possible impact of cultural values on the process of counseling. Specifically, counselors have to become aware of their worldview and assumptions about what constitutes successful counseling when working with Chinese American clients. Issues such as independence, the necessity of eliciting emotional reactions, and the equality of family members must be seen from a cultural perspective and not as a given. Group experiences can also be highly effective with Chinese Americans, especially when cultural influences on behavior are discussed.

References

Abbott, K. A. (1976). Culture change and the persistence of the Chinese personality. In G. De Vos (Ed.), *Responses to change: Society, culture, and personality* (pp. 87–119). New York: Van Nostrand.

Asian Americans: Are they making the grade? (1984, April 2). *U.S. News and World Report.*

Bourne, P. G. (1975). The Chinese student: Acculturation and mental illness. *Psychiatry, 38,* 269–277.

Bowen, M. (1978). *Family therapy in clinical practice.* New York: Aronson.

Chen, C., & Yang, D. (1986). The self-image of Chinese American adolescents. *Pacific/Asian American Mental Health Research Center Review, 3/4,* 27–29.

Cook, H., & Chi, C. (1984). Cooperative behavior and locus of control among American and Chinese-American boys. *Journal of Psychology, 118,* 169–177.

Fenz, W. D., & Arkoff, A. (1962). Comparative need patterns of five ancestry groups in Hawaii. *Journal of Social Psychology, 58,* 67–89.

Ho, M. K. (1987). *Family therapy with minorities.* Newbury Park, CA: Sage.

Hsu, F. L. K. (1953). *Americans and Chinese: Two ways of life.* New York: Abelard-Schuman.

Jung, M. (1984). Structural family therapy: Its application to Chinese families. *Family Process, 23,* 365–374.

Kitano, H. H. L., & Daniels, R. (1988). *Asian Americans: Emerging minorities.* Englewood Cliffs, NJ: Prentice Hall.

Kuo, S. Y., & Spees, E. R. (1983). Chinese American student life-styles: A comparative study. *Journal of College Student Personnel, 42*(2), 407–413.

Leong, F. T. L., & Tata, S. P. (1990). Sex and acculturation differences in occupational values among Chinese American children. *Journal of Counseling Psychology, 37,* 208–212.

Liu, W. T., & Yu, E. S. (1987). Ethnicity and mental health. *The Pacific/Asian American Mental Health Center: A decade review* (pp. 3–18). Chicago: University of Illinois.

Loo, C., & Ong, P. (1984). Crowding perceptions, attitudes, and consequences among the Chinese. *Environment and Behavior, 16,* 55–87.

Lorenzo, M. K., & Adler, D. A. (1984). Mental health services for Chinese in a community mental health center. *Social Casework, 65,* 600–610.

McLeod, B. (1986). The Oriental express. *Psychology Today,* pp. 48–52.

Nishi, S. M. (1982). The educational disadvantage of Asian and Pacific Americans. *Pacific/Asian American Mental Health Research Center Review, 1,* 4–6.

Saner-Yiu, L., & Saner-Yiu, R. (1985). Value dimensions in American counseling: A Taiwanese-American dimension. *International Journal for the Advancement of Counseling, 8*, 137–146.

Shon, S. P., & Ja, D. Y. (1982). Asian families. In M. McGoldrick, J. K. Pearce, & J. Giordano (Eds.), *Ethnicity and family therapy* (pp. 208–228). New York: Guilford Press.

Sue, D., Ino, S., & Sue, D. M. (1983). Nonassertiveness of Asian-Americans: An inaccurate assumption? *Journal of Counseling Psychology, 30*, 581–588.

Sue, D., Sue, D. M., & Ino, S. (1990). Assertiveness and social anxiety in Chinese-American women. *Journal of Psychology, 124*, 155–164.

Sue, D., Sue, D. W., & Sue, D. M. (1983). Psychological development of Chinese-American children. In G. J. Powell, J. Yamamoto, A. Romero, & A. Morales (Eds.), *The psychosocial development of minority group children* (pp. 159–166). New York: Brunner/Mazel.

Sue, D. W. (1981). *Counseling the culturally different: Theory and practice.* New York: Wiley.

Sue, D. W., & Kirk, B. A. (1972). Psychological characteristics of Chinese-American college students. *Journal of Counseling Psychology, 6*, 471–478.

Sue, D. W., & Sue, D. (1990). *Counseling the culturally different: Theory and practice* (2nd ed.). New York: Wiley.

Sue, S. (1985). Asian Americans and educational pursuits: Are the doors beginning to close? *Pacific/Asian American Mental Health Research Center Review, 4*, 25.

Sue, S., & Morishima, J. K. (1982). *The mental health of Asian Americans.* San Francisco: Jossey-Bass.

Sue, S., & Okazaki, S. (1990). Asian-American educational achievements. *American Psychologist, 45*, 913–920.

Sue, S., Sue, D. W., Zane, N., & Wong, H. Z. (1985). Where are the Asian American leaders and top executives? *P/AAMHRC Review, 4*, 13–15.

Sue, S., & Zane, N. W. S. (1985). Academic achievement and socioemotional adjustment among Chinese university students. *Journal of Counseling Psychology, 32*, 570–579.

To America with skills. (1985, July 8). *Time*, pp. 42–44.

Tong, B. R. (1971). The ghetto of the mind: Notes on the historical psychology of Chinese-America. *Amerasia Journal, 1*, 1–31.

Tseng, W., & Hsu, J. (1972). The Chinese attitude toward parental authority as expressed in Chinese childrens' stories. *Archives of General Psychology, 26*, 28–34.

U.S. Department of Commerce, Bureau of the Census. (1980). *Census of the population: Supplementary report. Race of the population by states.* Washington, DC: U. S. Government Printing Office.

Chapter 8
COUNSELING JAPANESE AMERICANS: FROM INTERNMENT TO REPARATION

Satsuki Ina Tomine

Subsequent to the Japanese attack on Pearl Harbor on December 7, 1941, President Franklin D. Roosevelt issued Executive Order 9066, which enabled the military, in absence of martial law, to circumvent the constitutional safeguards of American citizens of Japanese descent. The order authorized the mass evacuation of 110,000 Japanese Americans residing on the West Coast, who were interned from 1 to 5 years without due process of law. Although implemented as a "military necessity," it has been documented that "The grave injustices were perpetrated in spite of the fact that our government had in its possession proof that not one Japanese American, citizen or not, had engaged in espionage, not one had committed any act of sabotage" (Weglyn, 1976, p. 29). It has also been documented that in this bleak period in American history, the decision to create concentration camps, bounded by barbed wire and guard towers, was, in fact, a result of hysteria, racism, and economic exploitation (Weglyn).

Almost 50 years later, through the indefatigable efforts of leaders and advocates of the Japanese American community, the Civil Liberties Act of 1988 was passed. Popularly known as the Japanese American Redress Bill, this bill mandated Congress to pay each victim of the internment $20,000 in reparation for a most grievous error perpetrated on Americans of Japanese descent.

The following is a story written by a 45-year-old Japanese American woman who participated in an intensive group therapy session that focused on the internment experience during World War II:

> Once upon a time there was a little soldier girl who grew up surrounded by barbed wire. She was scared, and so were her mommy and daddy and brother. But they all marched together

and pretended to be unafraid. The father wrote poems about guard towers and guns while the brother played with his toy tank made with broken checkers for wheels. Then one day, the little soldier girl's daddy was taken away and no one could pretend to be unafraid anymore. No one knew where her daddy was. And when she grew up she kept searching for her daddy. She often recognized him because he always went away when she needed him. And she still today, sleeps in her soldier clothes, trying to be unafraid.

This story captures the "quiet trauma" of this woman's internment camp experience and the impact of this event on her later development. Like the other participants, this woman presented the classic image of the successful Japanese American. She was highly educated with a successful career and all the outward appearances of the so-called "model minority." And yet, like the others as well, she suffered from the invisible consequences of low-grade depression and psychosomatic illness. Lack of spontaneity, low risk taking, workaholism, and difficulty in interpersonal relationships were issues with which all participants in the group were able to identify.

The psychological consequences of having been born a political prisoner in her own country was something this woman was reluctant, and yet compelled, to explore within the safety of a supportive group of men and women who had also been Children of the Camps. This term, "Children of the Camps," coined by the author, is used to identify individuals who were either born or spent some portion of their formative years in the United States Internment Camps during World War II. This intensive therapy process will be presented in detail as a means of highlighting the social, political, and cultural issues that affect the psychological development of the Japanese American client.

Traditional Japanese Values and Norms

In order to acquire an in-depth understanding of the matrix of traditional Japanese values and norms that influence the Japanese American personality and family structure, the reader is referred to the resources at the end of the chapter. However, a brief sketch of significant cultural variables may help to clarify the process and content issues in counseling Japanese Americans. Keeping in mind variations due to social class, geographical origin, and generation in the United States, some common themes can be identified in terms of cultural values and norms.

Much of traditional Japanese culture can be traced to the philosophical precepts of life that were dictated by Confucianism and Buddhism. Within this system of thought, the individual is superseded by the family, specific hierarchical roles are established for all family members, and rules of behavior and conduct are formalized; an individual's adherence to this code of conduct is a reflection not only on the immediate family, but on the extended kinship network as well.

Regarding the nuclear family, Shon and Ja (in McGoldrick, Pearce, & Giordano, 1982) described the father as the leader and decision maker. His authority is unquestioned. The welfare of the family rests squarely on the father's shoulders. He enforces family rules and is the primary disciplinarian. The successes or failures of the family and its individual members are viewed essentially as the father's responsibility. The traditional role of the mother is that of the nurturant caretaker of both her husband and children. The mother is clearly the emotionally devoted, nurturant parental figure. The strongest emotional attachments, therefore, tend to be with the mother.

Highly developed feelings of obligation govern much of the interpersonal relationships of Japanese Americans. Shame and loss of face are frequently used to reinforce adherence to prescribed sets of obligations. The interdependent quality of relationships suggests that harmony in these relationships is best achieved through proper conduct and attitudes. The often unspoken obligatory reciprocity within relationships is a serious consideration in the life of a Japanese American. Respect and obedience to parents and others in authority positions reflect the indebtedness of the individual and serve to express affection and gratitude.

In a social structure where interdependence is so highly valued, the fear of losing face can be a powerful motivating force for conforming. The withdrawal of the family's, community's, or society's confidence and support, and the exposure of one's wrong actions for all to see, is a profound shaming experience to be avoided at all costs.

Harmonious interpersonal relationships are maintained by avoiding direct confrontation. Therefore, much of the communication style of the Japanese American is indirect and is characterized by talking around the point. Problem solving occurs within the prescribed family structure. There is a strong dictum that problems be kept within the family and solved there. The ability to endure hardships, demonstrate unflagging loyalty, and sacrifice for the good of the whole is often called upon for resolution of problems.

The Acculturation Variable

Empathic understanding of a client's experience is based on the principles of similarity and identification. Therefore, it is essential that counselors avoid projecting their unconscious stereotypes onto the culturally different client. This benevolent blindness can lead the counselor to discount or deny differences in values, behavior, family structure, and communication style that can serve as rich resources for change and growth. To minimize the dangers of assumed similarities or differences, a careful evaluation of the extent to which the client has adopted American mainstream values, attitudes, and behaviors must be made.

Japanese Americans typically identify themselves in terms of numbers of generations since immigrating to the United States. First generation "Issei," currently ranging in their 80s and older, are the immigrant group who arrived in the United States during the late 1800s. Targeted by the Oriental Exclusion Act of 1924, the Issei were prohibited from gaining citizenship or owning land (Kitagawa, 1967). Today they are the elderly in the community and the least likely cohort group to utilize Western mental health services. Due to the language barrier and traditional Japanese values of shame associated with having emotional problems, the Issei are more likely to cope with personal problems by relying on their religious beliefs and drawing on the cultural coping mechanisms of stoicism, privacy, fatalism, and family support (Maykovich, 1972). The Isseis interned in the camps during the war typically did not talk about the shame and humiliation they experienced nor of the guilt they felt about their children who had to be imprisoned because of their parents' nationality (Kiefer, 1974). Traditional loyalty, propriety, and fear of retribution were also likely factors that inhibited complaining or being openly critical of the government (Kitagawa, 1967). A recent study by Kiyoko Hallenberg (1988) of the Japanese American elderly who had experienced internment indicates that 55% of the subjects interviewed hardly ever talked about the internment even 15 years later, and 42% more than 40 years later.

Second generation "Nisei," currently ranging in age from 60 to 80 years, are the American-born children of the Issei. Educated in American schools, this cohort group tends to reflect a more bicultural approach to life. Some are bilingual, but due to the internment experience, most felt the social and familial press to acculturate and adopt American ways that would ensure success and acceptance in the larger community. The questioned loyalty and assimilability of the Japanese American raised by the wartime hysteria intensified the urgency to become "good Americans." Consequently, this generation of Japanese Americans, encouraged by their immigrant parents, were deeply committed to educational and professional achievement as the mechanism for being accepted by the dominant culture. Thus, the author feels that the unconscious influence of Japanese culture on the Nisei personality is more prominent than may be outwardly acknowledged.

In the group process, the Nisei and Sansei participants were asked to rate themselves on a scale of "very Japanese" to "very American." The

Nisei tended to rate themselves in the "very American" range along with their Sansei counterparts. Although the Nisei participants were older than the Sansei, and therefore during their early years were raised in a closed Japanese cultural system within the camps, they tended to deny the impact of this early Japanese socialization on their self-perception. However, in the discussion that followed regarding traditional Japanese values and coping styles, the Nisei participants often expressed surprise at how "Japanese" they really were.

The third generation "Sansei," who are now approximately 40 to 60 years old, may have been born in the camps or are likely to have experienced the reentry process after the internment as young children. This generation is, almost without exception, English speaking only. Though more fully acculturated, the intense striving to be "good Americans" has been perpetuated in the Sansei. Although national loyalty was no longer an issue, the Sansei in the group reflected the divided loyalty between familial expectations and personal desires.

Several of the Sansei participants in the group talked about their dissatisfaction with their jobs. In the discussion, it became clear that for some, their original career choice was fostered more by parental definitions of success and the more "accessible" or socially appropriate career paths for Asian Americans rather than by personal preference. When asked to describe any persistent problems in his life, a 45-year-old dentist reported:

> I have difficulty handling paper work, official forms, bookkeeping, business information and documents. I am easily distracted from priority work. I procrastinate. I am tentative and unclear as to my life's primary work.

Initially unable to label his feelings and understand the roots for his chronic state of depression, with the support of the group, he was eventually able to recognize the depth of his feelings of obligation to his parents, as well as his guilt for resenting his role as the dutiful son. Angry feelings surfaced as he described the faceless oppression that plays a part in his psychic dilemma.

This Sansei client was surprised to discover the extent to which he adheres to the values of filial respect and avoidance of losing face. His experience as a child internee, the possible internalized anxiety that his parents felt during the trauma of internment, and the subsequent discrimination and displacement led him to choose an "acceptable" career that would ensure his security and status in society. "It's hard work being Japanese, and it's damn painful to be a minority."

It is therefore important that the counselor be sensitive to the conscious and unconscious cultural identification processes operating in the Japanese American client. It is incumbent upon the counselor to have a working knowledge of traditional Japanese values and norms and to use this cultural information as the background from which the client emerges as a unique individual. McGoldrick et al. (1982) suggested that cultural information is best used as a filter to determine the extent to which cultural factors contribute to the presenting problem and as a resource in choosing clinical interventions.

The counselor's ability to appreciate the impact of social, cultural, and familial processes can help the client understand the source of his or her pain as well as enable the client to make more conscious choices about staying within or stepping outside of cultural and societal boundaries. A culturally sensitive counselor would thoroughly explore the possible social and psychological consequences of the client's choices.

Although generational identification of the Issei, Nisei, and Sansei can provide the counselor with a general sense of their degree of acculturation, other acculturation indicators can be helpful. Rural Japanese American communities tend to be more traditional in contrast to urban communities, which have been disturbed by urban renewal efforts. Affiliation with specific ethnic, social, civic, and religious organizations can also be a helpful indicator. Peer group affiliation in schools and dating preferences also help to determine the degree of acculturation. It is important to keep in mind, however, that the influences of culture and racial discrimination are often more unconscious than conscious, and the counselor would do well to explore these issues jointly with the client. Assessing the degree of acculturation will enable the counselor to clarify the presenting problem and to select appropriate culture-specific interventions.

The Presenting Problem

Human problems are at once unique and universal. What brings the client into therapy, however, is the inappropriate or ineffective ways in which he or she is coping with the problem. For ethnic minority clients, it is essential that these coping styles be understood in terms of both their cultural and defensive overlay. William Grier and Price Cobbs, in their classic text, *Black Rage* (1968), described the concept of the "paranorm" that can be applied to all minority group members who have been victims of racial bigotry and oppression. As a psychological defense against the dehumanizing effects of racism, minority subgroups develop a norm of appropriate paranoia against which they check their perceptions of safety and trust.

It would be impossible to ferret out how much of the client's coping style is cultural, defensive, or uniquely individual. Two types of errors in understanding the presenting problems, however, could bring the therapeutic process to a standstill. The first error is to assume that cultural or defensive factors are insignificant in influencing the client's coping style, and the second error is to assume the client's coping style can be explained completely by cultural or defensive factors, without consideration for individual uniqueness. Thus the workaholism some group participants describe would only be superficially understood if the clients' historical experience of being viewed as "unassimilable" as a race was not explored. Japanese Americans who experienced the confinement possess a group consciousness that should not be minimized. Fear of failure for this group would be understandably high. The counselor's task is to facilitate the client's awareness of this socially imposed defense mechanism to enable him or her to see the problem in the contextual as well as the uniquely personal framework.

To further illustrate this point, the participant whose story introduced this chapter spoke of her difficulty in finding lasting relationships with men. She typically picked men who tended to be emotionally unavailable to her. As an adult, she consciously understood that her father was taken away suddenly in the middle of the night and incarcerated in a separate prison for suspected dissidents. In the course of the group process, however, she realized that as a child she experienced her father's disappearance as abandonment and felt overwhelmed by the anguish and fear of her mother who was left to care for two small children alone behind barbed wires.

This early childhood trauma was then exacerbated not by a dysfunctional family's "no talk" rule, but by cultural mandates that discouraged discussion about what was internalized as a shameful experience. The precarious balance of maintaining dignity in the face of the loss of their personal freedom was a challenge to the Japanese American internees. As a coping style influenced by Japanese culture and reinforced by the larger society's amnesia about the camps, silence was used in an effort to heal the injury. The consequences of both the cultural and defensive coping mechanism are depicted in Hallenberg's study (1988), which found a significant relationship between not talking about the internment and chronic depression. The group helped the woman challenge her mistaken belief that somehow she was unlovable and that's why her father left her. She was also able to recognize how the silence into which she would withdraw mirrored the silence of her parents, the community, and the government regarding her internment experience.

The counselor's ability to attend to the personal, cultural, and defensive variables that influence the client's coping style enable the counselor to understand the backdrop for the presenting problem.

Intervention Strategies

In working with the Japanese American client, the entire range of clinical interventions may be considered for treatment. However, the counselor who has assessed the degree of acculturation, cultural constraints and prescriptions, and defense mechanisms against racism will be better able to make a sensitive choice of intervention. To minimize resistance in a cross-cultural therapeutic relationship, it is recommended that the interventions selected serve to challenge, not conflict with or negate, existing coping mechanisms. Consequently, the counselor must be willing to adapt interventions to the client's need. This requires the counselor to have a wide repertoire of clinical interventions from which to choose.

To better understand the psychological effects of the internment experience on Japanese Americans, a clinical analogy may be appropriate. Like the incest victim in a dysfunctional family, American citizens of Japanese descent were singled out and their fundamental rights to due process were violated by the very arm of the government designated to protect those rights. The social amnesia and denial subsequent to the internment further traumatized the victims and led to internalized shame and repressed anger. Not unlike the child victim, who manages to cope by developing psychic barriers against vulnerability, (Courtois, 1988), Japanese Americans as a group committed themselves to being good citizens and made every effort to be accepted by the larger society. After years of suppressing and denying the anger because of the dependency on the perpetrator, clients in this classic "incest bind" can experience symptomatic behaviors.

Creating a Safe Environment

The facilitator acknowledged and opened for discussion the cultural prohibitions against disclosing family problems and the open expression of feelings. The reluctance to reopen the painful experience of the internment required an extensive trust-building process. Participants were encouraged to be aware of their physical and emotional boundaries, and the facilitator modeled, with respect, each person's right to say "no." This was particularly crucial for people whose rights had been so blatantly violated. Participants were told that any level of self-disclosure was acceptable, and every member agreed to honor the confidentiality of the material presented by the group.

Telling Your Story

Not unlike the incestuous "family secret," the unacknowledged crime against the Japanese Americans was rationalized with euphemisms such as "wartime hysteria," "protective custody," and "national security." Consequently, many of the victims themselves, culturally primed to respect authority, and shamed by the experience, kept the story of their internment to themselves. Rather than complaining and revolting, they practiced silent endurance. Until recently, with the spectrum of reparation imminent, very little about the camp experience was acknowledged in the classroom, the media, or in government policy. For the participants, then, telling their story, talking about what they experienced and how they coped, was the beginning of the healing process. To have others in the group mirror back empathic acceptance, without judgment, served as an invaluable intervention in empowering the victim.

Prior to the session, each person was asked to talk to at least one other family member about his or her intention to participate in this group. This served not only to prepare the participants emotionally, but to begin effecting a challenge to the previous "no talk" rule to which the family may have adhered.

Often, implicit in the "minority" experience is the absence of acknowledgment and validation by the "majority" power structure. Just as in the family, when this validation is not provided, self-doubt prevails. Thus the facilitator's role was to model and support, emphatically and affirmatively, the acknowledgment of each participant's story. Participants were asked to bring photographs of themselves, share stories that were told about them, and describe what happened to their family. The participants expressed "shame" in terms of loss of face. Therefore, assisting the participant to look into the faces reflecting back acceptance and understanding served as a powerful shame reduction intervention. This section of the workshop was given no time limit. It was completed only after each person felt that he or she had finished.

Identifying Developmental Needs

Participants were encouraged to identify their developmental tasks and needs at the time of the internment and to consider how those tasks and needs were affected by the internment. Many participants were able to understand for the first time what it must have been like for their parents to have children behind barbed wire fences. One of the significant issues that surfaced was the disorganization of family roles and rules with the imposition of the military superstructure upon the family. Just the very physical structure of the barracks and mess hall affected family privacy, communication, and control. In addition, participants described the pervasive fear and anxiety that gripped their parents as they attempted to raise a family in a prison compound surrounded by tanks and armed guards standing on watchtowers.

Using the Adlerian Early Childhood Recollections process (Dinkmeyer, Pew, & Dinkmeyer, 1979), participants reexperienced that period of their development and identified what it was that they needed from their parents at the time. The group was then asked to respond to each individual's needs with verbal affirmations as the participant returned to the early experience, but this time with an empowered parental source. Cultural injunctions against violating filial piety carry a heavy burden of guilt. Therefore, during the debriefing, the facilitator actively reframed blaming of parents for their child's unmet needs as limitations compounded by external forces.

One woman described the images that came up for her as she regressed to her early infancy. She was born in the camps. She recalled that as she looked up from her straw mat "crib" she saw her parents' faces. Rather than being joyful at her birth, she realized that what she saw were faces that were fearful and anxious. She wept as she recognized that her arrival was not a welcome blessing. She realized that her need for security was only tenuously provided because her parents were likely to have been ambivalent about having an offspring when their own security was in question. With the help of the group, she further realized that the egocentric "child" decided that somehow she was the source of her parents' fear and anxiety.

Themes that emerged from these early recollections and consequent decisions included issues of trust, abandonment, powerlessness, fear of risk, pessimism, and self-discounting. Participants were able to relate these issues to current persistent problems in their work and love relationships.

Expressing the Unexpressed

Having identified the source of the hurt that had been so long buffered by culturally and socially induced guilt and shame, the participants were encouraged to express the emotions that had been suppressed so long. Anger directed at parents could be identified; anger directed at an amorphous government that had violated their right to freedom, however, was difficult to identify and justify. It was expressed as anger without a target, a diffuse, unlabeled rage.

Because of cultural prescriptions of emotional constraint, anger-release techniques were presented in progressive steps of intensity from passive to more active forms of release. Participants were invited to participate at a level that was just over their comfort zone and no more. The first step was to discuss the effects of suppressed emotions on the body and the relationship of this suppression to somatic illnesses and depression. People were then encouraged to relate their experiences to these concepts. The next step was to listen to music written and performed by Japanese Americans that expressed the trauma and humiliation of the internment experience. This process enabled participants to hear the feelings of others poignantly and emotionally expressed. For many, this released tears and feelings of affirmation.

Each step progressively intensified the release of feelings. To reduce anxiety about the public display of emotions, people were paired up for each exercise, and partners were instructed to affirm and nonverbally support the other person's feelings. Most preferred to pair up and go to separate rooms to have some privacy. Participants were then encouraged to move their bodies using Bioenergetic (Lowen, 1975) movements and to vocalize their feelings.

Debriefing was extensive, and inhibitions were discussed and acknowledged. The facilitator explained that reluctance or refusal to participate was honored as a choice and was not a sign of emotional inadequacy. Participants were assured that no judgment or clinical assessment would be assigned as a result of their choices. For all victims, choice without judgment is crucial to the healing process.

Grieving the Losses

As anger gave way to sadness, participants identified their grief over their losses. One man said, "When my parents lost their freedom, I guess I lost some of my childhood." Participants recalled discussion about material losses, but rarely about emotional losses. Children grew up or were born into a family environment where parents had lost the dignity of self-determination. Though most of the internees faced the situation with courage, the experience took away 2, 3, sometimes 4 years from the lives of innocent people. Participants were encouraged to identify ways to continue to heal the wounds of the inner child. Personal work, family work, and even political work was discussed.

Personal work was the need to acknowledge the losses that the child had experienced and to work to fulfill unmet needs. One man said, "I really need to let the child in me play joyfully and without guilt." Another woman said, "I'd like to let the fearful child in me have new experiences."

Family work included discussion of the detrimental effects of the "no talk" rule and how beginning to talk to parents and learning about their experiences could help participants integrate these feelings and experiences into their personal history. Discovering how parents had coped, how the internment had affected their relationships, and their feelings about their children were all issues that remained cloaked in silence for members of the group.

At the political level, of course, the pending monetary reparation of $20,000 for all the surviving internees was discussed. Many participants felt that the reparation represented a symbol of the long-awaited acknowledgment of the crime against the Japanese Americans. The guilt and loss of face shrouded in government silence could now be lifted and guilt assigned to the appropriate perpetrator. Foremost, acknowledgment and a formal apology would facilitate the healing of an insidious wound.

Termination

The group grew very close. A simulated family had been created where the pain could be identified, shared, and·validated. The grief work could be completed and the participants could move forward in their development. For most, the group experience was just the beginning of a therapeutic journey. One participant closed the final session with, "Now, maybe I can really do something with my freedom!"

Nuts and Bolts

In attempting to replicate this group experience, it is highly recommended that at least one of the facilitators be a member of the Japanese American community because of the highly sensitive nature of the issues involved and the cultural constraints against involving "outsiders." A facilitator who had also been an internee can facilitate some of the more difficult processes through self-disclosure and role modeling. Ideally, a male and female cotherapy team would be helpful. Because fewer men than women are likely to participate, the presence of a male role model can serve to validate the different gender perspectives. A small group size of five or six can serve to minimize the "public" quality of the group and also allow each member as much time as needed to tell his or her story and express deeply buried emotions that are likely to surface. A tight, safe context is essential for trauma victims; therefore, a weekend intensive with a 1-month and 6-month follow-up was adopted in order to prevent time disruption and screen out possible dropouts.

Because it is not generally acknowledged by the Japanese community or the community at large that people suffer today from the consequences of the internment, this group experience is not likely to be one that a participant would want to publicize. Therefore, participation is more likely to be enhanced by working within the community through notifying key people such as clergypersons, education and medical personnel, and social service providers who can, by word of mouth, inform people about such a group experience.

As with other groups, it is essential that the group leader conduct an individual intake to assess the psychological well-being of potential participants. Due to the social, cultural, and political influences that have caused much of the emotions around the internment experience to be suppressed, it is important that individual members possess the necessary ego strength to process intense emotions and that they have a relatively supportive environment to which they will return. Because an essential feature of the healing process is the ability to bond and experience acceptance, individuals with personality disorders that could interfere with this process are referred for individual therapy to deal with internment issues.

Conclusion

Because the evacuation of the Japanese Americans in 1942 occurred on the West Coast of the United States and Canada (Weglyn, 1976; Daniels, 1971), not every Japanese American client will have the direct experience of the internment as did those participating in the group discussed in this chapter. This description of the group experience, however, can help counselors to understand the acculturation process, cultural constraints and resources, and defensive strategies for coping with racism and discrimination when working with Japanese American clients. Additionally, the group process presented in this chapter can serve to demonstrate methods for modifying traditional interventions to make them culturally appropriate for the Japanese American client.

Implications of the internment experience on subsequent generations of Japanese Americans need to be addressed. Possible clinical issues to be considered include the intergenerational effects of cultural coping mechanisms with respect to the trauma of internment.

References

Courtois, C. A. (1988). *Healing the incest wound: Adult survivors in therapy.* New York: Norton.

Daniels, R. 1971. *Concentration camps USA: Japanese Americans and World War II.* New York: Holt, Rinehart & Winston.

Dinkmeyer, D. C., Pew, W. L., & Dinkmeyer, D. C. (1979). *Adlerian counseling and psychotherapy.* Monterey, CA: Brooks/Cole.

Hallenberg, K. (1988). *Internment experience of the Japanese/American. Elderly and their emotional adjustment.* Unpublished master's thesis.
Kiefer, C. W. (1974). *Changing cultures, changing lives.* San Francisco: Jossey-Bass.
Kitagawa, D. (1967). *Issei and Nisei. The internment years.* New York: Seabury Press.
Lowen, A. (1975). *Bioenergetics.* New York: Penguin Books.
Maykovich, M. (1972). *Japanese American identity dilemma.* Tokyo, Japan: Waseda University Press.
McGoldrick, M., Pearce, J. K., & Giordano, J. (1982). *Ethnicity and family therapy.* New York: Guilford Press.
Weglyn, M. (1976). *Years of infamy: The untold story of America's concentration camps.* New York: Morrow Press.

Additonal Resources

Armor, J., & Wright, P. (1989). *Manzanar.* New York: Vintage Books.
Broom, L., & Reimer, R. (1949). *Removal and return: The socioeconomical effects of the war on the Japanese Americans.* Berkeley: University of California Press.
Chuman, F. F. (1976). *The bamboo people: The law and Japanese Americans.* Chicago: Japanese American Citizens League.
DeVos, G. A. (1955). A qualitative Rorschach assessment of maladjustment and rigidity in acculturating Japanese Americans. *Genetic Psychology Monograph,* No. 52, p. 51.
Doi, T. (1973). *The anatomy of dependence.* Tokyo, Japan: Kodansha International.
Executive Order 9066. 7 Fed Reg 1407 (1942). As of March 31, 1942 Public Law 503, 18 USC Section 47(a) (1942).
Grier, W. H., & Cobbs, P. M. (1968). *Black rage.* New York: Basic Books.
Hosokawa, B. (1969). *Nisei: The quiet Americans.* New York: Morrow.
Ishigo, E. (1972). *Lone Heart Mountain.* Los Angeles: Anderson, Ritchie, & Simon.
Kashima, T. (1980). Japanese American internees' return, 1945 to 1955: Readjustment and social amnesia. *Phylon* (The Atlanta University), *41*(2), 107–115.
Kikumura, A. (1981). *Through harsh winters: The life of a Japanese immigrant woman.* Novato, CA: Chandler & Sharp.
Kitano, H. (1969). *Japanese Americans: The evolution of a subculture.* Englewood Cliffs, NJ: Prentice-Hall.
Kogawa, J. (1983). *Obasan.* Harmondsworth, England: Penguin Books.
Nishi, S. M., Bannai, L., & Tomihiro, C. (1983). Bibliography on redress: Wartime relocation and internment of Japanese Americans. *P/AAMHRC Research Review,* *2*(1), 6–8.
Ogawa, D. M. (1971). *From Japs to Japanese: The evolution of Japanese American stereotypes.* Berkeley, CA: McCutchan Press.
Okubo, M. (1946). *Citizen 13660.* New York: Columbia University Press.
Sone, M. (1953). *Nisei daughter.* Seattle: University of Washington Press.
Sue, S., & Morishima, J. K. (1982). *The mental health of Asian Americans.* San Francisco: Jossey-Bass.

Sue, S., & Wagner, N. N. (1973). *Asian-American psychological perspective*. Palo Alto, CA: Science and Behavior Books.

Takaki, R. (1989). *Strangers from a different shore*. Boston: Little, Brown.

Thomas, D. S., & Nishimoto, R. S. (1946). *The spoilage*. Berkeley, CA: University of California Press.

Tsukamoto, M., & Pinkerton, E. (1987). *We the people*. Elk Grove, CA: Laguna Publishers.

Wake, M. N. (1983). Acculturation and clinical issues affecting the mental health of Japanese Americans. *P/AAMHRC Research Review*, 2(4), 5–7.

Wilson, R. A., & Hosokawa, B. (1980). *East to America: A history of the Japanese in the United States*. New York: Morrow Press.

Yamamoto, J., Machizawa, S., & Steinberg, A. (1986). The Japanese American relocation center experience. *P/AAMHRC Research Review*, 5(3/4), 17–20.

Chapter 9

COUNSELING AMERICANS OF SOUTHEAST ASIAN DESCENT: THE IMPACT OF THE REFUGEE EXPERIENCE

Rita Chi-Ying Chung and Sumie Okazaki

The Southeast Asian refugee population is one of the fastest-growing ethnic minority groups in the United States. It is also a population with a particularly urgent mental health care need (Asian Community Mental Health Services, 1987). In order to counsel this population effectively, the counselor needs to be aware not only of the common presenting complaints and symptoms, but also of the cultural background and circumstances that brought Southeast Asian refugees to this country. This caveat is often issued for counseling the culturally different or immigrant population, but because the clients' refugee experience is out of the ordinary and their cultural background foreign to many counselors, the presenting problem can often be confusing and overwhelming both to the counselor and to the clients. Furthermore, it is difficult to discern how much of the present difficulties a particular refugee client faces is due to the refugee experience itself and how much is due to preexisting problems he or she may have had prior to the move. The purpose of this chapter is twofold: (1) to familiarize readers with the background and psychosocial adjustment issues the Southeast Asian refugee population face, and (2) to offer some practical suggestions from which the counselor can select those that respond to the needs of a particular client population.

This project was supported by the National Research Center on Asian American Mental Health (NIMH #R01 MH44331) and by the Medical Research Council of New Zealand.

Background

Since 1975, more than 1.5 million people have fled from their homes in Cambodia, Laos, and Vietnam; their mass exodus was precipitated by war, revolution, genocide, invasion, internal political turmoil, and famine. The United States has received far more refugees from Southeast Asia for permanent resettlement than from any other country. As of September 1988, nearly 900,000 Southeast Asians have resettled in the United States (Rumbaut, in press). According to the U.S. Committee for Refugees (1988), Vietnamese account for about 60% of this refugee population, Laotians for 20%, and Cambodians for 20%. The report also indicated that 56% of the refugees were men and 44% were women.

The age distribution of the refugee population is notably skewed toward the young, the median age being 23.9 years. Twenty-eight percent were school-aged children (6–17 years) and 19% were young adults between ages 18 and 24. Approximately 6% of the refugees were preschoolers, not including children born in the United States to refugee families. Only 2.5% were aged 65 or over. Rumbaut and Weeks (1986) estimated that over 200,000 children have been born in the United States to the refugee population.

Southeast Asian refugees have settled in every state in the United States. The population is especially concentrated in 14 states including California, Texas, and Washington. Although an initial effort was made by the U.S. government to scatter the refugees throughout the country so as not to overburden any particular community, California has by far the greatest concentration, accounting for about 40% of the total number of Southeast Asian refugees in the United States. This phenomenon is due to the second migration of the refugees, who moved from their original resettlement area to California in search of warmer weather, better job opportunities, close family ties, and a larger refugee community (Nguyen, 1982b).

Before discussing the refugees' migration to the United States, let us first clarify the definition of refugee status. The Southeast Asian refugees, like other refugee groups, must be distinguished from voluntary immigrants. The refugees were displaced from their countries by events outside of their control such as war and turbulent political situations; circumstances were such that it was no longer viable for them to remain in their home countries and lead their customary way of life. Consequently, the acquisition of the refugee status was involuntary and sudden, and they were practically and psychologically ill-prepared for the sudden departure from their familiar world.

Southeast Asian refugees entered the United States in two waves. The first wave covered the period from about April 1975 to December

1977, following the fall of Saigon. This first wave of refugees consisted mainly of Vietnamese who were targeted by the Vietcong movement because of their close associations with the American or South Vietnamese forces. Thus the Vietnamese were hastily evacuated by helicopters or by sea-lift, with the assistance of the American government. The Cambodians were bused to Thailand before entering the United States. Only a small number of Laotians came to the United States in 1975, but they did so by first going to Thailand and then applying for admittance on humanitarian grounds. These first-wave refugees tended to be well educated and were able to speak some English.

As the political repression intensified in Cambodia, Vietnam, and Laos, a new wave of refugees attempted to escape by sea or across the jungle. The exit of this second wave of refugees covered the period between 1978 and 1980 and included Vietnamese, Laotians, Hmong, and Cambodians. Those from Vietnam left their homeland on small, overcrowded, unseaworthy boats (thereby acquiring the label of the "boat people") and encountered brutal attacks by Thai pirates. It has been estimated that 77% of the boats that left Vietnam and eventually landed in Thailand were attacked by pirates (U.S. Committee for Refugees, 1984). More than 50% of the "boat people" were subjected to severe violence. Many were beaten, raped, or killed in such attacks. Those who were fortunate enough to reach the shores of Malaysia, Singapore, Indonesia, Hong Kong, or the Philippines were forced to wait months or even years in overcrowded and unsanitary camps before they were permanently resettled.

For Cambodians, Hmong, and Laotians, the journey across the jungle was no less traumatic and tragic than that of the Vietnamese by sea. They escaped by taking the land route (thus being called the "land refugees"), crossing mine fields, avoiding ambushes, and traversing jungles. They faced communist soldiers and suffered from tropical diseases. Death, hunger, starvation, and exhaustion were common. This second wave of refugees included a great number of the poor and illiterate, especially among the Hmong and Laotians. A small number of the "boat people" were middle-class, educated ethnic Chinese. However, in contrast to the first wave, the second wave of refugees were generally less educated and much less able to speak English. Furthermore, some of the second-wave refugees, especially those from rural areas, had virtually no exposure to Western culture prior to arriving in the United States.

Common Beliefs and Practices

In addition to the refugee experience, the Southeast Asians brought with them their cultural heritage. In order to place the presenting symptoms and complaints in a cultural context, it is vital to be aware of the Southeast Asian refugees' conception of mental health and help-seeking behavior. Due to the limited space allocated to this chapter, a comprehensive description of the cultural heritage of the many ethnic, linguistic, religious, tribal, and socioeconomic subgroups of Southeast Asians will not be covered. This information can be found elsewhere (Nguyen & Kehmeier, 1980; Olness, 1979; Scott, 1982; Whittaker, 1973). Here, we will briefly highlight the cultural beliefs and practices related to the conception of mental health that are relevant to understanding the refugees' help-seeking patterns and presentation of mental health problems.

Researchers have suggested that many culturally based attitudes influence Southeast Asian refugee help-seeking behavior (Van Deusen, 1982; Vignes & Hall, 1979). Tung (1983) found that traditional beliefs, superstitions, and the belief in the supernatural are common barriers to mental health care. This certainly is true of this population. Southeast Asian views on what constitutes mental disorders are also different from Western views.

Studies suggest that Southeast Asian refugee patients behave similarly to Chinese American patients in that they express depression and other psychological problems predominantly through somatic symptoms such as headaches, weakness, pressure on the chest or head, insomnia, and tenseness (Lin, Tazuma, & Masuda, 1979; Mollica, Wyshak, & Lavelle, 1987). The argument that Asian Americans tend to somatize psychological problems has created considerable controversy. For instance, Rumbaut (1985) characterized the concept of somatization as a Western stereotype of Asian Americans' inability to express themselves psychologically. Many have argued the importance of recognizing that although Southeast Asian Americans may present initially with somatic complaints, they are capable of discussing their problems in psychological terms (Cheung, 1982; Kinzie et al., 1982; Mollica et al., 1987; Mollica, Lavelle, & Khuon, 1985; Rumbaut, 1985).

In general, people from Asian cultures tend to believe that mental disturbance is associated with organic or somatic factors; they view mental and physical health as closely interrelated (Sue & Morishima, 1982). Mental disturbances are highly stigmatized in most Asian cultures. Mental illnesses are believed to reflect poorly on one's family and one's heredity because they are regarded as signs of personal weakness. These beliefs cause Asian Americans to avoid seeking advice outside the family for psychological problems. Southeast Asian Americans are no exception to holding such beliefs.

Southeast Asian American communities often rely on indigenous healers and folk medicine (Egawa & Tashima, 1982; Muecke, 1983; Yeatman & Dang, 1980). It has been suggested that a Western physician can assume that Southeast Asian patients are concurrently utilizing a traditional cure for their symptoms along with Western medical treatment (Mollica & Lavelle, 1988). Many indigenous healing practices involve beliefs in possession, soul loss, and witchcraft. Rituals for exorcism involve calling back the "souls" of individuals believed to be suffering from soul loss and asking local guardian gods for protection. These rituals are performed by shamans and Taoist priests in Vietnam (Hickey, 1964) and by Buddhist monks in Laos and Cambodia (Westermeyer, 1973). Fortune-telling with cards and coins, the Chinese horoscope, and physiognomy (palm reading and reading of facial features) are also popular.

Chinese medical practices have influenced the belief systems of most people from Southeast Asian cultures. Chinese folk remedies are widely practiced among the Vietnamese, Cambodians, and Hmong (but not among Laotians), and they include use of herbal concoctions and poultices, forms of acupuncture, massage, and the dermabrasive practices of cupping, pinching, rubbing, and burning. Coin rubbing leaves bruises on the skin that are often mistaken for child abuse (Nguyen, Nguyen, & Nguyen, 1987). Acupuncture is often used as a remedy for mental illness (e.g., depression, psychoses) because mental illness is seen as a disturbance of the internal vital energy.

It is important to recognize that many Americans of Southeast Asian descent are unfamiliar with Western mental health concepts (Lin & Masuda, 1983). Laos never had psychiatrists, whereas in South Vietnam there were only a handful in 1975. It is doubtful that there were any mental health professionals in Cambodia. Accordingly, when Americans of Southeast Asian descent seek treatment from Western doctors, they expect a quick relief of symptoms. They often request injection or medication because they view mental illness as a physical disorder. Indeed, mental illnesses are seen as a subcategory of life misfortunes (such as war and theft), and no clear differentiation between psychological and physical problems is made.

It is also important to be cognizant of the religious beliefs of Southeast Asian refugees. The religious beliefs and health practices of this population often cannot be distinguished from one another, given the refugees' conviction that religious beliefs influence health ideas and practices, which in turn affect this population's subsequent use of the medical system. Religious beliefs differ among various Southeast Asian cultures.

Vietnamese religious beliefs are a combination of Buddhism, Taoism, and Confucianism, but Buddhism plays a more peripheral role for the Vietnamese than it does for Cambodians. The Confucian concepts (such as filial piety; ancestor worship; hierarchical, yet reciprocal interpersonal relationships; high regard for education, social status, and material welfare; family orientation, loss of face, and shame) play prominently in

Vietnamese values and are similar to concepts in the Chinese culture. Cambodians' beliefs are derived from Thervada Buddhism, and religion plays a central role in every aspect of their life. Cambodians place importance in attaining personal spiritual enlightenment rather than in achieving material success. Laotians strongly believe in animism, which is a set of beliefs in the supernatural, gods, demons, and evil spirits as an essential part of everyday life. Illnesses are often treated by a shaman rather than by a medical professional. For example, "string tying" is a common practice in which a cord is tied around the wrist to enable a person to communicate with the spirit of decreased ancestors or to prevent the loss of a sick person's soul. The string may be perceived as a symbol of a patient's spiritual wholeness and his or her social and familial support system (Muecke, 1983).

In addition to cultural barriers for seeking counseling, several social factors also prevent the refugees from obtaining help. Many refugee groups are largely unaware of the types and availability of mental health services (Van Deusen, 1982). It has also been suggested that a possible cause of low service utilization is that many Southeast Asian refugees have experienced difficulties in sharing their health complaints because of the inadequacy or unavailability of interpreters (Mollica & Lavelle, 1988).

Furthermore, when Southeast Asian clients do finally present at a counseling setting, their presentation may be of a mixed psychological and medical nature that may require a medical evaluation (Kinzie, 1985). A number of reports indicate a high prevalence of medical problems in the Southeast Asian refugee community (Catanzaro & Moser, 1982; Hoang & Erickson, 1985; Mollica, Wyshak, Coelho, & Lavelle, 1985). These problems add to the refugees' financial and psychological difficulties. Thus, in understanding the context in which Southeast Asian refugees present their counseling needs, it is important to recognize the extent of their medical, social welfare, spiritual, and psychological needs.

Psychosocial Adjustment

Two major factors contribute to the psychosocial maladjustment of the Southeast Asian refugees. One is the trauma they experienced in the process of leaving the country of origin, and the other is a set of problems related to resettlement and adjustment in the United States. Mollica, Wyshak, Coelho, & Lavelle (1985) identified the types of major trauma events refugees have commonly experienced and found that Cambodians had experienced an average of nine traumatic events during the war, the escape, and the refugee camp stay. Mollica and his colleagues

(1987) then reclassified the types of trauma events into four general categories: (a) deprivation (e.g., food and shelter), (b) physical injury and torture, (c) incarceration and reeducation camps, and (d) witnessing killing and torture. The Hmong, Laotians, and Vietnamese groups were found to have experienced traumatic events in three categories on the average. Some also experience survivor's guilt in regard to those who were lost, killed, or left behind.

Many refugees experienced or witnessed torture, rape, and other human atrocities, and they survived emotionally by acting "dumb." This phenomenon is a common reaction not particular to Southeast Asians, but also among other survivors of atrocities. The term *Tiing Mooung* ("dummy" personality, puppet, or scarecrow) was commonly used by the Khmer to describe behavior of refugees under the Khmer Rouge Regime (1975–1979). In order to survive, individuals acted as if they were deaf, dumb, foolish, confused, or stupid, and learned to obey orders obediently without asking questions or complaining because they knew that if they seemed "smart" they would be tortured or executed. This fear of death and punishment has remained in the minds of many Khmer refugees. They continue to be afraid to speak up or show their true feelings, and continue to act like a *Tiing Mooung* even in this country (Mollica & Jalbert, 1989). In addition, Rożee and Van Boemel (1989) documented high incidences of nonorganic blindness among older Cambodian refugee women who had experienced severe trauma during and after the fall of Cambodia in 1975. The authors found that the degree of subjective visual impairment was significantly related to the number of years the women were under internment in communist camps where they experienced forced labor, starvation, physical and sexual abuse, and the execution of significant others.

Moreover, the resettlement process poses additional challenges for the Southeast Asian refugees. In an initial resettlement period of 1 to 2 years, the refugees seek to fulfill basic, concrete needs such as employment and housing (Tayabas & Pok, 1983). During this period, the refugees display an impressive drive to recover what has been lost and to rebuild their lives. Because most of the educational qualifications obtained in Southeast Asia do not transfer to this country, the socioeconomic status of the more educated refugees drops considerably when they first arrive in the United States. Some of the initial drop in status can be recovered over time, with increased acculturation, language improvement, retraining programs, hard work, and determination. However, most refugees remain underemployed. The results of a longitudinal study on the psychosocial adjustment of first-wave Vietnamese refugees (Lin, Masuda, & Tazuma, 1982; Lin, Tazuma, & Masuda, 1979; Masuda, Lin, & Tazuma, 1980) indicated that over a 3-year period, the refugees made remarkable progress in all aspects of resettlement. But regardless of their prior social class background in Vietnam, most held skilled and semiskilled working-class jobs. Only 2% of those with prestigious, professional jobs in Vietnam had regained their former status after 3 years.

During the resettlement period, many refugees also change jobs, attend English as a Second Language (ESL) classes, or relocate from their initial placement area to an area of greater refugee concentration. It has been indicated that the first-wave refugees seem to be adjusting more successfully than second-wave refugees because they tend to have been better educated, more wealthy, and possessed more resources (Nguyen, 1982a).

After the initial period of resettlement, emotional and psychological problems begin to appear as the refugees start to confront the loss of their culture, identity, and habits. What had once been routine in their home country is now a major ordeal. For example, using a telephone, going to a bank, or going shopping are some of the new tasks they must master. They also experience increased problems within the family, and the level of mental dysfunction is likely to increase (Lin et al., 1979). Strains begin to surface at home because the unemployment or underemployment of men commonly forces wives to work; such changes in gender roles present a conflict between the values of their home culture and those of the host country. Furthermore, children and adolescents acculturate faster than do parents to the host culture and show less respect for traditional Southeast Asian values. Such frustrations and family tensions often lead to an increase in domestic violence that may not have occurred in the home country. For many families, the refugee experience may change a previously pathological family dynamic in a dramatic way. For example, survivor's guilt for some individuals is compounded by what may have been a dysfunctional family situation in the old country prior to the move. For others, the shared refugee experience may have strengthened family ties so that previous dysfunction within the family no longer exists. Some refugees experience nostalgia, depression, anxiety, survivor's guilt, and frustration so acutely that they toy with the idea of returning to their home country. Such ideations are common, especially among those who did not make the decision to leave, namely adolescents.

Despite the progress the Vietnamese have made in adapting to the United States, Lin and his colleagues (1979, 1982) and Masuda et al. (1980) found a consistently high level of life stress and emotional disturbances over the initial 3-year period. About half of the refugees consistently showed signs of severe psychological distress. It was suggested that this was related to stressors such as financial problems and conflict within the family.

Because of the compounding problem of their memory of the trauma and their less-than-optimal daily living conditions, the Southeast Asian refugees are at high risk for mental disorders. Indeed, high prevalence of serious depression has been reported in the clinics serving Southeast Asian refugees (Kinzie & Manson, 1983; Mollica, Wyshak, Coelho, & Lavelle, 1985; Mollica & Lavelle, 1988). Recent studies have revealed that many Southeast Asian patients suffer from both depression and posttraumatic stress disorder (PTSD) (Kinzie, Frederickson, Ben, Fleck, & Karls, 1984; Mollica, Wyshak, Coelho, & Lavelle, 1985; Mollica et al., 1987). This finding is not unexpected considering the serious multiple traumas (e.g., torture, witnessing executions) that many Southeast Asian refugees experienced.

Within the Southeast Asian population, specific subgroups have been identified as being at high risk for developing serious psychiatric disorders, primarily due to their high level of traumatic experiences and low level of resources. Refugee women and children are the most seriously traumatized. Many young girls and women were seriously victimized in the attacks by pirates; many were raped, kidnapped, and sold into prostitution. In addition, a large percentage of the refugee women (especially the Cambodians) were widowed, or they lost their children to starvation, kidnapping, or death.

Older men (above age 45) and younger single men (below age 21) also have been found to be highly distressed because of the lack of familial and social support (Lin et al., 1979). Older men particularly have difficulty finding jobs because most of them had been well established back home. In the United States they are considerably disadvantaged in terms of having to learn a new language, acquire new skills, and get meaningful jobs relative to their status and expectations. They tend to experience more social isolation because the pace of acculturation is slower for them (Maidow, cited in Beiser, 1988).

Refugee adolescents in particular suffer from identity problems. According to Tobin and Friedman (1984), refugee adolescents live not in two cultures, but in three; the American culture they see in school and on television, the culture of their childhood sustained in their memories and in their parents' nostalgic stories of the "old world," and the refugee culture of war, flight, and camps. Southeast Asian adolescents often manifest their difficulties in behaviors typical of troubled adolescents, such as suicide, social deviance, depression, substance abuse, or membership in gangs. For the Southeast Asians, however, the underlying causes of such behavior are likely to be associated with their unique refugee experience and must be understood as such.

In addition, refugee children and adolescents often face problems with adaptation in school. Racial tension and brawls are a regular aspect of school life for many Southeast Asian children in California, where many report being punched, mimicked, harassed, or robbed by non-Asian students (Huang, 1989). Intergenerational conflicts are also common. During the resettlement period, refugee children and adolescents witnessed the transformation of their parents from previously competent, autonomous caretakers to depressed, overwhelmed, and dependent individuals. Adolescents' confidence in their parents is inevitably undermined when the parents become dependent on the children, who acquire the new language and customs more quickly.

Children and adolescents who were not accompanied by close family members in their resettlement are at a particularly great risk for mental health problems (Nidorf, 1985; Williams & Westermeyer, 1983). Those who left Southeast Asia without parents may feel that their parents rejected them, despite the fact that they acknowledge parental sacrifice. Those who encountered trauma during the escape may blame their parents for arranging the escape or for not protecting them. Certain events may trigger increased anxiety or feelings of guilt and depression, such as receiving letters from home or on ethnic holidays. American school holidays also may intensify the refugee youth's loneliness and isolation because they provide much unstructured time to think about personal losses and to worry about the future and the family back in Asia (Huang, 1989).

The unaccompanied minors often live with older adolescent siblings who are ill-equipped to offer parental guidance, warmth, and attention. In other cases, they live with distant relatives, who have few emotional bonds to them but are acting as caretakers out of familial duty or for an opportunity to earn additional welfare money. Nidorf (1985) observed that this group of minors also do not have meaningful support from close adult family members, and they often manifest symptoms of severe depression, hysterical conversion reactions, high levels of agitation, and antisocial and acting-out behaviors. They also tend to experience intense feelings of loneliness, isolation, "not belonging," and homesickness. Furthermore, due to the notion of family and filial piety as the main ingredient of the Southeast Asian family structure, their lack of family brings shame, confusion, general despair, humiliation, and self-denigration. These youths are also at high risk for joining gang activities as a way of belonging to a closely-tied unit (Nidorf).

Preparation for Counseling

Southeast Asian clients' expectations for social service assistance are high. Presentation of psychological complaints and counseling needs are often coupled with requests for concrete social services, which may include assistance with housing, employment, welfare, and so on. Priorities for responding to these requests should be established to develop trust and credibility. On the other hand, the need for concrete services can assume a magnitude of desperation so severe that receiving these services may overshadow any other counseling issues. This section highlights some common issues and considerations that precede the actual counseling sessions.

The major social problems that Southeast Asian refugees often present fall into "the resettlement triad"—language, housing, and employment. Because such problems are often presented to counselors and many counseling issues involve daily living problems, there is an urgent need for a linkage between existing resettlement programs, social service providers, and the mental health or counseling services. The plight of many refugee women illustrates this point. Refugee women express feeling isolated more often than do refugee men (Rumbaut, in press). Their difficulties seem to arise largely from their reluctance to attend ESL programs; knowing the language of the host country is often the first step in adapting to the culture. The women do not want to attend ESL classes because they feel they cannot understand anything. It has been suggested that their memory and concentration have been greatly impaired by trauma experiences (Mollica, Lavelle, & Khuon, 1985). They also do not attend the classes because of transportation problems and lack of child care facilities. Without the knowledge of English, the refugee women remain isolated and incapable of functioning effectively in American society.

To begin solving the problems presented in counseling, establishing liaisons with other service delivery systems or community agencies (such as public health/medical clinics, schools, and work and social rehabilitation programs) is crucial. In addition, linkages between the counseling agent and community leaders, spiritual leaders, elders, monks, priests, herbalists, and shamans seem to be helpful. As a case in point, one mental health agency that serves predominantly Southeast Asian refugees has a Buddhist monk on the counseling staff, and this has increased the credibility of the agency among the Cambodian refugee clients (Chan, 1987).

In counseling Southeast Asian Americans, language is a major barrier in the communication between the client and the counselor. A method commonly used to overcome this obstacle is the use of translators or interpreters. In most cases, however, these translators and interpreters are untrained. Usually family or community members who can understand some English, such as children, relatives, or neighbors, are used as translators. Because of their lack of training, errors in translation are common. The translators may not fully understand the counselor and may be too embarrassed to say so. Some translators often answer for the client without posing the question to the client because the translator feels that he or she knows the answer. Difficulties also arise in confidentiality, poor paraphrasing of questions, and inadequate translation of medical and psychological terms into the client's language.

Furthermore, many misdiagnoses occur because of cultural misunderstanding. In one instance, a Southeast Asian man was committed to a psychiatric institution and was heavily medicated because his sponsor reported that he kept referring to dead relatives appearing and speaking to him. What the sponsor failed to realize was that referring to the dead is a common and accepted behavior among people from Southeast Asian cultures.

As one can see, training translators and interpreters is crucial for effective counseling. If available, consultation with trained Southeast Asian paraprofessionals is strongly recommended. Southeast Asian mental health paraprofessionals are not just interpreters or translators, but specialized mental health clinicians who are familiar with both Western models of disease and the unique medical and psychiatric worldview of their own culture. They will know how to convey adequately subtle medical and cultural meanings between clients and physicians (Mollica & Lavelle, 1988). Hence, bilingual/bicultural clinicians not only bridge the gap between language and treatment, but they also help to establish a culturally sensitive treatment milieu.

Approaches to Counseling

Once some of the more pressing daily living needs are met, the counselor may proceed in dealing with psychological issues. Two main issues in counseling Southeast Asian refugee clients will be outlined in this section. First, we are concerned with the nonspecific factor of the counseling relationship; that is, in establishing the therapeutic relationship with the refugee clients. Second, we offer some techniques and examples in dealing with specific counseling content of this special population. However, the following guidelines must be tempered with various needs of the particular population. In efforts to provide culturally sensitive service, the counselor must also beware of being "too Asian," as in the case of counseling a parent-child conflict. While showing respect for the Southeast Asian culture, the counselor should educate the parents in the customs and laws of this country as well. For example, corporal punishment is commonly practiced among the Southeast Asians as a means of disciplining a child or an adolescent. The counselor must communicate to the parents that severe physical punishment is not acceptable in this country and that there are laws concerning child abuse.

Generally, in establishing a counseling relationship with Southeast Asian refugee clients, many principles for counseling Asian American clients apply. Sue and Zane (1987) suggested that a counselor needs to maintain both ascribed and achieved credibility with Asian American clients in order to engage them in the counseling or psychotherapy process and to prevent premature termination. Ascribed credibility is governed by the counselor's position or role factors such as age, sex, or expertise in traditional Asian cultures, whereas achieved credibility comes from what the therapist or counselor actually does in the session to gain the trust and confidence of the client. Even if the counselor has an initially low ascribed credibility with a Southeast Asian client, he or she may achieve credibility by being culturally sensitive. The first step toward achieving credibility is the counselor's effort in gaining familiarity with the client's cultural and personal background.

Some suggestions for achieving credibility follow. First, the counselor should be aware of the refugee clients' unfamiliarity with the Western style of "talk" therapy, and be flexible with the format of the sessions. The refugee clients should be made as comfortable as possible, for example, by conducting the session sitting on a floor mattress rather than in chairs, or by serving Chinese tea instead of coffee. As trivial as such accommodations in physical settings may seem, they serve to gain the trust of the refugee clients. Physical settings are also important in understanding cultural norms for personal space. Many Asian cultures do not condone physical touching or hugging.

In interacting with Southeast Asian clients, the counselor must recognize the importance of establishing sufficient trust and confidentiality before probing for what is disturbing the client. This process may take longer with Southeast Asian clients than with more acculturated Asian clients, because the ascribed credibility of "talk therapy" is low. With refugee clients particularly, a good way to initiate interaction would be to discuss everyday survival issues, such as asking the clients if they have sufficient medical care, housing, and income. The purpose of such discussion is not necessarily to offer them actual assistance in solving such problems, but to show concern about their overall well-being.

When working with specific problems that refugee clients bring in, the general goal is to (a) alleviate hopelessness, (b) instill in clients faith in themselves and hope for the future, (c) provide strategies for coping with stress, and (d) help clients attain a sense of mastery. To achieve these ends, the principle is to use whatever materials and techniques the counselor possesses in his or her background to help the clients express their concerns, and not be limited by the traditional "talking" approaches. A useful rule of thumb is to concretize or to act out the feelings and the goals through various mediums such as art, dance, and music. The aim is to empower the refugee clients and to make them self-sufficient because what they often lack is the resources. Once they are given the resources (which often can be as little as providing them with a meeting space for support groups), many clients can begin to help themselves.

A good starting point in the counseling process is to find out what coping skills the refugee clients possessed or used in Southeast Asia. Then the counselor may proceed to restore and to reinforce those skills so that new coping strategies can be built on them. Group work has been found to be effective with many Southeast Asian clients to achieve these ends and to normalize the refugee experiences. Refugee clients may come to realize that seeking help from others is an acceptable way of coping with stress and that they can be of support to each other. In addition, group counseling can offer clients socially acceptable ways to act out their feelings (such as hitting a pillow to provide a catharsis for anger). Starting the sessions with such physically oriented activities, rather than launching right into discussions of experiences and feelings, serves as a good ice breaker.

An effective exercise for discussing coping and adaptation issues with refugee clients (individually or in a group) is to have them list the cultural differences between themselves and the new environment and what they see as the concrete tasks for adapting to the new culture (Tran, 1988). Both the process of compiling the list and the list itself are informative to the counselor in assessing how the individual is adapting, the willingness of the individual to adapt, and whether the barriers to adaptation are self-imposed or not. Once the list is completed, the counselor may direct the discussion toward how the distance between the two cultures can be bridged. A similar exercise in discussing the adaptation process is to have the clients draw a "tree of life," in which the roots signify the skills and the resources they possess (e.g., being Asian, being bilingual, having a supportive family), the trunk is the process (e.g., education, job training), and the branches bear the fruits of life—past and present achievements such as current job and aspirations for the future. In mapping out their resources and aspirations concretely, the Southeast Asian refugee clients can begin to see where they are in the adaptation process, what strengths they have, and what barriers they need to overcome in order to achieve their goals. In one instance, a refugee man in his mid-20s, who was fluent in five languages, revealed that his aspiration was to work as a nurse in this country as he had done back in Asia, but that he had given up his hopes for doing so because his English language skills were inadequate. Once his personal resources and aspirations were concretely laid out in front of the group, the group and the counselor helped him to gain the confidence he needed in order to take steps toward attaining his goals.

Another useful group technique, which engages the refugee clients and also serves to illustrate the concepts of coping, is the use of simple stories that include Eastern concepts and philosophies (e.g., Buddhist,

Confucian, or Taoist) that are familiar to the clients. Some examples of the stories are included following the conclusion of this chapter. Many of these stories illustrate the concept of yin and yang; the moral of the stories illustrates that the best strategy for coping with stress is by "going with the flow" and by counteracting with the opposite force rather than resisting the stress head-on. In using such stories, it is often effective to have members of the group enact the parables physically. By using the concept of yin and yang familiar to the Southeast Asian clients, and also by dramatizing, the counselor is literally illustrating for the client a way to cope with stress.

At some point in the counseling process, the counselor should also be prepared to listen to the client's trauma story, which some refugees may be willing to share once the counseling relationship has been established. This is an area where the counselor's "doing the homework" by learning about the experiences of the refugee population becomes crucial. Without proper awareness of the refugees' background, an untrained counselor's initial reaction to the Southeast Asian client's "horror story" is commonly shock and awe at the degree of appallingly inhumane cruelty to which the client has been subjected. Such a reaction on the counselor's part, although understandable, is often not helpful to the client urgently seeking help from an authority.

Studies demonstrate that clients' hopelessness is a major presenting symptom (Mollica & Lavelle, 1988). Mollica, Wyshak, Coelho, and Lavelle (1985) found that feelings of hopelessness affect not only the patients but also the staff addressing the refugee problems. It is vital to be aware that even experienced counselors are frequently overwhelmed and revolted by the horror of their clients' personal stories and can become easily infected by the hopelessness of their clients. Many counselors trained in the Western model have had no training to help them prepare for the strong emotional reactions they may develop in reaction to trauma stories. The taxing nature of listening to such stories often leads to the counselor's reluctance to probe too deeply into their clients' life experiences. Therefore, it is in the best interest of all concerned to refer clients with extreme trauma experiences to clinicians who are trained to deal with traumas in a culturally sensitive manner.

In working with most refugee clients, however, it is of foremost importance for the counselor first to normalize both the trauma experience and the reaction by acknowledging that the client's experience is not an isolated incident and that his or her present state (e.g., feelings of isolation, nightmares) is a normal reaction. Second, the counselor must point out that it is the client's resources (i.e., courage and strength) that got the client this far.

As mentioned earlier, many refugee clients suffer from severe demoralization, in addition to depression and PTSD. Both depression and

PTSD can impair the clients' memory, which makes even the daily routine difficult for them and in turn increases their feeling of being out of control and insufficient. To illustrate the extent of memory deficit, F. Chan (personal communication, April, 1990) reported that on the Digit Span test of the Wechsler Adult Intelligence Scale-Revised (WAIS-R), the refugee PTSD patients could remember on the average only 3 digits forward and 2 digits backward. In order to combat memory deficits, Chan uses memory training with the refugee patients by giving them mnemonic techniques (especially those that use visual imagery) to help them remember day-to-day events. Regaining some control over their memory gives the refugees a sense of hope, mastery, and control. It also restores self-esteem, improves their mood, and relieves other depressive symptoms. Moreover, memory training may be used as a preparation for ESL classes.

Conclusion

Counseling Americans of Southeast Asian descent is a task that presents an enormous challenge to the existing mental health and counseling systems. With this population, cultural sensitivity is not an added nicety, but rather a prerequisite in order to begin to help them. A counselor's task of becoming familiar with the cultural and historical background of the refugees is difficult even for counselors who are of Asian, but not Southeast Asian, descent.

There has been some research on the efficacy of parallel mental health services (i.e., services that are tailored specifically to meet the particular needs of the ethnic population they serve) for ethnic minority clients (Flaskerud, 1986; Snowden, Ulvang, & Rezentes, 1989; Zane, 1989). However, establishing such elaborate services and training multilingual, multicultural counselors are long-term goals; many communities lack the resources, and the counseling needs of the refugees are urgent. Thus, we have attempted to outline some background information, guidelines, and suggestions essential for counseling Southeast Asian refugees. Yet, this represents only the beginning of a process in working with this population. Of course, nothing can substitute for the actual experience of and interactions with the refugee population. The key is to recognize the courage and strength in the refugees that brought them to this country and to engage those powers in their adaptation and growth process.

Stories Adapted From Old Chinese Tales

Story of the Bamboo

During a fierce storm, the bamboo bends every which way the wind blows, while the other trees (e.g., oak) stand straight and resist the wind. But after the storm the bamboo tree stands proudly, looking into the heaven and reaching for life, dreams, and hopes. The other trees lie on the ground lifeless and without hope because they resisted the wind; they were not flexible and did not move with the wind.

The Frog

A frog sitting at the bottom of a well looks up toward the opening of the well and asks, "Oh! That's the size of the sky?" In reality the frog will not know how big the sky is until it steps out of the well. The frog in a well is limited in its knowledge by a narrow vision.

References

Asian Community Mental Health Services. (1987). *California Southeast Asian mental health needs assessment*. Oakland, CA: Author.

Beiser, M. (1988). Influence of time, ethnicity, and attachment on depression in Southeast Asian refugees. *American Journal of Psychiatry, 145*(1), 46–51.

Catanzaro, A., & Moser, J. R. (1982). Health status of refugees from Vietnam, Laos and Cambodia. *Journal of American Medical Association, 244*(24), 2748–2749.

Chan, F. (1987, April). Survivors of the Killing Fields. A paper presented at the Western Psychological Association Convention, Long Beach, CA.

Cheung, F. H. (1982). Psychological symptoms among Chinese in urban Hong Kong. *Social Science and Medicine, 16*, 1339–1344.

Egawa, J. E., & Tashima, N. (1982). *Indigenous healers in Southeast Asian refugee communities*. San Francisco: Pacific Asian Mental Health Research Project.

Flaskerud, J. (1986). The effects of culture-compatible intervention on the utilization of mental health services by minority clients. *Community Mental Health Journal, 22*(2), 127–141.

Hickey, G. C. (1964). *Village in Vietnam*. New Haven: Yale University Press.

Hoang, G. N., & Erickson, R. V. (1985). Cultural barriers to effective medical care among Indochinese patients. *American Review of Medicine, 36*, 229–239.

Huang, L. N. (1989). Southeast Asian refugee children and adolescents. In J. T. Gibbs & L. N. Huang (Eds.), *Children of color: Psychological interventions with minority children*. San Francisco: Jossey-Bass.

Kinzie, J. D. (1985). Overview of clinical issues in the treatment of Southeast Asian refugees. In T. C. Owan (Ed.), *Southeast Asian mental health: Treatment, prevention, services, training, and research* (pp. 113–135). Washington, DC: NIMH.

Kinzie, J. D., Frederickson, R. H., Ben, R., Fleck, J., & Karls, W. (1984). Post-traumatic stress disorder among survivors of Cambodian concentration camps. *American Journal of Psychiatry, 141*(5), 645–650.

Kinzie, J. D., & Manson, S. (1983). Five years' experience with Indochinese refugee psychiatric patients. *Journal of Operational Psychiatry, 14*(3), 105–111.

Kinzie, J. D., Manson, S., Do, V., Nguyen, T., Anh, B., & Pho, T. (1982). Development and validation of a Vietnamese Language Depression Rating Scale. *American Journal of Psychiatry, 139*(10), 1276–1281.

Lin, K. M., & Masuda, M. (1983). Impact of the refugee experience: Mental health issues of the Southeast Asians. In *Bridging cultures: Southeast Asian refugees in America* (pp. 32–52). Los Angeles: Special Services for Groups— Asian American Community Mental Health Training Center.

Lin, K. M., Masuda, M., & Tazuma, L. (1982). Adaptational problems of Vietnamese refugees: Part III. Case studies in clinic and field: Adaptive and maladaptive. *Psychiatric Journal of University of Ottawa, 7*(3), 173–183.

Lin, K. M., Tazuma, L., & Masuda, M. (1979). Adaptational problems of Vietnamese refugees. *Archives of General Psychiatry, 36*, 955–961.

Masuda, M., Lin, K. M., & Tazuma, L. (1980). Adaptation problems of Vietnamese refugees: II. Life changes and perception of life events. *Archives of General Psychiatry, 37*, 447–450.

Mollica, R. F., & Jalbert, R. R. (1989). *Community of confinement: The mental health crisis on Site Two: Displaced persons' camps on the Thai-Kampuchean border.* Boston, MA: Committee on World Federation for Mental Health.

Mollica, R. F., & Lavelle, J. (1988). Southeast Asian refugees. In L. Comas-Diaz & E. H. Griffith (Eds.), *Clinical guidelines in cross-cultural mental health* (pp. 262–303). New York: Wiley.

Mollica, R. F., Lavelle, J., & Khuon, F. (1985, May). *Khmer widows at highest risk.* A paper presented at the Cambodian Mental Health Conference: A day to explore issues and alternative approaches to care. New York, NY.

Mollica, R. F., Wyshak, G., Coelho, R., & Lavelle, J. (1985). *The Southeast Asian psychiatry patient: A treatment outcome study.* Boston: Indochinese Psychiatric Clinic.

Mollica, R. F., Wyshak, G., & Lavelle, J. (1987). The psychosocial impact of war trauma and torture on Southeast Asian refugees. *American Journal of Psychiatry, 144*(12), 1567–1572.

Muecke, M. A. (1983). Caring for Southeast Asian refugees in the U.S.A. *American Journal of Public Health, 73*(4), 431–438.

Nguyen, D. L., & Kehmeier, D. F. (1980). The Vietnamese. In J. F. McDermott, Jr., W. Tseng, & T. W. Maretzki (Eds.), *People and cultures of Hawaii: A psychocultural profile.* Honolulu: University of Hawaii Press.

Nguyen, N., Nguyen, P. H., & Nguyen, L. H. (1987). *Coin treatment in Vietnamese families: Traditional medical practice vs. child abuse.* Unpublished manuscript.

Nguyen, S. (1982a). Psychiatric and psychosomatic problems among Southeast Asian refugees. *Psychiatric Journal of the University of Ottawa, 7*(3), 163–172.

Nguyen, S. (1982b). The psycho-social adjustment and the mental health of Southeast Asian refugees. *Psychiatric Journal of the University of Ottawa, 7*(1), 26–35.

Nidorf, J. F. (1985). Mental health and refugee youths: A model for diagnostic training. In T.C. Owan (Ed.), *Southeast Asian mental health: Treatment, prevention, services, training, and research* (pp. 391–429). Washington, DC: NIMH.

Olness, K. (1979). Indochinese refugees: Cultural aspects in working with Lao refugees. *Minnesota Medicine, 62,* 871–874.

Rożee, P. D., & Van Boemel, G. (1989). The psychological effects of war trauma and abuse on older Cambodian refugee women. *Women and Therapy, 8*(4), 23–50.

Rumbaut, R. G. (1985). Mental health and the refugee experience: A comparative study of Southeast Asian refugees. In T. C. Owan (Ed.), *Southeast Asian mental health: Treatment, prevention, services, training, and research* (pp. 433–486). Washington, DC: NIMH.

Rumbaut, R. G. (in press). The agony of exile: A study of the migration and adaptation of Indochinese refugee adults and children. In T. L. Aheam & J. Garrison (Eds.), *Refugee children: Theory, research and practice*. Baltimore: Johns Hopkins University Press.

Rumbaut, R. G., & Weeks, J. R. (1986). Fertility and adaptation: Indochinese refugees in the U.S. *International Migration Review, 20*(2), 428–466.

Scott, G. M., Jr. (1982). The Hmong refugee community in San Diego: Theoretical and practical implications of its continuing ethnic solidarity. *Anthropological Quarterly, 55,* 146–160.

Snowden, L. R., Ulvang, R., & Rezentes, J. (1989). Low-income Blacks in community mental health: Forming a treatment relationship. *Community Mental Health Journal, 25*(1), 51–59.

Sue, S., & Morishima, J. K. (1982). *The mental health of Asian Americans*. San Francisco: Jossey-Bass.

Sue, S., & Zane, N. (1987). The role of culture and cultural techniques in psychotherapy: A critique and reformulation. *American Psychologist, 42*(1), 37–45.

Tayabas, T., & Pok, T. (1983). The arrival of the Southeast Asian refugees in America: An overview. In *Bridging cultures: Southeast Asian refugees in America* (pp. 3–14). Los Angeles: Special Services for Groups—Asian American Community Mental Health Training Center.

Tobin, J. J., & Friedman, J. (1984). Intercultural and developmental stresses confronting Southeast Asian refugee adolescents. *Journal of Operational Psychiatry, 15,* 39–45.

Tran, M. T. (1988). In the eyes of the beholders: Indochinese views on culture values and changes. *Journal of Vietnamese Studies, 1,* 47–51. Melbourne, Australia.

Tung, T. M. (1983). Psychiatric care for Southeast Asians: How different is different? In T. C. Owan (Ed.), *Southeast Asian mental health: Treatment, prevention, services, training, and research* (pp. 5–40). Washington, DC: NIMH.

U.S. Committee for Refugees. (1984). *Vietnamese boat people: Pirates' vulnerable prey*. Washington, DC: American Council for Nationalistic Services.

U.S. Committee for Refugees. (1988). *Refugee Reports, 9*(12), 1–15.

Van Deusen, J. (1982). Part 3. Health/mental health studies of Indochinese refugees: A critical overview. *Medical Anthropology, 6,* 213–252.

Vignes, A. J., & Hall, R. C. W. (1979). Adjustment of a group of Vietnamese people to the United States. *American Journal of Psychiatry, 136*(4A), 442–444.

Westermeyer, J. (1973). Lao Buddhism, mental health, and contemporary implications. *Journal of Religion and Health, 12,* 181–187.

Whittaker, D. P. (1973). *Area handbook of the Khmer Republic.* Washington, DC: U.S. Government Printing Office.

Williams, C. L., & Westermeyer, J. (1983). Psychiatric problems among adolescent Southeast Asian refugees. *Journal of Nervous and Mental Disease, 171*(2), 79–85.

Yeatman, G. W., & Dang, V. V. (1980). Cao Gio (coin rubbing): Vietnamese attitudes towards health care. *Journal of American Medical Association, 247,* 1303–1308.

Zane, N. (1989). Pacific-Asian American mental health intervention. *Asian American Psychological Association Journal, 13*(1), 93–99.

Additional Resources

Farmbry, K. (Compiler). (1989). *The string bracelet: Reflections of and by the young people of Southeast Asia.* Washington, DC: Intercultural Productions.

Howard, K. K. (Compiler). (1990). *Passages: An anthology of the Southeast Asian refugee experience.* Fresno: Southeast Asian Student Services, California State University.

Chapter 10

ISSUES IN COUNSELING 1.5 GENERATION KOREAN AMERICANS

Julie C. Lee and Virginia E. H. Cynn

Korean Americans share many of the same cultural values as other Asian American groups (e.g., Chinese Americans, Japanese Americans) in the United States, but they encounter different adjustment problems because of their unique immigration pattern to the United States. One particular subgroup, the 1.5 generation Korean Americans, is especially vulnerable to the difficulties of immigration transitions. Also known as the transgeneration or knee-high generation (Yu, 1988), the 1.5 generation consists of bicultural, bilingual Korean Americans who are foreign-born, but have spent the majority of their developmental years in the United States.

The 1.5 generation faces the inherent challenges of adjustment and the demands of two conflicting cultures (Cheung, 1980; Abe & Zane, in press). Unlike their immigrant parents, they are young and mobile, and quick in adapting to American cultural values, attitudes, and life-style. Differences in the rate of acculturation between parent and child can be a source of great distress. What is uniquely disturbing and of concern for this group is that these pressures are amplified by their young age. The majority are adolescents who experience the normal difficulties of teenage years. The confusion of physical and emotional changes, the desire to be independent and mobile, and the questions of identity are all too common for young Korean Americans. It is imperative that mental health professionals identify the implications of their particular experiences for their psychological well-being.

This chapter was supported by the National Research Center on Asian American Mental Health (R01 44331).

Profile of Korean Immigrants

Demographic Characteristics

Between 1970 and 1980, the population of Korean Americans rose from 70,000 to 357,393, a percentage increase of over 400% (Park, Fawcett, Arnold, & Gardner, 1990). By the year 2000, it is estimated that there will be well over 1.3 million Korean Americans in the United States (Yu, 1988). Korean Americans are described as family-oriented, highly educated, hardworking, and ambitious. Approximately 85% are married, and 74% of them maintain a nuclear family (Kim, 1987). In a study of Asian Americans in the greater Chicago area, it was estimated that up to 70% of the Korean families had children under 10 years of age (Kim & Condon, 1975). Approximately half of the U.S. Korean population are 19 years old and under (Pai, Pemberton, & Worley, 1987). Park et al. (1990) found that Korean immigrants come to the United States to reestablish contact with family members and to take advantage of educational and occupational opportunities.

In several studies, recent Korean immigrants have been identified as a highly educated group (Hurh & Kim, 1980; Park et al., 1990). In 1980, the average Korean American household income was $22,500; the majority were living in the cities of Los Angeles, New York, and Chicago (in rank order). Approximately 50% had dual incomes, and 24% were self-employed in small businesses (U.S. Census, 1980). The difficulties in learning a new language hinder many immigrants from seeking salaried employment commensurate with their education (Park et al.). Therefore, with the desire to increase income and regain some control over their lives, many recent Korean immigrants gravitate to small self-owned businesses.

Cultural Values

The pervasive influence of Confucian ideology and teachings is seen in present-day Korean culture, philosophy, and social structure. Great value is placed on the concepts of hierarchical relations and obedience to authority. With regard to family and interpersonal relations, the basic tenets of Confucianism prescribe filial piety, submission of self to family, proper order between elders and youth, and obedience to the husband. The Korean family structure is a prime example of Confucian influence on culture. Roles between husband and wife, father and child, mother and child, and among siblings are strictly defined. The father is head of the family; he is expected to be authoritative, strict, and to provide for and protect the family. The maternal role allows for more intimacy between the mother and child. Her primary role is to be the healer and the family emotional monitor (Rohner & Pettengill, 1985). Because the eldest son is expected to inherit his father's role and carry on the family name, he is more valued than the daughter, who is raised to become a member of another family upon marriage. The hierarchical nature of relationships is not only reflected in role structure and expectations, but also in language. "Even the structure of the language changes in regard to syntax, word endings, and terminology depending upon the gender, generation, and relationship attributes of the individuals involved" (Shon & Ja, 1982). For example, the communication patterns between parent and child are unidirectional and move from the elder to the youth.

The Korean culture has a relationship/group orientation, which contrasts with the American cultural values of individuality and independence. This particular orientation stems from "the culturally stipulated ideology stressing the cardinal importance of the family, obedience to its authority, and deference to its elders" (Rohner & Pettengill, 1985). Korean philosophy emphasizes that an individual's independence or autonomy of self is superseded by family needs. Thus, one's responsibility is such that "personal actions reflect not only on the individual and nuclear family and extended families, but also on all of the preceding generations of the family since the beginning of time" (Shon & Ja, 1982).

To maintain the valued concept of harmonious and peaceful relations, Korean culture reflects a restrained, rather than an expressive, orientation. In accordance with Confucian teachings, any form of communication, expression, and behavior undermining harmony in relationships is viewed as undesirable. Therefore, confrontive, directive, or harsh behavior is avoided at all times. For example, in the presence of elders, one should remain silent and be attentive to cues for proper behavior.

Korean culture is highly collectivistic, a direct contrast to the American values of individuality (Gudykunst, Yoon, & Nishida, 1987). At the psychological level, collectivistic tendencies involve strong ingroup (e.g., family) identity, in which the ingroup is viewed as an extension of the self (Triandis, Leung, Villareal, & Clack, 1985). Yu and Kim (1983) argued that the Korean tradition of emphasizing obedience and conformity has great psychosocial developmental implications for Korean American children, who must contend with a host society that encourages self-determination and individuality. For many in the 1.5 generation, the process of adaptation or acculturation is compounded by the contradictory nature of the two cultures. This often precipitates overwhelming anxiety, confusion, and distress.

Issues of the 1.5 Generation Korean American

Pressures to Succeed

Because Korean American parents are determined to provide for their children economically, they have high expectations that their children will succeed. These expectations are often above and beyond the 1.5's capabilities or desires. In a study of 564 preadolescent and adolescent Korean Americans by Pai et al. (1987), 71% of the youths interviewed reported school performance as their primary concern, 88.3% considered making parents proud as "quite important" to "top of my list," and 90.1% reported doing well in school. These youths also had a tendency to have very high expectations and goals for their future. Although high aspirations can be viewed in a positive light, counselors must regard this with caution. Korean American children see their parents as having unreasonably high expectations for them. The 1.5 generation Korean Americans may be at risk for setting unrealistic goals and expectations for themselves. Afraid that they will be unable to perform to the standards laid out for them, many 1.5 generation Korean Americans suffer significant levels of achievement anxiety.

Also, with respect to pressure to succeed, this particular generation often find themselves in a "no-win" situation. This situation reflects the contradictory expectations of family and social context. Their families strongly encourage success and support the hard work ethic. Yet, recently many Korean Americans have been criticized for being too extreme in their ambitious nature. Thus, as adolescent Korean Americans, they must handle the difficult choice of siding with the expectations of either the social context (for example, peers) or those of family.

Communication Barriers

Language and communication difficulties often create a generational gap between members of the 1.5 generation and their parents. These young people often come from bilingual settings in which English is spoken outside the home, and Korean is predominantly used inside the home. It has been suggested that many Koreans, especially members of the 1.5 generation, lack fluency in both languages (Yu, 1988). The language barrier is a primary obstacle in the communication between members of this generation and their parents. Establishing and maintaining open communication is difficult for the Korean-speaking parent and English-speaking child. Outside the home, the individual may experience language difficulties at school, and thus be unable to compete academically at expected levels. The individual may be ostracized by peers due to his or her limited English skills, and thus lose interest in school. Because of the inability to communicate effectively with both parents and friends, 1.5 generation Korean Americans often experience feelings of alienation. They are unable to seek support from and identify positively with any of their social networks. As a result, these young people may isolate themselves from the family and the general social context.

Communication barriers are not limited to language skills for the immigrant family. Parental warmth (acceptance-rejection) and parental control (permissiveness-strictness) are two major dimensions of parenting styles that exist in all human societies (Rohner & Ronher, 1981). Rohner and Pettengill (1985) assessed the parenting style of Korean parents in Korea and that of Korean American parents. Results showed a sharp contrast between Korean American and Korean perceptions of parents. Korean youths associated both paternal and maternal control with parental warmth and low neglect, whereas Korean American youths viewed strict parental control as hostility and rejection. Yu and Kim (1983) argued that Korean American parents, especially recent immigrants, raise their children according to traditional Korean child-rearing practices based on their own upbringing and desire for their children to maintain the Korean cultural heritage. These findings imply that as Korean American youths become more acculturated while parents remain traditional in child-rearing practices, they may begin to misinterpret their parents' strictness as overall rejection and hostility, thus becoming emotionally distressed.

Ethnic Identity Development Conflicts

For the 1.5 generation Korean American, high parental expectations and communication difficulties can be compounded by ethnic identity problems. Spencer and Markstrom-Adams (1990) suggested that "the complexity of identity formation may increase as a function of color, behavioral distinction, language difference, physical features, and long-standing, although frequently unaddressed, social stereotypes." Because Korean immigrants come from a highly collectivistic culture (Gudykunst et al., 1987), they may insist on a collectivistic approach in the United States. Hurh (1980) argued that the United States is a nation in which race is still one of the most powerful factors "limiting structural assimilation;" thus, remaining collectivistic may be a strategy for these immigrants to maintain a sense of belonging to community.

Fearful their children will lose touch with the Korean heritage, Korean parents and families in the United States will insist that the younger generation maintain ties with Korea. However, it is sometimes difficult for members of the 1.5 generation to share their parents' attachment to Korea. Some may experience guilt and a tremendous sense of obligation to feel and to acknowledge Korea as part of their identity. The 1.5 generation member recognizes the importance of a Korean identity, but many express feelings of ambiguity toward Korea or being Korean (Pai et al., 1987). During adolescent development, defining a self-identity may be the single most important task at hand (Rosenthal, 1987), but with the "absence of a sense of belonging to a vital and nourishing milieu of contemporary American society, and a sense of disconnectedness with their own original ethnic heritage" (Yu & Kim, 1983), members of this generation are at risk for psychological distress and maladjustment.

Culturally Responsive Counseling

Acculturation

The 1.5 generation Korean American is expected to succeed without compromising any of the traditional Korean values. Leong (1986) defined this process of adaptation (acculturation) as the degree to which an individual has identified with and integrated into the dominant mainstream culture. The primary challenge for the 1.5 generation is somehow to integrate the contradictory values of the two cultures into a unified identity.

Hurh (1980) outlined a typological scheme of acculturation for Korean Americans: a "traditionalist" is one who is more Korean than American; the "integrationist" is one who is still Korean but tries to become more American; the "isolationist" is one who is neither American nor Korean; and, the "pluralist" is one who is both Korean and American. . Hurh's concepts of integrationist and isolationist are similar to Sue and Sue's (1971) marginal individual. Described as ambivalent, insecure, self-conscious, isolated, lonely, and frustrated (Park, 1928; Stonequist, 1935) the marginal individuals' dysfunctional aspects receive more attention than their positive attributes. But, Hurh (1980) suggested that marginality may be a necessary developmental stage in becoming a pluralist/biculturalist/Asian American. "Americanism" and "Koreanism" are not mutually exclusive, and a synthesis of both cultures results in a new Korean American identity via successful resolution of marginality (Hurh).

This model provides a developmental framework and does not imply that all 1.5 generation Korean Americans go through these stages in sequence. Various factors, such as age at immigration, parental values, and geographical location of residence will influence the 1.5's pattern of identity development. Nevertheless, the last stage of biculturation may provide a wider repertoire of behaviors and options for the 1.5 generation and relieve the pressures to choose one culture over the other.

Acculturation-Consistent Strategies

Because many 1.5 generation Korean American families are unfamiliar with the concepts of Western "talk therapy" and medical approaches, mental health paraprofessionals must use treatment that is culturally appropriate. Sue and Zane (1987) cited various strategies to establish cultural competence in psychotherapy and counseling. For example, credibility can be increased by striving to have a clear understanding of how the client and the counselor identify and conceptualize presenting problems and the means for their solution (Sue & Zane; Sue, 1981). It is not prescribed that counselors attempt to match clients on these dimensions, but that they be aware of incongruencies, which can lead to reducing a counselor's credibility (Sue & Zane).

In striving to attain credibility in the eyes of a Korean family, one counseling strategy may be to define and to respect the family members' roles. A democratic counseling approach may undermine the parental authority over the children. The counselor may choose to handle the initial sessions primarily by addressing and deferring to the father as a sign of respect, while also being cautious not to compromise the credibility of the counselor as the expert. It is likely that the mother will be more involved in counseling, thus the counselor should always allow the father to make the final decisions by letting the mother consult her husband before making any counseling commitments.

The second strategy is the concept of "gift giving." It is advised that the client's immediate perception of benefits from counseling will prevent early termination, demonstrate credibility, and address skepticism of Western methods of counseling (Sue & Zane, 1987). For many Korean Americans, the normalization of family problems as a typical acculturation process may be the most valuable gift possible. Normalization gives the client an opportunity to ease the magnitude of the problem by the counselor's suggestion of how common the presenting issues are (Sue & Zane; Sue & Morishima, 1982). Also, this allows the family to save face and to limit the shame the family has endured for seeking help, thus encouraging the family to have a positive outlook on counseling. The intricacies of how to counsel a culturally diverse population are not limited simply to acknowledging culture. When the treatment is concerned with the client's intrapsychic processes, the counselor must account for the role of culture above and beyond superficial considerations. A counselor's cultural sensitivity remains distal to treatment outcome when cultural responsiveness is not taken beyond the point of "concrete operations and strategies" (Sue & Zane). The single most important method to implement in providing culturally responsive counseling is to develop acculturation-consistent treatment strategies. This is the most effective technique of addressing what and how culture is contributing to the client's presenting issues. The counselor must be actively aware of a client's position on the continuum of acculturation and stage of ethnic identity development. If a culturally responsive strategy of treatment is being implemented, and yet the client is very acculturated, culturally responsive counseling may become culturally nonresponsive treatment.

The following is a composite description of several possible cases that highlight the relevant issues of family expectations, communication barriers, and conflicts of ethnic identity development that were introduced above. The purpose of the discussion that follows the case study is to illustrate a therapeutic process that may be helpful in counseling the 1.5 generation Korean American. It is important to note that this is only an example intended to emphasize the more pressing issues for members of this generation; counselors must always individualize any of the strategies suggested in this chapter.

The Case of Jack

Jack is a 17-year-old male Korean American. He is the eldest of three children. Jack's parents made the decision to immigrate to the United States 9 years ago in hopes of providing their children with better opportunities and better lives in the new country. Both of Jack's parents are college educated. Due to their limited English skills, the parents could not find jobs commensurate with their education. After finding economic stability, Jack and his family moved to a small middle-class suburban city. Jack is now a high school senior. There are only a handful of ethnic minorities in his school and Jack is the only Korean American. Jack has developed a close-knit circle of friends, all of whom are Caucasian.

Jack's parents are very strict and maintain control over the children's daily school and homework schedules. The children must receive permission from their father if they wish to do any nonacademic activities. The parents choose all of the children's school courses. They have begun to choose the colleges that Jack will apply to for next year. His parents want him to apply only to schools with competitive premedical programs. Yet, Jack is not sure what he would like to be. His parents tell him he will be a successful doctor, and make them proud. Jack initially accepts these expectations because he is afraid to express his hesitations about medicine, and does not want to make any waves. Recently, Jack has become very anxious about his college applications because he is afraid he will be unable to live up to his parents' expec-

tations. He feels that his parents do not really care about him, but only about how well he does in school. He finds it difficult to concentrate and has no drive to do his schoolwork.

Jack's parents have always taught the children to be proud of their Korean heritage. Jack does not consider Korea his homeland, and at times feels guilty for such thoughts. Lately, he has become very resentful of his father and his lectures on being Korean and knowing Korean culture. Jack is embarrassed by his parents' broken English and Korean ways. Jack was invited to several banquets honoring him as an outstanding high school achiever, but never told his parents of these events, afraid they would attend and embarrass him in front of his friends.

During this past month, Jack and his parents have been struggling with their relationship. Jack's relationship with his father has become especially strained. There have been several confrontations between the two. Jack has made several remarks to his parents about how he wished he weren't Korean. He has demanded that his parents let him live his own life. The last confrontation ended with Jack's father threatening to disown such a shameful son. His father suggests that Jack's disrespectful behaviors are a sign of the bad influence his American friends have had on him.

Jack has withdrawn from his family and friends, unable to discuss his problems with anyone. He wishes his parents could be like his friends' parents. Jack presents a depressed mood, loss of appetite, and insomnia. As a result, his schoolwork is suffering. The teacher observes the changes in behavior and requests to see Jack and his parents. Upon realizing the many issues that are present, she refers them to a counselor.

Complicated by different levels of acculturation of the adolescent and the parents, this case study highlights the 1.5 generation Korean American's struggle through normal adolescent development. Two major causes of Jack's depression are the conflicts of ethnic identity and the high parental expectations. Although family systems therapy may seem to be the desirable therapeutic technique, Jack's very traditional parents may not be open to this type of intervention at this time. It is important for counselors to recognize the parents' limitations of actively participating in counseling. The parents may find counseling a difficult process to understand, especially with their limited English skills. Under these circumstances, rapid and significant changes cannot be expected. It is likely that Jack, and especially his parents, will focus their goals of therapy on alleviating physiological symptoms of depression and addressing the decline in academic achievement. These goals must be addressed initially in therapy so that the counselor's credibility will not suffer and premature termination will not occur. Counselors need to be prepared to set a long-range goal and gradually work toward involving the parents in family systems therapy. This may not happen before Jack leaves for college, but his younger siblings may benefit. For Jack, the most efficacious therapeutic method seems to be individual counseling with parental consultation.

The primary goal of parental consultation is to alleviate the tensions between Jack and his parents, as well as to provide educational information on the acculturation process and the causes of depression. For Jack, both problem-solving therapeutic and educational approaches can be beneficial. Because both of these strategies are more culturally congruent, they may be the most effective strategies to use in this particular case. One common goal of these two interventions is to introduce insight to Jack's problems at hand to enable his self-growth. Because of the limited scope of this chapter, we will highlight only the individual approach with Jack. The following will outline the counseling process suggested for this case study.

The very first session should involve both Jack and his parents. This is an opportunity for them to come together on neutral ground, and it also allows the counselor to assess the dynamics of the family. (For discussion purposes, "family" will refer to Jack and his parents from this point on.) To prevent premature termination, it is essential that the family feel they have benefited from the very first session. Normalization of family problems and issues may be the most valuable "gift" possible during the first stage. This can accomplish two things. One is to save "face" and limit the shame the family has endured for seeking treatment. The second is to allow the family to realize that their problems are not so unusual and can be attributed to a normal process in immigration adjustment. This is particularly important because the family is geographically isolated from other Koreans.

Once the counselor has assessed the family dynamics and identified the actual problems and issues involved, he or she should inform the family of the depression diagnosis and outline the treatment plan with the family. Informing them that depression is a common reaction to pressures and that it has excellent prognosis will help to alleviate their anxieties and keep the diagnosis in perspective. Inform the family that there are many strategies that will counter depressive symptoms, and that Jack can learn them in individual sessions. Because most of the counseling sessions will be with Jack, the counselor should stress the importance of the family meeting periodically. It may be beneficial to reframe the request of family involvement by suggesting that the counselor will rely on the family's strength and support throughout Jack's therapy.

A primary goal in individual counseling is to alleviate Jack's depressive symptoms of withdrawal, appetite loss, and insomnia, after his suicidal potential has been assessed. This can be achieved by teaching him skills to deal with his external pressures. For example, progressive relaxation techniques can be introduced to counter anxiety and increase stress management skills. At the more internal level, the counselor should be prepared to address his personal conflicts of self-concept and ethnic identity. The counselor can further build credibility by acknowledging Jack's difficulties (high parental pressures and expectations) as the first-born male child in a traditional Korean household. Let Jack know that such expectations may affect self-concept, and focus on building Jack's self-efficiency and self-reliance skills throughout the counseling process.

The severity of Jack's depression can increase because of decreased social support due to his withdrawal from friends and family. It will be important to emphasize that the problems he is facing are not unusual among his peers and that many have coped effectively. One of the first steps to help Jack overcome his depression is to explore various types of effective coping strategies. Different exercises can be incorporated to help him gain awareness of self and regain interest in his schoolwork. For example, Jack can keep a daily schedule. This will allow him to structure his day and gain interest and control over his activities. Another exercise may be to have him keep a diary of his daily thoughts and feelings, thus enabling him to identify and become aware of his feelings of self and feelings toward his parents. As Jack begins to come to terms with his problems, counseling can begin to relieve his symptoms.

To address the issues stemming from conflicts in self-concept, it is important for Jack to be able to accept that there are difficulties in developing an ethnic identity. He may need to be reminded that he may not be able to rely on his family or friends because they may not be able to empathize with him nor understand his conflicts. However, the counselor may point out that this can be a challenging process with rewarding outcomes. The counselor should be candid with Jack and encourage him to take responsibility for reaching a resolution.

A strategy to help resolve Jack's identity issue is to have him list what he feels are the positive and negative aspects of being very traditionally Korean, very American, and bicultural. At the same time, Jack should identify whose definition (e.g., self, family, or mainstream culture) of identity he is internalizing under different situations. These methods may help him to clarify the external and internal forces influencing his identity development. This provides Jack with the opportunity to choose and to define his own unique identity. Throughout the process, the counselor should help Jack to realize the importance of understanding both cultures without any value judgments attached to them.

The counselor should inform Jack that self-identity may change over time due to normal development; however, it is important that Jack feel comfortable with his current decisions. Also, suggest to Jack that if he does not feel comfortable doing so, he does not necessarily have to choose one identity over the other. Explain to him that he may feel more comfortable in moving between different cultural roles depending on social context. For example, he can be very Korean or traditional in a family situation by not openly contradicting his parents, but be very American in a school situation where he wants to be assertive. The counselor may need to emphasize to Jack that he is empowered to make the final choice as long as he is aware of and prepared for the consequences of his decision. For example, it may be important to let Jack know that taking premedicine courses in the first couple of years of college does not necessarily mean that he has to go to medical school. Later, he can make the decision to do something else, as long as he knows that his decision is worth the negative reactions his parents may have toward his choice.

We will now turn to a brief discussion of giving educational information as a counseling strategy for Jack's parents. Two goals for this component of counseling are to enlist Jack's parents' support for continuing therapy for Jack and to increase their confidence in therapy so that they will be more open to future interventions (e.g., family systems therapy). It would be helpful to provide educational information on Jack's symptoms (e.g., depression, loss of appetite, insomnia) by informing the parents of the definition and the causes of depression. Emphasize the interaction between physiological (e.g., neurochemical) and psychological (e.g., depressive symptoms) stresses to counter the stigma they may hold about "mental disorders." In addition, identifying the negative effects of stress and pressure on people may bring insight to how they may relieve some of Jack's presenting difficulties. To decrease their fears that Jack is going to be "too Americanized" it is important to let them know that it is normal to swing from one extreme (e.g., traditionally Korean) to another (e.g., too American) before adolescents find a balance that will allow them to retain their Korean identity, but acculturate enough to succeed in the American culture. It may be necessary to praise the parents by pointing out how well Jack has done because of their efforts. However, let them know of the magnitude of the pressure that Jack is under and the counterproductive nature of overwhelming stress, such as aspirational conflict. To enhance the possibilities of compromise, inform them of the availability of career advisors in exploring various career options. The decisions the family makes can be a collaborative effort in which the advisor acts as a mediator. This particular task may open the lines of communication between Jack and his parents and help to alleviate the existing conflicts.

It is important to note that this particular case study was only an example; therefore, the limitations of the recommendations given should be recognized. As previously stated, the strategies and techniques advised throughout the chapter should always be individualized for each client.

Conclusion

The conflicts between two often contradictory cultures can be an overpowering stressor causing much struggle and pain for many 1.5 generation Korean Americans. When a counselor is called upon to address these problems, he or she must be active in understanding the influences of culture and the unique immigration patterns on this population. By recognizing the expectations of the two diverse cultures in counseling, a counselor is better able to help the client successfully integrate both cultures. The attempts to find a balance between these two cultures can be eased by the counselor's acknowledging the great faith and courage these families have shown in immigrating to the United States. Incorporating Korean Americans' ability to aspire and hope for the future into counseling strategies is likely to lead to successful counseling with the 1.5 generation Korean Americans.

References

Abe, J. S., & Zane, N. W. S. (in press). Psychological maladjustment among Asian and Caucasian American college students: Controlling for confounds. *Journal of Counseling Psychology.*

Cheung, F. K. (1980). The mental health status of Asian Americans. *Clinical Psychologist, 34*, 23–24.

Gudykunst, W. G., Yoon, Y. C., & Nishida, T. (1987). The influence of individualism-collectivism on perceptions of communication in ingroup and outgroup relationships. *Communication Monographs, 54*, 295–306.

Hurh, W. M. (1980). Towards a Korean-American ethnicity: Some theoretical models. *Ethnic and Racial Studies, 3*, 444–464.

Hurh, W. M., & Kim, K. C. (1980). Social and occupational assimilation of Korean immigrant workers in the U.S. *California Sociologist, 3*, 125–142.

Kim, B. L., & Condon, M. (1975). A study of Asian Americans in Chicago: Their socioeconomic characteristics, problems, and service needs. Washington, DC: NIMH, HEW.

Kim, K. C. (1987). Adaptation of Korean immigrants. In W. T. Liu (Ed.), *The Pacific/Asian American Mental Health Research Center: A decade review*. Chicago, IL: The Pacific/Asian American Mental Health Research Center, University of Illinois at Chicago.

Leong, F. T. L. (1986). Counseling and psychotherapy with Asian-Americans: Review of the literature. *Journal of Counseling Psychology, 33*, 196–206.

Pai, Y., Pemberton, D., & Worley, J. (1987). *Findings on Korean-American early adolescents and adolescents*. Kansas City, MO: School of Education, University of Missouri-Kansas City.

Park, I. H., Fawcett, J. T., Arnold, F., & Gardner, R. W. (1990, March). *Korean immigrants and U.S. immigration policy: A predeparture perspective*. Honolulu, Hawaii: East-West Population Institute.

Park, R. E. (1928). Human migration and the marginal man. *American Journal of Sociology*, *6*, 881–983.

Rohner, R. P., & Pettengill, S. M. (1985). Perceived parental acceptance-rejection and parental control among Korean adolescents. *Child Development*, *56*, 524–528.

Rohner, R. P., & Rohner, E. C. (1981). Parental acceptance-rejection and parental control: Cross-cultural codes. *Ethnology*, *20*, 245–260.

Rosenthal, D. A. (1987). Ethnic identity development in adolescents. In J. S. Phinney & M. J. Rotheram (Eds.), *Children's ethnic socialization* (pp. 156–179). Newbury Park, CA: Sage.

Shon, S. P., & Ja, D. Y. (1982). Asian families. In M. McGoldrick, K. Pearce, & J. Giordano (Eds.), *Ethnicity and family therapy* (pp. 208–228). New York: Guilford Press.

Spencer, M. B., & Markstrom-Adams, C. (1990). Identity process among racial ethnic minority children in America. *Child Development*, *61*, 290–310.

Stonequist, E. V. (1935). The problem of the marginal man. *American Journal of Sociology*, *13*, 1–12.

Sue, D. W. (1981). *Counseling the culturally different: Theory and practice*. New York: Wiley.

Sue, S., & Morishima, K. (1982). *The mental health of Asian Americans*. San Francisco: Jossey-Bass.

Sue, S., & Sue, D. W. (1971). Chinese-American personality and mental health. *Amerasia*, *1*, 36–49.

Sue, S., & Zane, N. (1987). The role of culture and cultural techniques in psychotherapy. *American Psychologist*, *42*, 37–45.

Triandis, H. C., Leung, K., Villareal, M., & Clack, F. (1985). Allocentric vs. idiocentric tendencies. *Journal of Research in Personality*, *19*, 395–415.

U.S. Department of Commerce, Bureau of the Census. (1988). *Asian and Pacific Islander population in the United States: 1980* (Report No. PC80–2–IE). Washington, DC: U.S. Government Printing Office.

Yu, E. Y. (1988, December). *Critical issues of the Korean community in the future*. Paper presented at the meeting of the United Way, Metropolitan Region, Los Angeles, CA.

Yu, K. Y., & Kim, L. I. C. (1983). The growth and development of Korean-American children. In G. J. Powell, J. Yamamoto, A. Romero, & A. Morales (Eds.), *The psychosocial development of minority group children* (pp. 147–159). New York: Brunner/Mazel.

Additional Resources

Choy, B. Y. (1979). *Koreans in America*. Chicago: Nelson-Hall. *Korean Culture*. (published quarterly). Los Angeles: Korean Cultural Services.

Korea Times Magazine. (published quarterly). Los Angeles: Korea Times Newspaper.

THE LATINO
AMERICAN EXPERIENCE

Latino is a generic term that identifies a culture shared by several ethnic groups in the United States—Mexicans, Puerto Ricans, Cubans, as well as other ethnic groups with origins in Central and South America. Latino culture developed as a result of the fusion of Spanish culture (brought to the Americas by missionaries and conquistadors) with American Indian and African (the result of the slave trade) cultures in Mexico, South America, and the Caribbean Basin. Commonality among Latino American ethnic groups is found in the use of the Spanish language, the influence of Roman Catholic traditions, differential sex-role socialization, and strong kinship bonds between family members and friends. However, there is a wide variety within each Latino American group based on variables such as level of acculturation, socioeconomic status, language use, and generation in the United States.

Chapter 11

COUNSELING LATINAS

Patricia Arredondo

As members of the second largest ethnic minority group in the United States (20 million as of March 1989), Latinas are becoming a highly visible force. In 1985, there were 8.5 million Latinas in the United States—1 of every 17 women (U.S. Bureau of the Census, 1985a). They are present in different sectors of the work force, are U.S.-born and immigrants, are bilingual or monolingual in English or Spanish, represent all races and ages, and are products of their primary as well as U.S. cultural norms. In effect, Latinas are a diverse, evolving population, and as a result must be understood for the developmental issues they introduce. This is acknowledged through a growing field of research and literature about Latinas. A special issue with a focus on mental health concerns of Hispanic women (Amaro & Russo, 1987) and an edited text about Puerto Rican women (Garcia-Coll & Mattei, 1989) serve as sources of updated data and discussion for counseling professionals.

It is significant to note that there are both scientific and political concerns about the generic category *Hispanic* or *Latino*. In the United States, the term *Hispanic* is a governmental designation. People from Central and South America and Mexico, although preferring to identify according to their national origin, such as Dominican or Colombian, are more responsive to the term *Latino*. With the recognition of the limitations of both terms, *Latinas/Latinos* will be used in this presentation. A further clarification is that *Latinas* refers to women and therefore the word stands by itself. For this author, Latinas is more inclusive.

These preliminary comments indicate the formidable challenges that confront counseling professionals who are trying to provide culturally sensitive services to this group of women. To intervene effectively, counselors will require more than a theoretical understanding of counseling practices as they are pervasively taught in most training programs. Counselors must have a working knowledge and understanding of Latino culture, its role in socializing women, and the social, economic, political, and historical forces that affect their development in a society where they confront racism and sexism. The issues are ones of surviving and thriving. Perhaps the latter might be perceived as too ambitious, but to

143

this writer, Latina well-being will be a nutrient to United States social and economic development in general.

Before discussing counseling considerations, it is necessary to provide background information about Latinas that highlights their similarities and differences. This will include demographics, comments about the historical, social, economic, and political contexts that shape their realities, and a discussion about Latino culture in terms of values, sex roles, and mental health. From this broad context, the reader can appreciate the complexity of the issues that will be identified.

The second part of the chapter will focus on a group intervention. This example demonstrates the need to work from a strength versus a deficit perspective when counseling Latinas and the benefits of addressing culture-specific values rather than denying them. Emphasis is given to the relative importance of the needs of a particular population of Latinas—immigrants—and what would be practically and emotionally valuable.

Who Are the Latinas?

What distinctions can be made among Latinas and what do they have in common? This section will have specific references to Latinas and information about Latinos in general. The latter also illuminates the Latino context that surrounds these women.

Census data specify population figures for the four subgroups that are classified as Hispanic. Nationally, 61% are Mexican; 15% are Puerto Rican, 6% are Cuban, and 18% are other Latinos from Central and South American countries and Spain (U.S. Bureau of the Census, 1985b). People from El Salvador, Guatemala, Honduras, and the Dominican Republic are a growing population who have been emigrating for political reasons. Demographic data are not consistently available about this group nor are they accurate with reference to undocumented workers.

Regional residence is not accidental. Latinos live in every state, but ethnic groups are concentrated in specific regions. This localization reflects the historical and political relationship between the particular ethnic group and the U.S. government.

Mexican Americans are concentrated in the Southwest. Prior to the 1848 Treaty of Guadalupe Hidalgo, this territory was Mexico. Generations of Mexican Americans have their roots in the Southwest and reflect a range of differences in acculturation. Some have become monolingual English speaking and "Americanized" whereas others have maintained strict linguistic and cultural practices. In contrast, most Puerto Ricans live in the Northeast. Their entry to the U.S. mainland began at the onset of World War I when Puerto Ricans became citizens in 1917, and increased after World War II as they sought economic betterment. The plan for most was to return to the island eventually. Its relative closeness encourages regular travel between home and the mainland. The largest Puerto Rican settlements are in New York City and New Jersey, with population growth currently strong in Connecticut and Massachusetts.

The smallest identified subgroup but greatest in economic power are the Cubans. Their migration coincided with the rise to power of Fidel Castro (1956–1959) and the seizure of American-owned sugar plantations, cattle ranches, oil refineries, and other businesses (Axelson, 1985). The Southeast, particularly Florida, is home to the majority of Cubans in the United States. The fourth segment of the Latino population includes people from Central and South America and Spain, as previously mentioned. Although dispersed throughout the country, they are principally urban dwellers. Refugees fleeing the warfare and economic chaos of Central American countries are also locating in urban centers. This allows them to have a community of relatives and friends who can serve as resources, and to become lost more readily and avoid being easily detected as illegal entrants.

Salgado de Snyder (1987), Espin (1987), and Arredondo-Dowd (1981, 1985) described differences among Latinas due to experiences of migration/immigration and cultural adaptation issues. Legal or illegal status, bilingual ability, color, and specific subgroup membership are further points of distinction among the women, but also factors that have significant implications for mental health. For many immigrants, racism is a new phenomenon, as is classification as a "minority" group member. Initially this labeling may be perceived with confusion but eventually it is taken as an insult. The message is that one's group membership is a liability. Different rates of acculturation within a family affect family relations as well. School or employment experiences may serve to improve bilingual ability and familiarity with the new cultural norms. However, if these experiences are contrary to cultural sex-role or age-specific expectations, they can create interpersonal strain and stress.

Latinas are found in all segments of the life cycle, though there are notable differences in age distribution. As a group, they are younger (median age = 26 years) than women in the general population (median age = 32 years) (U.S. Bureau of the Census, 1985b). In terms of age distribution, the following differences are noted: Mexican American women are the youngest (median age = 24), Puerto Rican women are next (median age = 26), and then Central/South American women (median age = 28). As a group, Cuban women are older (median age = 41) than those in all other Hispanic groups, and even older than Anglo women (median age = 33) (U.S. Bureau of the Census, 1985c).

Educational attainment for Latinas is lower than that of Blacks and Anglos. In 1985, the median for years of education among Latinas 25 years and older was 11.5, compared with 12.7 for non-Hispanic women (U.S. Bureau of the Census, 1985b). Given the current reports about high dropout rates for Latino youth, it can be projected that educational attainment is likely to decrease.

Historically, labor force participation by Latinas has been low. The maintenance of traditional family roles, limitations of educational opportunities, and racism have prevented Latinas from being gainfully employed. They are typically employed as operators, fabricators, and laborers in service occupations. The 1985 employment figures documented that there were 2.8 million (5.7%) Latinas in the labor force (U.S. Bureau of the Census, 1985b). This puts their labor force participation at 49.4%; nearly one in two Latinas are employed (U.S. Bureau of Labor Statistics, 1986). In contrast, their unemployment rate is higher (11% versus 3.9%) than that of women in general. Another related fact is that Latinas are found in the lowest paying low-status jobs. In 1981, over half were found in nonagricultural industries as clerical and kindred workers (28%) and private household workers (12%). Only 4% were managers compared with 7% of all women. In 1984, the figure for Latinas in managerial and professional specialty occupations rose to 12% (U.S. Department of Labor, 1985). State and local government provided employment to another 17% of Latinas (U.S. Bureau of the Census, 1983). Poverty has become a source of stress for women in general and more critically for Latinas. In 1984, 25.2% of Latino families lived below the poverty line, compared with 9.1% of Anglo families. Largely because Latinos have larger families, their mean income per family member ($4981) is lower than that for all families ($7943) (U.S. Bureau of the Census, 1983). Changes in family size and composition are affecting Latinas in a new way. There are increases in the population of never-married women (26%), of women 15 years and older, and of women aged 30 to 34 (10.5%, compared to 10.4% for women in general) (U.S. Bureau of the Census, 1981a). Figures for divorce and separation among Latinas were 14.1%, compared to 9.8% of other women. Also in 1981, only 52.6% of Latinas 15 years and older were in families with a husband present (U.S. Bureau of the Census, 1981b). These data highlight the point that the traditional intact family model is suffering. Within-group differences are also evident. There are younger Puerto Rican women as heads of households compared to the older Cuban women in married couple families.

This section describing the Latina population is not exhaustive. It briefly introduces characteristics and circumstances of a social, historical, economic, and political nature. These data indicate that Latinas in general are overrepresented among lower socioeconomic classes and young in age. Mental health professionals, however, must be cautious not to generalize this information to all Latinas, nor assume that only cultural values explain the data. The forces of social class, economics, age, race, linguistic ability, migration and acculturation must be considered in order to avoid stereotyped attributions. Concomitantly, the data reflect the status quo of the Latina population in general as well as the complexities based on individual and group membership.

Cultural Value Orientations and Sex Roles

Latino values and traditions are rooted in a complex culture based on historical events replete with colonization, religious conversions, interracial marriages, and migrations. African, Indian, Asian, and European ancestry have shaped the global population. While Latinos share Spanish as a common language, differences in terminology and accent will vary depending on country of origin, regional residence in the United States, and degree of acculturation. The contemporary life-styles of Latinos in the United States may reflect to some degree the traditional culture as described by historians, psychologists, and other social scientists (Pescatello, 1976; Stevens, 1973; Padilla, 1981; Garcia-Coll & Mattei, 1989; Amaro & Russo, 1987). It is difficult to describe succinctly the Latino culture, therefore this discussion is limited to values orientation in the context of family structure and attendant sex roles. This is considered the most informative perspective for the counseling professional.

Padilla (1981) described the extended family structure that typically includes: "(a) formalized kinship relations such as the *compadrazgo* (godfather) system; and (b) loyalty to the family which takes precedence over the social institutions" (p. 199). Children learn early about unquestionable parental authority and loyalty. *Respeto* (respect) and cooperation are expected and accorded. "Familism" is supported by reciprocal obligations even when individuals have established their separate families (Vale, 1977). Within this context, sex roles are demarcated and individuals are socialized to behave accordingly. Latino culture is hierarchical and patriarchal, placing expectations on boys to be independent and to perform outside of the home. Paid work is valued and boys are encouraged at an early age to find jobs. Girls, on the other hand, are taught to be selfless and to sacrifice. "Aguantando" (enduring) is embedded in a process that rewards passivity and deference to male authority. Although women are seen as the perpetuators of the culture, they are still caught in the interface of family structures that reinforce their dependence and subordination (Julia, 1989).

Machismo has been popularized as a desirable male characteristic. Stevens (1973) defined it as the "cult of virility . . . arrogance and sexual aggressiveness in male-to-female relationships" (p. 315). In contrast, Stevens stated that marianismo describes the idealized woman. It is "the cult of female spiritual superiority which teaches that women are semi-divine, morally superior to, and spiritually stronger than men" (p. 315). Marianismo is directly connected with the veneration of the Virgin Mary in Latino Catholicism (Shirley, 1981). This cultural attitude with respect to sex roles places Latinos in a double bind because of the social and structural pressures that support expected behavior. Studies across different Latino ethnic groups (Mintz, 1956; Shirley, 1981) have found that a husband's authority varies by region and socioeconomic class. "Middle and upper class husbands exercise less authority over their wives than do some of the men in the lower socioeconmic class" (Vazquez-Nuttall & Romero-Garcia, 1989, p. 63).

Perceptions about Latinas as powerless, submissive, and self-sacrificing have created many stereotypes that diminish the true essence of the individual woman. Experiences of racism and sexism have continuously stressed Latinas' mental health. Their strengths as reliable, responsible caretakers, loyal first to family, have been minimized rather than valued, leading to differential treatment of Latinas in educational and work settings (Vazquez-Nuttall & Romero-Garcia, 1989; Amaro & Russo, 1987), further affecting their self-esteem and access to avenues of personal growth.

The forces of socialization have left their imprint on Latinas, creating at times confusion and frustration. As women strive to define themselves, they are subjected to family pressures and societal oppression due to pejorative stereotypes. They are exposed primarily to non-Latina female models of achievement and success and at the same time are expected to satisfy the traditional gender-specified roles in their families. They are told to be more Anglo/successful (not always in reference to Anglos), and at the same time to stay in their place (be submissive and self-sacrificing). Coping in silence (aguantando) does not work for all women. Although self-disclosure outside of the home is discouraged, Latinas approach counseling with mixed feelings of relief, embarrassment, and apprehension. Responsibility lies with the counseling professional to assess sensitively the issues at hand, to separate the facts from the stereotypes, and to develop culturally appropriate treatment strategies. Because all Latinas are different, even basic assumptions about self-definition as a Latina or of being Spanish speaking must be questioned. The distinctions within the group and some of the prevailing issues will be discussed next.

Conflicts Latinas Face at Different Stages

The values and sex roles of Latinas in the context of changing roles for women in the United States are affecting the Latinas' sense of identity and esteem. This is seen in counseling through different conflicts the women present. Some of the issues introduced by women will be described briefly.

1. Immigrants Attempting to Manage a Work and Home Life

Issues: Stress reactions due to multiple demands and pressures to perform successfully in both arenas. Guilt about not being able to be a full-time mother and spouse as the culture has taught them; fears for children in a new culture; self-doubts about ability to manage all. Linguistic and educational ability may aid or limit workplace communications. Time constraints limit access to a support network.

2. First-Generation Women Attending College Away From Home

Issues: Disloyalty to family by moving away; selfishness for putting one's goals first; and betrayal/abandonment of mother for leaving her to do it all. Ethnic identity confusion in new cultural and social settings; new/different experiences of racism; and social pressures to find friends and fit in.

3. Graduate Students

Issues: Discomfort about being an older student with doubts about abilities to achieve. International students' stress of managing new culture, studies, and at times family responsibilities. Homesickness. Guilt about being away from the family.

4. Professional Women in the Workplace

Issues: Stress reactions in attempting to balance family and professional roles. Experiences of discrimination and role demands with limited support from supervisors. Pressure on relationship with spouse based on ethnicity of spouse (Amaro & Russo, 1987). Balancing career goals (i.e., advancement, career change, or relocation) with cultural values and roles.

5. Women in Interethnic Marriages

Issues: Unresolved feelings of inferiority in reference particularly to "Anglos" may deem one powerless or subservient to spouse. Spouses' nonacceptance of one's family, or ethnic group pressures to choose sides. Gaining self-esteem and acceptance in association to spouse by devaluing self. Also, the woman's family may not accept the husband because he is not of the same ethnicity.

Un Grupo de Apoyo Para Mujeres*
(*A Support Group for Women)

This section describes a group for a particular Latina population—**recent immigrants**. They presented many of the conflicts described for women in transition who must face multiple changes simultaneously. There were many considerations specific to this group as there would be for another specialized population, and these guided the planning and implementation. Some aspects of this program may work for other groups, but some aspects may not be suitable for adoption in alternative situations.

Background

Access to services has been underscored as a factor that lowers utilization rates among Latinos (Task Force on Black and Minority Health, 1986; Padilla, Ruiz, & Alvarez, 1975). Even if a mental health center is in the community, this does not mean it can provide services to all who need them or at a convenient time. So it was that in planning a group for Latinas, primarily immigrants of lower socioeconomic status, careful consideration was given to location, day and time of the week, and child-care services. Additionally, cultural values and practices were perceived as essential to make the Latina population receptive. Religion, specifically, the Catholic church, became the cultural and practical point of reference.

Religion plays a key role in the lives of Latinos. The majority are Christian, particularly Roman Catholic, and religion and family life go hand in hand. This is particularly evident among the lower socioeconomic communities. For the immigrants in this Boston area community, the church had become an integral part of their new beginnings. The "cura" (the priest) holds speical status as God's representative on earth. Often, religious personnel perform social service functions that range from finding housing and medical resources to making home visits—a missionary approach. In this endeavor, the community outreach workers included the parish priest in planning the support group for the Latinas.

Previous studies (Todd, 1980; Walker, MacBride, & Vachon, 1977) have found evidence for a strong relationship between mental health and social networks. In her study with Puerto Rican women, Mattei (1989) found the importance of social relationships in women's autonomous decision making. Nazario-Crespo (1986) concluded that although the migratory process separates women from their social support network (SSN), it also "gave them the opportunity to look around and select members to comprise their SSN" (p. 132).

This writer had previously led support groups for immigrant women graduate students and observed the ease with which the participants communicated about issues they held in common. The topics discussed ranged from the formation of study groups to identity confusion due to multiple changes. The exchange of information and sharing of personal experiences created an educationally oriented social support system for the Latina immigrants.

Design of the Group

The group was scheduled to meet for eight sessions for 1 hour following the Sunday Mass. It was open to all women regardless of age and was conducted in Spanish. The three outreach workers, two women and a man, were bilingual and Latino (Puerto Rican, Colombian, and Venezuelan). This writer is Mexican American. Older children supervised the younger ones; spouses generally left, some with the children, following the Mass. To facilitate participation, the planners recommended that child care be provided. The priest was instrumental in identifying older children, some siblings of the younger ones. This was the key to allowing the women uninterrupted participation, though they would have attended even without it (from this writer's past experiences). The group met in the main dining room of the parish rectory attached to the church. Though formal, it was a comfortable space that allowed for chairs to be put in a circle.

Educational Content

The group was based on psychoeducational principles—the promotion of personal development through systematic, educational experiences (Mosher, 1974). The goal was to empower the women in their new roles and functions in a new community/country. The meetings provided a forum for the dissemination of relevant information through minipresentations and written material, and also invited the women to share their questions, experiences, and support with one another. The sessions were organized around personal and life-management topics to life change. A summary of the program, the interconnection of the topics, and the writer's observations on the process will be discussed.

Topic I. Personal Introductions
Who are the women in the community/in the room, and what do they identify as work and home life issues? Following brief introductions, and an overview by the group facilitators of the purpose of the group, an oral needs assessment was conducted. Although the relevant issues for the Latina immigrants were anticipated, it was also deemed important that they identify the priorities. Some of the following sessions were based on this input.

Topic II. Health Services

A brief presentation was made by a Latina medical doctor from the local community health center. Her purpose was to introduce the range of services and also inform the women about required innoculations for school-age children, emergencies, and pregnancy-related services, among other topics. The women's primary concern was health care for their children. For those who were undocumented, fears about privacy and the release of personal information were also addressed.

Topic III. Community Resources/Services

For many women, the time to access the services was critical. They wondered how they could accomplish tasks without missing work. Knowledge about Saturday services and the availability of assistance by the Latino community agencies proved helpful. The outreach workers addressed practical necessities and how to access services, such as water, electricity, housing, and immigration services. Maps and phone lists were provided. Bilingual information prepared by the state transportation system was also made available.

Topic IV. Dealing With Change

This session was an opportunity to acknowledge the many losses and changes the women were experiencing. They talked about topics such as urban versus rural living, the need to work up to two jobs, and the difference in the school day, all due to immigration. An outline of the Kübler-Ross model was presented in Spanish. We wanted the women to recognize the feelings they were experiencing as normal. This could entail two sessions.

Topic V. Schools and Teachers

Representatives from the bilingual school department provided information about the programs offered. They also described the schools' expectations about parent involvement and how that could be accomplished. This topic tapped many of the women's conflicts. The differences in the school program created unease; parents expected longer school days. They also found that work hours limited their access to school personnel. This discussion raised concerns about their new role responsibilities.

Topic VI. Parenting

The majority of the participants were married and mothers of school-age children, making a discussion about parenting issues very stimulating. U.S. cultural norms regarding corporal punishment were explained, and questions about children's moods and behaviors were addressed by the outreach workers. Generational differences in the group were introduced in a supportive way. Mothers of older children shared their experiences with the younger women.

Topic VII. Stress

Stress was evident in the changing lives of the women. There was a minilecture on the symptoms of stress and how to deal with stressful situations—"la ansiedad/la angustia." The women were asked to share examples of how they manage stress. Examples included getting up before everyone and drinking coffee alone to taking a long, hot bath. The sharing made for a lively session.

Topic VIII. Self-Care and Support Networks

The intention was to emphasize the connection between personal well-being and communication with others. A written exercise that identifies an individual's personal support system was introduced. The women were encouraged to share phone numbers with one another, to maintain connections through the church, and to contact the outreach workers as needed.

Summary of Group Experience

An average of 10 to 15 women attended the weekly sessions. The eight topics generated by the participants in the first session and by the group leaders' experiences are those of greatest concern. The initial sessions were mostly informational in nature. They were a bridge from the community agencies to the women. Beginning with more concrete and relevant facts allowed for some trust building to occur. The participants realized we were responsive to their concerns and they also became more comfortable with the leaders and other members of the group. Topics 4 to 8 were considered more personal and involving value orientations. We wanted to be sensitive to the women's readiness to self-disclose feelings as well as their beliefs and assumptions about their role in relationship to their children and the schools. By the time we reached topic 8, the women were speaking of the value of a support/educational group experience. Participants' high level of verbal participation was an indication that the group served their needs: to give and receive information, to give and receive support, and to feel more in control of the life management issues resulting from the impact of immigration. Based on communication among the participants, it seemed that relevant informational and interpersonal connections were made that would continue when the group ended. The outreach workers reported later contact by the women as well.

Summary

The examples have highlighted different conflicts of Latinas in different settings and personal endeavors. These conflicts may be experienced or expressed in many forms. Typical symptoms are somatization (migraines to immobilization of a limb), anxiety or panic attacks, and depression or other stress reaction behaviors. The themes that emerge are ones of loss, role conflict, ethnic identity confusion, and loss of control. The women's lives are stress-filled, confused, and often lack the support system a family typically provides. The value of "personalismo" cannot be readily expressed when Latinas find themselves in detached, noncaring environments. A sense of aloneness and isolation can develop.

Individuals undergoing life changes typically experience a range of normal feelings—from sadness to anger—and different coping mechanisms—from "superwoman" behavior to immobilization. Intervening individual variables that affect the Latina client must be considered so as not to erroneously pathologize or blame the culture for the person's condition. Counseling Latinas cannot be approached exclusively from a cultural perspective. The Latina client seeks an authentic counseling relationship; she does not want to be treated based on stereotyped thinking.

The counselor is cautioned about the tendency to overlook a woman's strengths and life management skills because she speaks with an accent or is an immigrant. The Latina client must be supported for her accomplishments and her decision to seek self-care. Being empathic does not equate with patronizing or condescending behavior. To be effective, counseling professionals must examine their own biases and assumptions and be willing to ask for assistance if they do not understand how to proceed. This prevents an unintentional oppression of the client and serves as an opportunity for the therapist to learn from another resource or professional.

Conclusion

Counseling Latinas can take many forms and approaches. Of primary importance is designing a treatment plan or intervention that is culturally, linguistically, and socially appropriate. What works for some immigrant Latinas of a lower socioeconomic background might not be relevant for those in college or for professional Latinas concerned about career advancement. The differences and distinctions are many, as pointed out throughout this chapter. Latinas have both a group and individual identity, and it must be respected by the mental health professional.

References

Amaro, H., & Russo, N. F. (Eds.). (1987). Hispanic women and mental health. *Psychology of Women Quarterly, 11*(4), 393–407.

Amaro, H., Russo, N. F., & Johnson, J. (1987). Family and work predictors of psychological well-being among Hispanic women professionals. *Psychology of Women Quarterly, 11,* 505–521.

Arredondo, P. (1986). Immigration as an historical moment leading to an identity crisis. *Journal of Counseling and Human Services, 1,* 79–87.

Arredondo-Dowd, P. (1981). Personal loss and grief as a result of immigration. *Personnel and Guidance Journal, 59,* 376–378.

Axelson, J. (1985). *Counseling and development in a multicultural society.* Monterey, CA: Brooks/Cole.

Espin, O. (1987). Psychological impact of migration on Latinas: Implications for psychotherapeutic practice. *Psychology of Women Quarterly, 11,* 489–503.

Garcia-Coll, C. T., & Mattei, M. L. (Eds.). (1989). *The psychosocial development of Puerto Rican women.* New York: Praeger.

Julia, M. T. M. (1989). Developmental issues during adulthood: Redefining notions of self, care, and responsibility among a group of professional Puerto Rican women. In C. T. Garcia-Coll & M. L. Mattei (Eds.), *The psychosocial development of Puerto Rican women* (pp. 115–140). New York: Praeger.

Mattei, M. L. (1989). A contradiction in ties: Autonomy and social networks of adult Puerto Rican women. In C. T. Garcia-Coll & M. L. Mattei (Eds.), *The psychosocial development of Puerto Rican women* (pp. 214–242). New York: Praeger.

Mintz, S. (1956). Canaveral: The subculture of a rural sugar plantation proletariat. In J. Steward (Ed.), *The people of Puerto Rico* (pp. 314–418). Urbana, IL: University of Illinois Press.

Mosher, R. L. (1974). Knowledge from practice: Clinical research and development in education. *Counseling Psychologist, 4,* 73–82.

Nazario-Crespo, T. I. (1986). *Social support networks of migrant Puerto Rican women.* Unpublished doctoral dissertation, Boston University.

Padilla, A. M. (1981). Pluralistic counseling and psychotherapy for Hispanic Americans. In A. J. Marsella & P. B. Pedersen (Eds.), *Cross-cultural counseling and psychotherapy* (pp. 195–227). New York: Pergamon Press.

Padilla, A. M., Ruiz, R. A., & Alvarez, R. (1975). Community mental health services for the Spanish-speaking surnamed population. *American Psychologist, 30,* 892–905.

Pescatello, A. M. (1976). *Power and pawn: The female in Iberian families, societies and cultures.* Westport, CT: Greenwood Press.

Salgado de Snyder, N. (1987). Factors associated with acculturative stress and depressive symptomatology among married Mexican immigrant women. *Psychology of Women Quarterly, 11,* 475–488.

Shirley, B. Z. (1981). A study of ego strength: The case of the Hispanic immigrant woman in the United States. (Doctoral dissertation, Boston University). *Dissertation Abstracts International, 42,* 258314–2584A.

Stevens, E. P. (1973). The prospect for a woman's liberation movement in Latin America. *Journal of Marriage and the Family,* 313–320.

Task Force on Black and Minority Health. (1986). *Report of Secretary's Task Force on Black and Minority Health. Volume VIII: Hispanic health issues.* Washington, DC: U.S. Department of Health and Human Services.

Todd, D. (1980). Social networks, psychosocial adaptation, and preventive/ developmental interventions: The support development workshop. *ERIC Reports*. Microfilm No. ED 198420.

Vale, P. (1977). *Apreciacion socio-historica de la familia puertorriquena*. Unpublished paper presented to the Institute of the Family, Rio Piedras, Puerto Rico.

Vazquez-Nuttall, E., & Romero-Garcia, I. (1989). From home to school: Puerto Rican girls learn to be students in the United States. In C. T. Garcia-Coll & M. L. Mattei (Eds.), *The psychosocial development of Puerto Rican women* (pp. 60–83). New York: Praeger.

Walker, K. N., MacBride, A., & Vachon, M. L. (1977). Social support networks and the crisis of bereavement. *Social Science and Medicine, 44*, 35–44.

U.S. Bureau of Labor Statistics. (1986). *Employment and earnings*. Volume 33. Washington, DC: U.S. Government Printing Office.

U.S. Bureau of the Census. (1981a). *Age, sex, race, and Spanish origin of the population by regions, divisions, and states: 1980*. Supplementary Reports: 1980 Census of the Population. Washington, DC: U.S. Government Printing Office.

U.S. Bureau of the Census. (1981b). *Marital status and living arrangements: 1980*. Current Population Reports, Series P-20, No. 365. Washington, DC: U.S. Government Printing Office.

U.S. Bureau of the Census. (1983). *Money income of households, families and persons in the United States: 1981*. Current Population Reports, Series P-60, No. 137. Washington, DC: U.S. Government Printing Office.

U.S. Bureau of the Census. (1985a). *Consumer income*. Current Population Reports, Series P-60, Nos. 149, 150. Washington, DC: U.S. Government Printing Office.

U.S. Bureau of the Census. (1985b). *Persons of Spanish origin in the United States: March, 1985. (Advance Report)*. Current Population Reports, Series P-20, No. 403. Washington, DC: U.S. Government Printing Office.

U.S. Bureau of the Census. (1985c). *Persons of Spanish origin in the United States: March, 1985*. Unpublished data.

U.S. Department of Labor. Women's Bureau. (1985). *Facts on U.S. working women, 1920–1985*. Fact Sheet No. 85–11. Washington, DC: U.S. Department of Labor.

Chapter 12

CUBAN AMERICANS: COUNSELING AND HUMAN DEVELOPMENT ISSUES, PROBLEMS, AND APPROACHES

Gerardo M. Gonzalez

Cubans in the United States are a diverse group. Most arrived here in successive immigration waves following Fidel Castro's revolution and takeover of power in Cuba in 1959. Although some of the initial waves of Cuban immigrants were overrepresented by professionals and upper-middle class people, later arrivals closely paralleled the demographics found in the Cuban population at large. It is important for counselors and other helping professionals who work with this population to dispel the myth that Cubans are a privileged, affluent minority with no special needs. The fact is that Cuban Americans experience many of the problems associated with immigration and social deprivation found among other Latino groups in the United States.

In order to assist and work effectively with Cuban Americans, their unique culture and its traditions must be understood. Many in the United States have a vaguely defined, often erroneous, and stereotypical perception of the Cuban American community. Cubans are a heterogeneous people. Because of its European, African, and Indian roots, Diaz (1981) described traditional Cuban culture as "ajiaco" (a typical stew of vegetables, roots, and meat). This stew has been further complicated by the pervasive influence of American institutions, language, and culture upon Cuban American life. As Cubans here struggle to retain some of their mores, values, language, and traditions, Cuban culture in the United States displays elements of Cuban traditional culture that may be disappearing in Cuba itself (Diaz).

Population Characteristics

Cuban migrations to the United States predate this century. By the late 1800s there were about 100,000 Cubans concentrated mainly in New

York City as well as in Tampa, Key West, and other Florida cities. Fleeing the Cuban wars of independence (1868–1895), people who were part of this first massive exodus established the tobacco industry in southern Florida and largely remained there to become the first large enclave of Cuban Americans (Diaz, 1981). However, the majority of Cubans residing in the United States today arrived in six stages of migration between 1959 and 1980 following the Cuban revolution, during which time some 600,000 Cubans immigrated to the United States. Perez (1985) presented an excellent, comprehensive summary of the most significant results of the 1980 U.S. census with respect to the population of Cuban origin residing in the United States. Much of the information on population characteristics presented here is based on these highlights of the 1980 U.S. census. According to the census of 1980, a total of 803,226 persons were identified as Cuban Americans, based on the respondents who indicated on the census forms that they are of "Cuban origin or descent." Today approximately 875,000 Cuban Americans live in the United States.

Most of the Cuban population in the United States are urbanites. The Cuban population surpasses the total U.S. population, as well as every other Latino group, in the proportion that resides in urban areas. The Miami-Fort Lauderdale area (Dade and Broward counties in Florida), greater New York, and Los Angeles combined contain more than three fourths of this population. In Miami alone, there are over 500,000 Cubans. Moreover, the trend is toward an accelerated concentration in Florida (Perez, 1985).

In comparison to other Latino populations, as well as with the total U.S. population, Cubans are the oldest group in terms of age. Middle-aged and elderly persons are overrepresented in the Cuban population, a totally atypical characteristic for a population largely composed of immigrants that have arrived within the last decade (Perez, 1985). The high proportion of the elderly has led to the relatively widespread existence among Cuban Americans of the three-generation family. However, as younger Cubans are assimilated into American culture and become more socially mobile, the traditional function of the extended family as a source of support and acceptance for older Cubans is likely to erode. In addition, the rapidly growing number of older Cubans in America, and the diminishing number of younger family members available for their care, will present a serious challenge to community agencies charged with the responsibility for services to this population. Not only is this a population that, like other older Americans, is concerned with the problem of failing health, but its members also experience the diminishing traditional importance of their position in the family.

Another important characteristic of the Cuban population in the United States is the overrepresentation of women. The sex ratio of the Cuban American population shows that there are only 90.8 men for every 100 women. This compares with 94.5 for the total U.S. population and 103.4 for the Mexican American population. Although a low sex ratio is typical of an older population, in the case of Cuban Americans it also reflects the restrictions the Cuban government imposes on the emigration of men eligible for military conscription (Perez, 1985). This has presented some special problems for divorced women who wish to remarry within the group. In comparison to other Latino groups and even with the total U.S. population, Cubans have the highest proportion of women in the divorced category.

Cuban American women also exhibit a high rate of participation in the labor force. According to the 1980 census, the percentage of all Cuban women 16 years of age and over in the labor force employed full-time all year was 47.1%. This compares with 40.1% of the total U.S. population and 35.0% of the Mexican American population. Given the tendency of Cuban women to be employed, it is not surprising that the Cubans led all other comparison groups (Mexican, Puerto Rican, other Spanish, and total U.S.) in the percent of families containing two workers. The impact of the high rates of female labor force participation among Cuban Americans is especially evident in the fact that the median income of Cuban married-couple families, with children under 6, is higher than the income of all such families in the United States. The majority of Cuban working women are employed in administrative support occupations as clerical workers and operators and fabricators in light manufacturing and textiles. Perez (1985) pointed out that apparently working in "la factoria" is indeed an important phenomenon among Cuban women.

The large number of elderly and working women, along with the presence of the three-generational family, raises some important questions about the future of the Cuban community as it continues to age. For example, Perez (1985) suggested that "A high proportion of persons over 40, combined with low fertility, points to a rapid aging of the population, a process that could severely tax the community resources for dealing with the dependent elderly. This may be a special problem if the younger and more acculturated Cubans prove to be reluctant to establish the type of three-generation households in which they themselves grew up" (p. 16).

Special Problems of Cuban Americans

Gonzalez (1988) reviewed the effects of immigration and acculturation on the Cuban American family, and also identified some other major problems confronting Cubans in the United States. In general, the problems can be categorized into five major areas: cultural adjustment problems, problems of acculturation, educational problems, career development problems, and special population problems.

Cultural Adjustment Problems

As mentioned earlier, the majority of Cubans in this country arrived in various stages of migration beginning in 1959 after the Castro revolution. Starting with the professionals, landowners, and businessmen in the early 1960s, successive waves of the migrant flow brought to the United States a virtual cross-section of Cuban society (Bach, Bach, & Triplete, 1981–1982). The largest migration occurred from 1965 to 1973 when over a quarter million Cubans were airlifted into the United States. The airlift group was larger than the group of Cuban immigrants who came to the United States between 1959 and 1965 (Azicri, 1981–1982). The airlift brought about a change in the characteristics of the Cuban American population. Whereas about one third of the early Cuban refugees were professionals and managers, that rate was reduced by half in the early 1970s and has not shown significant changes during the past decade. However, the image of a Cuban exodus composed of professionals, businessmen, and middle-class families prevailed until 125,000 Cubans migrated to Key West from the port of Mariel near Havana in the summer of 1980. In May 1980 alone, more Cuban refugees arrived in the United States than in all of 1962, the previous record year for Cuban immigration (Bach et al.).

The large influx of Cuban immigrants who arrived in the Mariel "Freedom Flotilla," as well as an estimated 7,000 criminals Castro sent to the United States with this group as a result of the post-Mariel prison riots and other events, gave rise for the first time to widespread anti-Cuban sentiment in the United States. Part of this sentiment was due to the changed conditions in the United States, which conflicted directly with the open Cuban admissions policy of historical precedent. Already besieged by high unemployment, inflation, and recession, many in the United States perceived this dramatic influx as yet another burden (Bach et al., 1981–1982). In addition, the well-publicized fallout from drug trafficking on the part of Cubans and other Latinos, and the swelling of Miami's Latino communities by refugees from Central American countries, has fueled this anti-Cuban sentiment. Thus, during the 1980s, for the first time since Castro's takeover, the United States ceased to grant automatic exile status to Cubans (Cuban American National Council, 1989).

Problems of Acculturation

One experience common to all immigrant groups is the process of acculturation. Acculturation refers to the problem of adjustment—the borrowing, acquiring, and adopting of cultural traits from a host society by people who have migrated from another society. According to Szapocznik, Ladner, and Scopetta (1979), clinical experience with the Cuban immigrant community in Dade County, Florida, indicates that the acculturation process has often resulted in family disruption within this population. Moreover, because youngsters acculturate more rapidly than their parents do, this process often exacerbates intergenerational differences. As an outgrowth of family conflict resulting from different rates of acculturation, Szapocznik et al. (1979) found an increased tendency for Cuban youngsters to participate in social networks characterized by antisocial activities, including drug abuse and other delinquent behavior. For instance, in the mid-1980s, the school dropout rate for Dade County's Latino students—most of whom are Cubans—neared 40%. At the same time, the number of youth gangs in the county increased to more than 60, and it is estimated that 8 out of every 10 gang members are Latinos (Cuban American National Council, 1989).

Understanding the concept of acculturation is crucial to counseling with Latinos generally, and Cuban Americans specifically (Ponterotto, 1987; Szapocznik, Scopetta, Kurtines, & Aranalde, 1978). In a study of acculturative differences in self- and family-role perception among Cuban American college students, Kurtines and Miranda (1980) found strong support for the hypothesis that one of the mechanisms that generate family disruption within migrant groups is the occurrence of intergenerational differences in rates of acculturation. According to the acculturation gap hypothesis, families who experience the greatest distress are those in which the levels of acculturation within the family unit are most discrepant. Furthermore, the mechanism by which the acculturation gap generates family disruption seems to be intrafamilial role conflict, both within and between family subsystems. Kurtines and Miranda reported that acculturative change was significantly related to a decline in the high esteem parental roles have traditionally occupied in the Cuban family. Based on their findings, Kurtines and Miranda suggested that when counseling migrants, treatment type and modality should be adjusted to deal with disruptive acculturative differences when they occur within families. In such cases, family therapy would provide a useful adjunct to individual therapy, and role play techniques would serve as a tool for reducing intrafamilial role conflict.

Perhaps the most extensive work with regard to the effects of acculturation on the Cuban family has been done by Szapocznik and his associates at the Spanish Family Guidance Center in Miami, Florida. Two innovative, culturally sensitive counseling approaches that have been developed and tested there for their effectiveness with Cuban families are Bicultural Effectiveness Training (BET) (Szapocznik, Santisteban, Kurtines, Perez-Vidal, & Hervis, 1986) and One-Person Family Therapy (OPFT) (Szapocznik, Kurtines, Foote, Perez-Vidal, & Hervis, 1983). BET is based on a model of adjustment that posits that individuals living in bicultural contexts tend to become maladjusted when they remain or become monocultural. In this model, Cuban Americans who fail to learn how to, or do not want to interact within the Anglo American context, tend to underacculturate and experience adjustment problems related to this phenomenon. On the other hand, individuals who reject the skills necessary to interact within the Latino context tend to overacculturate and lack the flexibility necessary to cope with their entire cultural milieu.

The One-Person Family Therapy approach is based on the hypothesis that it is possible to achieve the goals of family therapy (i.e., structural family change and symptom reduction) by working primarily with one person. This hypothesis is based on the notion underlying family therapy that says that changing a part of the system almost inevitably brings about changes in the whole system. In a study of the relative effectiveness of Conjoint Family Therapy (CFT) versus One-Person Family Therapy (OPFT) for a Cuban American population, Szapocznik et al. (1983) proposed a redefinition of family therapy as "a treatment modality in which the therapist's interventions target on changing family systems, regardless of who is present at a particular therapy session" (p. 890). The researchers concluded that OPFT would be preferred over CFT where there is particular difficulty in scheduling the whole family for therapy (as is often the case in working with Latino groups), when one family member requires a great deal of strengthening, or when family members are unwilling to participate in the therapy process.

One implication of these studies is that structural family therapy can be effective with a Cuban population. Furthermore, it was shown that participation by the entire family is not always required for this form of therapy. This is an important finding because Latinos generally, and Cuban Americans in particular, tend to underutilize mental health services. It is difficult to get full family participation even when some family members are willing to seek therapy. Moreover, because it is known that one of the outcomes of the acculturation gap within Cuban families is family stress and disruption, effective forms of family therapy can make an important contribution to the overall adjustment and assimilation of Cuban Americans.

One noteworthy characteristic of structural family therapy with regard to its use with Latinos is its focus on behavioral goals. Behavioral

approaches generally are more effective than intrapsychic types of therapies with this population (Ponterotto, 1987). Action-oriented, problem-
solving approaches are deemed more appropriate for Cuban Americans
who, when compared to Anglo Americans on a value orientation scale,
tend to have a greater present-time orientation and tend not to endorse
idealized humanistic values (Szapocznik, Scopetta, Kurtines, & Aranalde,
1978). Counseling with the Cuban American client should be present-
oriented. Cuban Americans are usually mobilized for treatment by the
onset of a crisis and expect the therapist to provide immediate problem-
oriented solutions to the crisis situation. Rather than being motivated to
seek treatment by the search for personal and spiritual growth, Cuban
Americans are more likely to be motivated to seek concrete and obtain-
able solutions to their problems.

Educational Problems

The majority of Cuban immigrants in the United States indicate
that their lack of knowledge of the English language is their principal
problem (Portes, Clark, & Lopez, 1981–1982). English comprehension
among Cuban exiles is surprisingly low, even after several years of residence in the United States. Only 24% of Portes's sample were fluent in
English, even when a liberal definition of fluency was adopted. This
finding is not entirely surprising when one considers the existence of a
large immigrant community where knowledge of the host country's language is not imperative for economic survival. However, the lack of
knowledge of the English language does present some rather serious
problems for economic advancement and school achievement.

It is impossible to say to what extent the lack of knowledge of the
English language is responsible for the excessive school dropout rates
that prevail among Spanish-speaking students. Despite the 1974 Supreme Court decision of *Lau v. Nichols*, which indicated that without
help, students who do not speak the school language are effectively
foreclosed from any meaningful education, there is still a lack of Latino
students enrolled in bilingual education (Wagenheim, 1981). This problem has been confounded for Latinos generally, and Cuban Americans
specifically, by the "English Only" national movement (Cuban American
National Council, 1989). This movement seeks to have the states and
the federal government adopt English as the official language of the
United States and its localities.

Because the Supreme Court did not prescribe any specific remedy
to the language problem of Spanish-speaking students in American schools,
many different approaches to bilingual education have been developed.
Most can be divided into two broad categories: transitional and main-

tenance. Under the transitional approach, the student's native language is used as a medium of instruction only until the student can function in an English language classroom. Under the maintenance approach, both the student's native language and English are used in instruction. Most Cuban American students who are enrolled in bilingual instruction are taught under the transitional approach. Students are expected to stay in these transitional programs for 1 to 3 years, until they can be "mainstreamed" into regular classrooms. Unfortunately, because the language most often spoken at home and outside the classroom is Spanish, many students never become sufficiently fluent in English to compete properly with their Anglo counterparts in the schools. The results are lower school achievement and increased dropout rates.

Greater sensitivity and special programs are needed to help Cuban American students cope with the pressures of a home and peer environment that promotes adherence to the native culture and language, and a school environment that demands optimal performance in the English language. Unfortunately, schools have not always been responsive to those needs.

Career Development Problems

Another pressing problem that Cuban Americans face in the United States is that of finding employment in areas where they have a particular skill or personal interest. Portes et al. (1981–1982) showed that the aspirations of newly arrived Cubans for new occupations in the United States were higher than their past attainments in Cuba. However, these high aspirations compared quite negatively with subsequent attainments. Almost half of the sample that Portes and his colleagues studied was found in the lower blue-collar category after several years in the United States. Those who reached professional or managerial occupations represented little more than half the population in that category in Cuba and much less than the percentage aspiring to it. Mean occupational prestige, as measured by a socioeconomic index, was 10 points below that at arrival, indicating significant downward mobility.

One of the major concerns for counselors who work with Cuban American clients is selecting appropriate interest inventories for measurement and assistance with career development goals. Very few studies have examined whether vocational development theories and interest inventories normed primarily on White Anglo samples have relevance to Spanish-speaking individuals (Harrington & O'Shea, 1980). The Spanish translations of English tests are not always appropriate. Butcher and Garcia (1978) warned that even when adequate translation is achieved, it cannot be assumed that the same constructs are being measured in a different culture. Being cognizant of these problems, Harrington and O'Shea conducted a study designed to determine the construct validity of Holland's hexagonal model with Spanish-speaking subgroups and to establish the construct validity of the Spanish form of their own Career Decision Making (CDM) instrument.

The subjects for this study were 267 Spanish-speaking persons who resided in the United States and indicated their ethnic background as Mexican American, Puerto Rican, Cuban, or South American. The intercorrelation matrix of the six CDM scales was compared with that of Holland's Vocational Preference Inventory. The results provided confirmation of the Holland hexagonal model in this diverse Spanish-speaking sample. According to the researchers, "This suggests that Spanish-speaking cultures have present work models whereby crafts, scientific, artistic, social, business enterprises, and business detail interest can develop" (p. 249). They also suggested that the vocational interests of the Spanish-speaking can be measured validly through the Holland scales. Therefore, the CDM Spanish form provides counselors with a Holland-based tool to explore career choices with the Spanish-speaking client. Research is needed to see whether the CDM scales can be used to help Cuban immigrants explore various career choices and obtain proper training for their choice of work in the United States. The key issue in career counseling with Cuban Americans centers on understanding the characteristics of this unique population and the vocational interests of their individual members. Career counselors must be sure that any technique or instrument they use to assess such interests be culturally sensitive and appropriate for use with this population. It cannot be assumed that materials and processes developed for use with an English-speaking population will automatically apply to a Spanish-speaking population.

Special Population Problems

As noted earlier, Cubans in the United States are a population older than the mean. There is a growing need for social services that are sensitive to two sets of characteristics unique to this population: (1) cultural background and (2) advanced age. The concept of matching services, particularly counseling modalities, to client characteristics has been well established in the mental health field. Recognition of the need for counseling approaches designed specifically for the elderly Cuban American population led Szapocznik, Santisteban, Kurtines, Hervis, and Spencer (1982) to develop a life enhancement counseling model that is culturally sensitive to the basic values of this group. This model makes therapeutic use of specific characteristics of elders, such as the tendency to reminisce, and employs an ecological approach to allow the therapist access to the elder's social environment. The overall goal of this form of therapy is to enhance the meaningfulness of life for elders. It conceptualizes many psychological difficulties and "disorders" of elders as potentially reversible rather than inevitable consequences of the aging process. The life enhancement counseling model was evaluated by Szapocznik, Santisteban, Hervis, and Spencer (1981) for its effect in the treatment of depression among Cuban American elders and was found to be effective both when used alone or in combination with pharmacotherapy. However, clients who received both medication and life enhancement counseling tended to improve more than those who received either form of therapy alone.

Validation of the efficacy of life enhancement therapy as an effective treatment model that is sensitive to both age and cultural characteristics of Cuban American elders, and which can be effective by itself or in combination with pharmacotherapy, has important implications for the treatment needs of this population. Cubans in general have a strong tradition of self-diagnosis and self-prescription. This tradition has been traced to the historical development of the pharmacist as a quasimedical practitioner in Cuba (Page, 1982). What began as a one-stop form of caregiving by physicians who diagnosed, treated, and dispensed medicines in the same place, later gave rise to the expectation that pharmacists would do the same. This expectation continues and is very much alive within the Cuban American community today. The one-stop pharmacist practitioner represents a convenient means for the self-diagnoser to obtain reassurance that the identified malady and chosen course of treatment are correct, according to an "authority." Thus, the potential over-reliance on legal drugs that are often obtained without a doctor's prescription should be taken into account when counseling with older Cuban Americans. Early in the development of the counseling relationship, the client should be encouraged to obtain a complete medical examination that includes an assessment of drugs being consumed. Based on the results of this examination, the counselor can develop a treatment plan that may include physician supervised pharmacotherapy in conjunction with life enhancement therapy, or life enhancement therapy alone as an alternative to self-medication.

Intervention Strategies

The problems of Cuban Americans are too complex and diverse for simple solutions. The need for cultural events and activities, such as festivals, parades, and art exhibits that celebrate Cuban culture, is important for individual cultural identity and community development.

Special programs designed to increase Cuban American participation in education, particularly higher education, are also important. Such educational programs might include special language enhancement initiatives, cultural sensitivity training for teachers and school counselors, and special institutional assessment techniques that might lead to comprehensive responses. In higher education, comprehensive institutional responses might include improved financial aid and articulation efforts, formation of special task forces and study groups to increase institutional awareness and responsiveness to specific problems, and increased recruitment and training of Latino educators.

Development of culturally sensitive counseling and development initiatives such as those discussed in this chapter to deal with acculturation issues, family adjustment, career development, and special population needs also is important. Additional efforts, including national political initiatives designed to combat the growing anti-Latino, anti-Cuban sentiment embodied in such movements as the "English Only" movement, are also essential. Initiatives such as "English Plus," where English remains the primary unofficial language of the nation, but other languages are encouraged rather than suppressed, should be supported by those concerned about human development issues.

All these issues are complex and require considerable creativity, involvement, and financial resources to produce solutions. As Latinos generally, and Cuban Americans in particular, grow in number and become more politically active, greater demands will be made for appropriate responses to these problems. Thus, the 1990s promise to be a decade of increasing calls for counseling and human development specialists to join the search for appropriate solutions to the problems affecting Cuban Americans and other Latino groups.

Summary

This chapter provided an overview of some of the major problems confronting Cuban immigrants and Cuban Americans in the United States. Issues related to population characteristics and cultural adjustment processes, as well as problems of acculturation, education, vocational development, and special population groups were explored. Ever since Homer's description of the wanderings of Ulysses and his weeping and rolling on the floor at the thought of home, many writers and investigators have been aware of the relationship between the process of cultural adjustment among immigrant groups and the presence of what has been termed "acculturative stress" (Santisteban, 1980). Cuban American immigrants are no exception. The popular misconception that

Cuban Americans are a privileged group and therefore need no special assistance should be dispelled. Cuban Americans face some difficult and unique challenges to their survival as a viable, productive minority group in the United States.

In this chapter several examples of approaches developed to respond to the most pressing needs of Cuban Americans were reviewed. These examples were selected because of their cultural sensitivity, creative approach, research basis, potential for replicability, and implication for further development and study. They do not represent an exhaustive review of effective approaches. Many other educational, therapeutic, and community responses must be explored and developed in order to meet the needs of the growing Cuban American population. The basic premise underlying any type of intervention developed for Cuban Americans, however, is that it must be sensitive to the particular needs, expectations, and values of this culture-rich, complex, and diverse population.

References

American Council on Education. (1989). *Minorities on campus: A handbook for enhancing diversity*. Washington, DC: Author.

Azicri, M. (1981–1982). The politics of exile: Trends and dynamics of political change among Cuban Americans. *Cuban Studies, 11 & 12*, 56–70.

Bach, R. L., Bach, J. B., & Triplete, T. (1981–1982). Flotilla "entrants": Latest and most controversial. *Cuban Studies, 11 & 12*, 29–48.

Butcher, J., & Garcia, R. (1978). Cross-national application of psychological tests. *Personnel and Guidance Journal, 56*, 472–475.

Cuban American National Council. (1989). *The elusive decade of Hispanics*. Miami, FL: Author.

Diaz, G. M. (1981). The changing Cuban community. In *Hispanics and grantmakers: A special report of Foundation News* (pp. 18–23). Washington, DC: Council on Foundations.

Gonzalez, G. M. (1988). *Cuban Americans*. In N. A. Vacc & J. Wittmer (Eds.), *Experiencing and counseling multicultural and diverse populations* (2nd ed.) (pp. 263–288). Muncie, IN: Accelerated Development.

Harrington, T. F., & O'Shea, A. J. (1980). Applicability of the Holland (1973) model of vocational development with Spanish-speaking clients. *Journal of Counseling Psychology, 27*, 246–251.

Kurtines, W. M., & Miranda, L. (1980). Differences in self and family role perception among acculturing Cuban American college students: Implications for the etiology of family disruption among migrant groups. *International Journal of Intercultural Relations, 4*, 167–184.

Page, J. B., (1982). A brief history of mind-altering drug use in prerevolutionary Cuba. *Cuban Studies, 12*, 55–71.

Perez, L., (1985). The Cuban population of the United States: The results of the 1980 U.S. Census of the Population. *Cuban Studies, 15*, 1–16.

Ponterotto, J. G. (1987). Counseling Mexican Americans: A multimodal approach. *Journal of Counseling and Development, 65*, 308–311.

Portes, A., Clark, J. M., & Lopez, M. M. (1981–1982). Six years later, the process of incorporation of Cuban exiles in the United States: 1973–1979. *Cuban Studies, 11 & 12*, 1–28.

Santisteban, D. (1980). *Acculturation/assimilation and psychological stress: A review of the literature.* Unpublished manuscript. University of Miami, Spanish Family Guidance Center, Miami.

Szapocznik, J., Kurtines, W. M., Foote, F. H., Perez-Vidal, A., & Hervis, O. (1983). Conjoint versus one-person family therapy: Some evidence for the effectiveness of conducting family therapy through one person. *Journal of Consulting and Clinical Psychology, 51*, 889–899.

Szapocznik, J., Ladner, R. A., & Scopetta, M. A. (1979). Youth drug abuse and subjective distress in a Hispanic population. In G. M. Beschner & A. S. Friedman (Eds.), *Youth drug abuse* (pp. 493–511). Lexington, MA: Heath.

Szapocznik, J., Santisteban, D., Hervis, O., & Spencer, F. (1981). Treatment of depression among Cuban American elders: Some validation evidence for a life enhancement counseling approach. *Journal of Consulting and Clinical Psychology, 49*, 752–754.

Szapocznik, J., Santisteban, D., Kurtines, W. M., Hervis, O. E., & Spencer, F. (1982). Life enhancement counseling: A psychosocial model of services for Hispanic elders. In E. E. Jones & S. J. Korchin (Eds.), *Minority mental health* (pp. 296–330). New York: Holt, Rinehart & Winston.

Szapocznik, J., Santisteban, D., Kurtines, W. M., Perez-Vidal, A., & Hervis, O. (1986). Bicultural effectiveness training: A treatment intervention for enhancing intercultural adjustment in Cuban families. *Hispanic Journal of Behavioral Sciences, 6*, 317–344.

Szapocznik, J., Scopetta, M. A., & Aranalde, M. (1978). Cuban value structure: Treatment implications. *Journal of Consulting and Clinical Psychology, 46*, 961–970.

Szapocznik, J., Scopetta, M. A., Kurtines, W. M., & Aranalde, M. A. (1978). Theory and measurement of acculturation. *Interamerican Journal of Psychology, 12*, 113–130.

Wagenheim, K. (1981). The Hispanic phenomenon. In *Hispanics and grantmakers: A special report of Foundation News* (pp. 49–53). Washington, DC: Council on Foundations.

Additional Resource

Cuban American National Council. (1987). *Miami mosaic: Ethnic relations in Dade County.* Miami, FL: Author.

Chapter 13
COUNSELING CHICANO COLLEGE STUDENTS

Augustine Barón, Jr.

Chicanos? Mexican Americans—with or without hyphen? Latinos? Hispanics? How does one refer to the American population having ethnic origins in Mexico? As will be discussed later, ethnic labels carry significant psychological meaning, which is important for counseling work. In this chapter, the terms *Chicano* and *Mexican American* (without the hyphen) will be used interchangeably, although there are regional, political, and generational variations in the acceptability of the terms.

Chicanos, according to the best forecasts using 1970 and 1980 census data (Hispanic Policy Development Project, 1984), will account in 1990 for about 69% of all Latino groups in the United States. This is roughly a 10% increase from the 1980 census, and translates into 17 million people, or about 7% of the total U.S. population. In some states, however, the percentages of Mexican Americans are already significantly higher, reaching almost 20%.

This chapter focuses on a specific subgroup of Chicanos, namely, those young Mexican American men and women attending colleges and universities. Based on 1980 census data, the percentage of Mexican Americans who had attended at least 1 year of college was about 19%. A recent report (U.S. Bureau of the Census, 1990) found that 3 out of 10 Latino high school graduates aged 18 to 24 were enrolled in college in 1988, about the same percentage as in 1978. Thus, there seems to have been little or no change over time in the overall college attendance rate for Latinos.

Embedded in these college figures is the rather high dropout rate among Chicanos. In a study on Latinos in general, the National Center for Education Statistics (1980) reported that 4 years after enrolling in college, about 10% of the men and 12% of the women completed a bachelor's degree. This compares to 38% of Anglo men and 42% of Anglo women. Astin (1972, 1975, 1982) highlighted high school dropout rates that further aggravate the situation for college achievement among Chicanos. Using 1980 census data, he found that the percentage of

171

Chicanos aged 20 to 25 who dropped out of high school was almost 50%. This figure is in sharp contrast with comparable dropout rates for African Americans (about 30%) and Anglos (almost 18%). In a similar study of 18- and 19-year-old Latinos, the National Council of La Raza (1990) found that, in 1988, 31% had dropped out of high school, compared to 18% of African Americans of the same age and 14% Anglos.

As these statistics indicate, a Mexican American college student who completes an undergraduate education has indeed achieved something noteworthy. The road to graduation is often a difficult one, which demands not only academic skills, but also sociopsychological tools to traverse it. This is where the role of the counseling professional clearly comes into play. Research by Sedlacek and colleagues (Sedlacek & Brooks, 1976; Tracey & Sedlacek, 1984, 1985, 1987; Sedlacek, 1987) indicated several noncognitive variables that have been found to be significant predictors of college success for African Americans, and that have intuitive validity for ethnic minority students in general. Among these are (a) having positive self-concept or confidence, (b) being able to conduct a realistic self-appraisal, (c) understanding and dealing effectively with racism, (d) being able to develop long-range goals rather than relying on short-term ones, and (e) having the availability of a strong support person.

Clearly, counselors are at their best when they address these factors through their individual, small group, and systemic/institutional interventions. This chapter will outline specific cultural concepts that are important to consider when planning a counseling intervention for Chicanos. Individual and group counseling examples that demonstrate the concepts in action will then be presented.

Key Cultural Concepts

Three key cultural concepts are useful to consider when formulating appropriate counseling interventions for Chicano college students: acculturation, ethnic identity development, and machismo (or more broadly, sex-role differences). Each plays a significant role in determining the focus, style, and scope of counseling methods.

Acculturation

The concept of acculturation has received increasing attention in the social science literature. Its importance is underscored by the fact that it has been identified as a significant moderator variable in a number of counseling-related processes for Chicanos. These include client dropout rates (Miranda, Andujo, Caballero, Guerrero, & Ramos, 1976), degree and content of self-disclosure (Castro, 1977), willingness to seek professional help (Ruiz, Casas, & Padilla, 1977), overall success of therapy (Miranda & Castro, 1977), and preference for an ethnically similar counselor (Sanchez & Atkinson, 1983).

Given these findings, the inclusion of acculturational status becomes an indispensable consideration for counselors in their early assessment, problem definitions, and goal setting with Chicano clients. Acculturation is best conceptualized as a multidimensional and multidirectional process whereby ethnic minorities learn, incorporate, and integrate both the overt and covert cultural characteristics of the dominant culture (Valdes, Barón, & Ponce, 1987). Mendoza and Martinez (1981) presented a model of acculturation that discussed the changes that occur across the primary modalities of cognitions, affect, and behavior. They outlined four core processes by which acculturation occurs: (a) **cultural resistance**, the active or passive resistance to incorporating dominant cultural patterns (i.e., lack of acculturation); (b) **cultural shift**, the substitution of one set of patterns for those of the dominant culture (i.e., assimilating new cognitions, affects, and behaviors while extinguishing the "old" ones); (c) **cultural incorporation**, the adaptation of patterns representative of both one's own cultural group and those of the dominant culture (i.e., retaining both cultures at once); and (d) **cultural transmutation**, the alteration of certain elements of both cultures to create a third, unique "hybrid" pattern (e.g., religious practices that fuse Christian religion with American Indian theology).

Overt cultural characteristics such as dress, language usage, eating habits, and celebrations are more easily incorporated into a new set of patterns and can be more easily observed than is the case for covert characteristics such as beliefs, attitudes, values, and feelings. This makes it challenging to assess acculturational status fully. Compounding the difficulties is the fact that acculturation occurs at different rates and along different developmental pathways for each individual, based on such factors as generational status, geographical location, personal motivations for assimilating into the dominant culture, and degree of contact with other groups.

Nonetheless, numerous methods for assessing acculturational status among Chicanos have now been developed and are available for use in counseling. Some of these measurement tools include the Measure of Acculturation for Chicano Adolescents (Olmedo, Martinez, & Martinez, 1978), the Behavioral Acculturation Scale (Szapocznik, Scoppeta, & Tillman, 1979), the Bilingualism/Multiculturalism Experience Inventory (Ramirez, 1983), and the Acculturation Rating Scale for Mexican Americans (Cuellar, Harris, & Jasso, 1980). These scales provide useful methods for understanding the intragroup diversity among Chicanos.

Acculturational status is perhaps the primary factor to consider early on in a counseling contact. The more closely a client identifies with his or her Mexican heritage to the exclusion of Anglo American culture, the more counseling methods may need to be altered. Using Ivey's (1971) microcounseling framework, the less acculturated a client is, the more a counselor may need to modify his or her attending and influencing skills. Eye contact, for example, on the part of the client may be indirect toward the counselor, indicating a sign of respect for an authority figure. As is the case for other minority groups, such "looking down" or "away" should not be misread as lack of respect for, or attention to, the counselor. In general, the less acculturated to American customs that a Chicano client is, the harder the counselor will need to work to maximize a sense of comfort, respect, and warmth in the sessions. This is particularly the case when the counselor differs from the client in ethnicity or acculturational status.

Ethnic Identity Development

Closely associated with acculturational status is the notion of ethnic identity development. Whereas acculturation is broadly concerned with the degree to which dominant cultural norms are accepted, rejected, or transformed by ethnic minorities, racial/ethnic identity development usually refers to attitudes, beliefs, and feelings for the dominant culture vis-à-vis one's own ethnic group. Such development is primarily focused on inter- and intrapersonal factors that have implications for healthy sociopsychological development. In a sense, ethnic identity development is a subset of the larger, all-encompassing notion of acculturation. There is an inextricable interaction between the two in that shifts in acculturation bring about changes in ethnic identity development and vice versa.

A variety of theoretical models have also been developed for this second key concept (Atkinson, Morten, & Sue, 1979; Christensen, 1986; Cross, 1971; Helms, 1985; Thomas, 1971). They are usually intended to account for developmental changes occurring in most, if not all, ethnic minorities.

Although some of these models are intended specifically for African Americans, they have also been applied to ethnic minority groups in general. What these models share in common is the view that ethnic minorities incorporate negative stereotypes about their own group in early childhood, which must be shed in order to arrive at a healthy state of self-affirmation and esteem. The process of replacing a negative self-concept may be precipitated by a variety of events, usually involving something traumatic, such as a discriminatory action perpetrated against the individual. The person is then brought to a greater sense of awareness about his or her own group's strengths and the dominant group's weaknesses, often culminating in the middle stages with anger toward, and isolation from, the dominant group. This is later resolved by developing a capacity to appreciate all cultures and to celebrate diversity.

Though the various models have mixed theoretical validity based on available current research, studies do indicate that ethnic identity development does play a role in successful client-counselor matching (Parham & Helms, 1981), degree of self-regard, self-esteem, and self-actualization (Parham & Helms, 1985a, 1985b), and degree of felt anxiety (Parham & Helms, 1985b).

As noted at the beginning of the chapter, ethnic labels carry significant psychological meaning, and it is from the perspective of minority identity development that such meaning is derived. In the case of Chicanos/Mexican Americans, for example, what term one chooses to use may say much about one's own political ideology, identity, and so forth. Within the same family, for example, a parent may self-identify as an "American of Mexican descent," a son may identify as a "Mexican American", and a daughter may describe herself as a "Chicana" or "Mexicana." Each family member is consciously or unconsciously making a statement about his or her identity.

The parent in this example wants to assert his or her affiliation with America first and Mexican ancestry second. Such an assertion is not uncommon for older Mexican Americans who are naturalized or first-generation citizens. The son who identified as Mexican American is making perhaps the most neutral (and therefore the most difficult to interpret) statement of the three. The term is widely used and accepted among members of the group. The last terms, Chicano(a) and Mexicano(a), are also strong statements indicating clear affiliation with Mexican heritage. This is so because the person is using the Spanish language forms of the labels. The term Chicano(a) was used pejoratively against Mexican Americans early in this century, and was transformed into a positive label by Mexican American activists in the 1950s and 1960s, much as occurred with the term *Black* for African Americans during the same period. Currently, *Black* seems to be giving way to *African American*, and in the Mexican American community, the terms *Hispanic* and *Latino* have come into use as inclusive terms for all people having ancestral roots in Cuba, Mexico, Puerto Rico, and Central and South America.

The main point here is that something as simple as an ethnic label can give the counselor a good deal of information about the client's minority identity development. This in turn will influence the counseling process. Available research on the ethnic identity development models indicates that when an ethnic minority individual is at the early stages of identity development, he or she has the most negative views of self and group, and may prefer a majority-group counselor or a counselor who is of a different ethnic group (Helms, 1985). At the middle stages of development, anger and militancy are key issues in counseling, and the client often requests a counselor of the same ethnic group who is seen as creditable and not a "cop-out." At the later stages, the ethnicity of the counselor is not as important a factor as is the counselor's overall capacity to appreciate cultural diversity and respect the client's unique worldview (Helms).

Machismo

With the advent of the women's movement and an increasing focus on sex-role differences, society has incorporated a Spanish word (and concept) into its vocabulary, namely, **machismo**, along with its variants (e.g., macho man). Because the term, as used in American society, is often equated with male chauvinism, its positive denotations and connotations in Latino culture are often lost. Although Anglo American culture tends to view the term mostly in the pejorative terms of sexism, machismo in Latino cultures is most closely aligned with the concept of chivalry. As such, machismo includes being gallant, courteous, charitable, and courageous. A Mexican man who is seen as macho is acting like a knight in the best sense of that term.

One Mexican American psychologist (Ruiz, 1981, pp. 191–192) captured this well when he wrote:

> It [machismo] connotes physical strength, sexual attractiveness, virtue, and potency. In this sense, the label "macho" has many of the same connotations it has in English. . . . At a more subtle level of analysis, "real" masculinity among Hispanics involves dignity in personal conduct, respect for others, love for the family, and affection for children. When applied by non-Hispanics to Hispanic males, however, "macho" often is defined in terms of physical aggression, sexual promiscuity, dominance of women, and excessive use of alcohol. In reaction to this abuse, Hispanic women are assumed to be submissive, nurturant, and virtuous; thereby maintaining the unity of the Hispanic family, despite all the disruption from their fathers, husbands, and sons.

Ruiz captured a core problem in the social science literature regarding the term. If machismo is seen only in pejorative terms from a non-Latino perspective, and Latinos are then seen as valuing such a concept, it must be concluded that the Latino culture condones the brutality engendered by male chauvinism. What is missing in the social research is an appreciation for the positive definition of machismo in the Latino culture.

The problem comes down to one of language, where a Spanish term and concept have been borrowed and incorporated into American culture and the English language, and thereby transformed from being largely positive into being mostly negative.

Without a doubt, sexism does indeed exist among Chicanos. Unfortunately, the concept of machismo, arising as it does from Latino roots, has tended to overestimate the presence of male chauvinism because it is assumed that the culture not only tolerates but fosters sexism to a greater degree than do other cultures. In a sense, Chicanos and other Latinos are often seen by non-Latinos as having "excessive" amounts of male chauvinism, precisely because of the misunderstanding surrounding the concept of machismo.

Many counseling questions arise from this concept, and these are important to explore with a client. For example, what negative definitions has a Mexican American client internalized about machismo? Does he or she understand and value the positive definition of machismo rooted in Latino culture? How do definitions of masculinity and femininity affect the client's romantic and work relationships, expectations for career development, and so on? Any discussion of sex-role issues with Chicano clients will invariably necessitate an exploration of machismo and how the concept is understood and internalized in everyday life.

Counseling Examples: The Concepts in Action

Two examples, one based on individual counseling and one involving a group counseling intervention, are presented below. Each captures the key cultural concepts noted above, along with related issues.

An Individual Counseling Case

Alberto (a pseudonym) was a 22-year-old, first-year graduate student in psychology. He came to the university counseling center complaining of being anxious and depressed over his schoolwork. On his intake form, Alberto had described his ethnic group affiliation as "Chicano." This led the counselor, who was also Mexican American, to believe that Alberto had some heightened awareness of his heritage, and possible affirmation of positive pride.

At the end of the first session, however, it became clear that Alberto was still at an earlier point in ethnic identity development. He stated that he felt "out of place" at the university, that he really did not belong in such a "high power" environment. When questioned more closely about this, especially in light of the fact that he had successfully obtained an undergraduate degree (the first in his family to do so), Alberto dismissed the accomplishment as all due to luck. He also belittled the college he attended as being second-rate. In so doing, Alberto was demeaning himself as well.

The core notion that the counselor highlighted in this first session was that of **entitlement**. The less positive an ethnic identity one has, the more likely one feels **un**-entitled to the benefits of the dominant culture, such as an advanced degree. A goal pinpointed in the first session was to help Alberto increase his self-esteem by improving his ethnic identity.

Succeeding sessions focused on exploring the overt and covert messages Alberto had received from family members, friends, peers, teachers, and others about his ethnicity. Some were quite positive, but the majority were very negative. The counselor employed a rational-emotive approach to confront Alberto supportively on his irrational beliefs about himself and his culture. Homework assignments included readings intended to underscore positive aspects of Mexican American culture, and personal checklists where Alberto was to write about his own positive qualities as a Chicano.

Perhaps the most poignant moment occurred when Alberto began the sixth session with tears welling up in his eyes, indicating to the counselor that he had something painfully embarrassing to disclose. Alberto proceeded to recall how he felt when he was told at the end of his intake session that he was being referred for ongoing counseling to a Mexican American psychologist on staff. His immediate reaction was disappointment and anger at being accorded what he considered to be "second-class" treatment. Alberto's internalized negativity toward his own ethnic group made it impossible for him to accept the idea that a Chicano counselor could be at all competent. Having experienced a caring and competent Chicano professional over the last six sessions had triggered strong feelings of shame as he confronted how deeply his internalized racism was embedded. To disclose this admission to the counselor directly was a testament to Alberto's courage and gradual emergence from the toxicity of his self- and group-deprecation.

In the next five sessions, a second major area of concern emerged, focusing on Alberto's sexual identity as a gay man. With comfort and trust firmly established in the sixth session, he was now able to explore the volatile issue of his gayness, especially within the context of Chicano culture. His beliefs about masculinity and his notions about machismo in relation to his gayness became the focal points for discussion. The first half of therapy strove to increase self-esteem through increasing a positive ethnic identity, and the second half endeavored to accomplish the parallel function of increasing self-affirmation through the formation of a positive gay identity.

Toward the end of his therapy (around the 10th session), Alberto had begun to explore a gay relationship and felt very positive about the experience. Therapy ended at the 12th session. Follow-up sessions indicated that Alberto's increased feelings of self-esteem had also translated into his being more at ease at the university. In short, he had a sense that he "belonged," that he was entitled to be there and to partake of all the university had to offer.

A Group Intervention for Hispanic Men

For several years now, a 12-session, process-oriented Hispanic men's group has been run at the Counseling and Mental Health Center at the University of Texas in Austin (Valdes, Barón, & Ponce, 1987). Though it carries the inclusive term of Hispanic, most, if not all, of the group members are usually of Mexican ancestry. Groups have typically ranged in size from five to eight members and have been coled by two Chicano counselors. The center's experience in recruiting members for the group indicates that this is a difficult first step. Many students, in general, are reticent about entering a group, and entry anxiety can be especially acute for ethnic minorities. Thus, the task of composing a group needs careful planning involving intensive publicity through print and other media, as well as through "word-of-mouth" networking. Pre-group interview sessions can be a helpful way to develop an early sense of safety and clarity for each potential member by reducing the ambiguity of the group's purpose and process.

Once the group begins, its development seems to follow some predictable pathways, involving core themes. In the beginning phase of the group, much time is spent clarifying the goals of the group along with the personal aims that each member has for himself. Writers in the area of counseling for Latinos often note the importance of developing behavioral, goal-oriented, prescriptive, and structured activities (Herrera & Sanchez, 1980). The groups that have been run thus far attest to the importance of this explicit approach, especially in the early phases of group development. Such a process allows each group member to develop criteria by which to monitor his progress and reduces the ambiguity of the group.

The members, then, are encouraged to share their goals and expectations in the first session, sometimes using structured exercises, but usually relying on open discussion. Perhaps the most important discussion point that arises involves a decision about the nature of the group itself. Will it be a "rap" group? Is it intended to be a political action group? A support group or a therapy group? Often members wish to define the group as a rap or support group because this is seen as less psychologically threatening. Although group leaders make it clear in pregroup interviews that the experience is indeed intended to be therapy, members will often attempt, nonetheless, to reduce their anxiety by changing the nature of the group.

A related issue concerns group attendance. Although this issue is also covered in pregroup meetings (i.e., members are expected to be on time and attend every session), discussion also arises that "tests" the conditions of the group. Seeking permission to come late or to skip certain sessions is often an indication of initial entry anxiety. These feelings are openly labeled and discussed by the group leaders, with an attempt to normalize the reactions while still adhering to the conditions set forth in the pregroup interviews.

Another issue that emerges is the ethnic identity of each group member. In one way or another, each member is testing out how "Mexican" he is by commenting on such issues as bilingual proficiency, skin color, dress, parents' socioeconomic background, the origins of his name or nickname, and in what part of the state or country he was born. This discussion can yield fruitful information that can be related to the ethnic identity development models discussed earlier. The group leaders often highlight for the group the basic developmental pathways noted in the identity models as a way of helping the members understand their thoughts, feelings, and actions in relation to themselves, other Mexican Americans, and the majority culture.

Because entering a counseling group carries some admission that a group member is seeking help, the concept of machismo arises early on as well. Help-seeking is contrary to the traditional male orientation of self-sufficiency and control. Thus, each member's perception of himself as a man who is now reaching out for help is also explored within the first three sessions. Again, the purpose is to normalize feelings of embarrassment or shame, while also beginning to explore the structures of rigid definitions regarding masculinity.

Other issues related to machismo, as well as acculturational status and ethnic identity formation, which arise in the beginning phase, include inter- and intragroup dating behavior (i.e., Latino vs. non-Latino partners), friendships with other men, entitlement concerns as students on a large, mostly Anglo campus, and experiences of covert and overt discrimination.

In the middle phase of group development (5th through 10th sessions), a variety of emotionally charged issues surface. With cohesion and trust firmly in place after the first four sessions or so, members begin to feel comfortable in disclosing anger, sadness, fear, and distrust related to oppression as ethnic minorities. These feelings usually focus on incidents of racism that group members have experienced. They also begin to delve into the toxic effects of internalized racism. For the first time in many cases, group members begin to share the negative thoughts and feelings they have against their own ethnic group. These are explored against the backdrop of societal oppression and the models of healthy ethnic identity development.

An important task of the group leaders is to help move the discussion away from scapegoating Anglos toward an exploration of personal power and responsibility. This is often a challenge, especially if one or more group members remain heavily centered on anger. While exploring empowering, suggesting constructive channels for the anger becomes a primary issue in the middle phase.

In the termination phase (11th and 12th sessions), the activity of the group shifts to assessing the progress of each group member toward his goals, future objectives, and plan of action beyond the group. A review of the group and its development over time is also conducted. Often group members will strategize on how to form supportive networks of fellow students, including how to stay in contact with group members.

Finally, members begin sharing their thoughts and feelings about ending. Because such sharing can be contrary to "conservative" male behavior, this can resurrect restrictive notions of masculinity. The resurfacing of male identity concerns is used as a way in which to recapitulate the key concepts of acculturation, ethnic identity development, and machismo. Summarizing this core trio helps to put a conceptual and emotional closure on the group.

In addition to this men's group, a second type of group designed for Hispanic women has also been successfully implemented at the University of Texas Counseling and Mental Health Center. Although intended for women from all Latino groups, the majority of women are of Mexican ancestry, as is the case for the men's group. The developers of the intervention, Vasquez and Han (1990), rely on a semistructured format incorporating the basic design elements of focused theme groups (Drum & Lawler, 1988). The group consists of nine sessions focusing on issues such as accultuturation, ethnic identity development, and sex-role/gender differences. Special focus is placed on the dual minority status of Latino women, thereby accentuating the difficulty in developing empowerment, entitlement, and overall self-esteem.

Summary

The concepts of acculturation, ethnic identity development, and machismo are central to the understanding of Mexican American college students involved in the counseling process. Although these concepts are enormous in scope, an increasing body of literature is helping to elucidate the complexities. The group discussed in this chapter, for example, provides a viable method for helping Chicano male students understand the intricate dynamics of their multifaceted identity formation. The intellectual and emotional insights gained through such a counseling intervention, along with positive changes in behavior, play important roles in maximizing a Chicano student's success in college. As such, these counseling groups are very much in line with interventions recommended by researchers (e.g., Sedlacek, 1987) who underscore the importance of psychosocial developmental factors as key predictors of academic achievement.

References

Astin, A. W. (1972). *College dropouts: A national profile*. Office of Research, American Council on Education, Research Report, 7(1).

Astin, A. W. (1975). *Preventing students form dropping out*. San Francisco: Jossey-Bass.

Astin A. W. (1982). *Minorities in higher education*. San Francisco: Jossey-Bass.

Atkinson, D. R., Morten, G., & Sue, D. W. (1979). *Counseling American minorities: A cross-cultural perspective*. Dubuque, IA: Wm. C. Brown.

Castro, F. G. (1977). *Level of acculturaion and related considerations in psychotherapy with Spanish speaking/surnamed clients* (Occasional Paper No. 3). Los Angeles: Spanish Speaking Mental Health Research Center, University of California.

Christensen, C. (1986). *Cultural boundaries*. Toronto: University of Toronto Press.

Cross, W. E. (1971). The Negro-to-Black conversion experience: Toward a psychology of Black liberation. *Black World, 20*, 13–27.

Cuellar, I., Harris, L. C., & Jasso, R. (1980). An acculturation rating scale for Mexican-American normal and clinical populations. *Hispanic Journal of Behavioral Sciences, 2*, 199–217.

Drum, D. J., & Lawler, A. C. (1988). *Developmental interventions: Theories, principles, and practice*. Columbus, OH: Merrill.

Helms, J. E. (1985). Toward a theoretical explanation of the effects of race on counseling: A Black and White model. *The Counseling Psychologist, 12*, 153–165.

Herrera, A. E., & Sanchez, V. C. (1980). Prescriptive group psychotherapy: A successful application in the treatment of low income Spanish-speaking clients. *Psychotherapy: Theory, Research, and Practice, 17*, 67–174.

Hispanic Policy Development Project. (1984). Washington, DC: *The Hispanic Almanac*.

Ivey, A. (1971). *Microcounseling: Innovations in interviewing training*. Springfield, IL: Charles C Thomas.

Mendoza, R. H., & Martinez, J. L. (1981). The measurement of acculturation. In A. Barón, Jr., (Ed.), *Explorations in Chicano psychology* (pp. 71–82). New York: Praeger.

Miranda, M. R., Andujo, E., Caballero, I. L., Guerrero, C., & Ramos, R. A. (1976). Mexican American dropouts in psychotherapy as related to level of acculturation. In M. R. Miranda (Ed.), *Psychotherapy with the Spanish-speaking: Issues in research and service delivery.* Los Angeles: Spanish Speaking Mental Health Research Center, University of California.

Miranda, M. R., & Castro F. G. (1977). Culture distance and success in psychotherapy with Spanish-speaking clients. In J. L. Martinez (Ed.), *Chicano psychology* (pp. 249–262). New York: Academic Press.

National Center for Education Statistics. (1980). *The condition of education for Hispanic Americans.* Washington, DC: U.S. Government Printing Office.

National Council of La Raza. (1990). *Hispanic education: A statistical portrait 1990.* Washington, DC: Author.

Olmedo, E. L., Martinez, J. L., & Martinez, S. R. (1978). Measure of acculturation for Chicano adolescents. *Psychological Reports, 42,* 159–170.

Parham, T. A., & Helms, J. E. (1981). The influence of Black students' racial attitudes on preferences for counselor's race. *Journal of Counseling Psychology, 28,* 250–257.

Parham, T. A., & Helms, J. E. (1985a). Attitudes of racial identity and self-esteem of black students: An exploratory investigation. *Journal of College Student Personnel, 26,* 143–147.

Parham, T. A., & Helms, J. E. (1985b). Relation of racial identity attitudes to self-actualization and affective states of black students. *Journal of Counseling Psychology, 32,* 431–440.

Ramirez, M. (1983). *Psychology of the Americas: Multicultural perspectives in personality and mental health.* New York: Pergamon.

Ruiz, R. A. (1981). Cultural and historical perspective in counseling Hispanics. In D. W. Sue (Ed.), *Counseling the culturally different: Theory and practice* (pp. 186–216). New York: Wiley.

Ruiz, R. A., Casas, J. M., & Padilla, A. M. (1977). *Culturally relevant behavioristic counseling.* Los Angeles: Spanish Speaking Mental Health Research Center, University of California.

Sanchez, A. R., & Atkinson, D. R. (1983). Mexican-American cultural commitment preference for counselor ethnicity, and willingness to use counseling. *Journal of Counseling Psychology, 30,* 215–220.

Sedlacek, W. E. (1987). Black students on white campuses: 20 years of research. *Journal of College Student Personnel, 28,* 484–495.

Sedlacek, W. E., & Brooks, G. C., Jr. (1976). *Racism in American education: A model for change.* Chicago: Nelson-Hall.

Szapocznik, J., Scopetta, M. A., & Tillman, W. (1979). What changes, what stays the same and what affects acculturative change? In J. Szapocznik & M. C. Herrera (Eds.), *Cuban Americans: Acculturation adjustment and the family* (pp. 32–44). Washington, DC: COSSMHO.

Thomas, C. W. (1971). *Boys no more.* Beverly Hills, CA: Glencoe Press.

Tracey, T. J., & Sedlacek, W. E. (1984). Noncognitive variables in predicting academic success by race. *Measurement and Evaluation in Guidance, 16,* 172–178.

Tracey, T. J. & Sedlacek, W. E. (1985). The relationship of noncognitive variables to academic success: A longitudinal comparison by race. *Journal of
College Student Personnel, 26*, 405–410.

Tracey, T. J. & Sedlacek, W. E. (1987). Prediction of college graduation using
noncognitive variables by race. *Measurement and Evaluation in Counseling and
Development, 19*, 177–184.

U.S. Bureau of the Census. (1990). *School enrollment—Social and economic characteristics of students: October 1987 and 1988.* (P-20, 443). Washington, DC:
U.S. Government Printing Office.

Valdes, L., Barón, A., Jr., & Ponce, F. Q. (1987). Counseling Hispanic men. In
M. Scher, M. Stevens, G. Good, & G. A. Eichenfeld (Eds.), *Handbook of
counseling psychotherapy with men* (pp. 203–217). Newbury Park, CA: Sage.

Vasquez, M. J. T., & Han, A. L. (1990). *Leader's manual for Hispanic women's group.*
Unpublished manuscript. Counseling and Mental Health Center, The University of Texas at Austin.

Additional Resources

Casas, J. M., & Vasquez, M. J. T. (1989). Counseling the Hispanic client: A
theoretical and applied perspective. In P. Pedersen, J. Draguns, W. Lonner,
& J. Trimble (Eds.), *Counseling across cultures* (pp. 153–175). Honolulu: University of Hawaii Press.

Gomez, D. F. (1973). *Somos Chicanos: Stangers in our own land.* Boston: Beacon
Press.

Levine, E. S., & Padilla, A. M. (1980). *Crossing cultures in therapy: Pluralistic counseling for the Hispanic.* Monterey, CA: Brooks/Cole.

McWilliams, C. (1968). *North from Mexico: The Spanish speaking people of the United
States.* New York: Greenwood Press.

Meier, M. S., & Rivera, F. (1972). *The Chicanos: A history of Mexican Americans.*
New York: Hill & Wang.

Meier, M. S., & Rivera, F. (1974). *Readings on La Raza: The twentieth century.* New
York: Hill & Wang.

Padilla, A. M. (1981). Pluralistic counseling and psychotherapy for Hispanic
Americans. In A. J. Marsella & P. B. Pedersen (Eds.), *Cross-cultural counseling
and psychotherapy* (pp. 195–227). New York: Pergamon.

Ponterotto, J. G. (1987). Counseling Mexican Americans: A multimodal approach. *Journal of Counseling and Development, 65*(6), 308–312.

Ruiz, R. A., & Casas, J. M. (1981). Culturally relevant behavioristic counseling
for Chicano college students. In P. G. Pedersen, J. G. Draguns, W. J. Lonner,
& J. E. Trimble (Eds.), *Counseling across cultures* (pp. 181–202). Honolulu:
University of Hawaii Press.

Chapter 14

PUERTO RICANS IN THE COUNSELING PROCESS: THE DYNAMICS OF ETHNICITY AND ITS SOCIETAL CONTEXT

Jesse M. Vázquez

Puerto Ricans in the United States: Historical and Political Overview

Although Puerto Rico has been a territory of the United States since 1898, many Americans still don't know where the island is geographically located, or that all Puerto Ricans have been American citizens since 1917, or that they are a racially heterogeneous population, or that Puerto Rican monetary currency is American currency, and so on. The degree of cultural illiteracy that exists among non-Puerto Rican Americans about Puerto Rico and the Puerto Ricans is astounding. Unfortunately, the lay public knows far more about the negative Puerto Rican stereotypes than it does about matters cultural, political, historical, and psychological.

Puerto Ricans now constitute the second largest (Chicanos are the largest) ethnically distinct Latino group in the continental United States. Over 2.5 million Puerto Ricans now live in the United States, and about 3.3 million still reside in Puerto Rico (U.S. Bureau of the Census, 1990). Although emigration from Puerto Rico to New York has been occurring since the early 1900s (and well before that under Spanish rule), the early and middle 1950s marked the most dramatic high point of the Puerto Rican migration to the United States. During that high watermark of migration, approximately 80% of the migrants settled in New York City (Fitzpatrick, 1987). Since that time, for well over 40 years, Puerto Ricans have continued to migrate not only to New York, but to other major urban centers in the northeastern and midwestern parts of the United

States (e.g., Philadelphia, Boston, Chicago, Newark, Trenton, and other urban centers across the country). New York City, however, continues to be home to the greatest number of Puerto Ricans in the continental United States, including Hawaii and Alaska. A significant colony of Puerto Ricans had taken root in Hawaii beginning in about 1902; Puerto Rican workers were sent to the Hawaiian Islands to cut sugar cane and pick pineapples (Centro de Estudios Puertorriqueños, 1977; Silva & Souza, 1982). According to recent estimates, one out of every eight New Yorkers is Puerto Rican. Puerto Ricans make up approximately 12.6% of New York City's population (Rodriguez, 1989).

For many Puerto Ricans, however, the pattern of migration is circular (between the U.S. and Puerto Rico), a phenomenon that sustains cultural, linguistic, and family connections and loyalties. And according to Bonilla (1989), the circular migration—the dynamics and causes of which he places into the larger framework of an advanced international capitalism—is also creating a startling similarity in worldviews and problems shared between those who reside on the island and those who, for a time, find themselves in the United States. This phenomenon is greatly facilitated by Puerto Ricans' U.S. citizenship, ease of travel, the island's political and economic connection with the United States, as well as the place that Puerto Rico occupies in the larger network of the global economy.

The first-person chronicles of the earlier migrants, the work of novelists, and the studies of historians, sociologists, anthropologists, and community activists reflect a toughness of the spirit and intellect of those Puerto Ricans who served as the pioneers and formed the first *barrios*, or colonies, in New York City and in other cities throughout the United States (See Colon, 1982; Iglesias, 1984; Fitzpatrick, 1987; Mohr, 1985; Morales, 1986; Padilla, 1958; Padilla, 1987; Pantoja, 1989; Rivera, 1982; Rivera, 1987; Rodriguez, 1989; Sanchez-Korrol, 1983).

There is a history of struggle among Puerto Ricans, both on the island and in the United States. It is a struggle against the abuses and oppression of colonialism and imperialism of the Spanish and then the North Americans; it is a struggle to maintain a unique cultural heritage and identity amidst technological change, and the overwhelming external and internal pressures to adopt and adapt to things "American"; and for the Puerto Ricans in the United States, it is also a struggle to survive economically, culturally, linguistically, and psychologically. Counselors who choose to work with Puerto Rican clients must begin to appreciate the complexity and legacy of this social and historical reality. Unquestionably, the impact of these historical events has played a critical role in shaping the collective social, economic, and psychological worlds of the Puerto Ricans who continue to live on the island, as well as of those who have chosen to build communities in the United States.

Puerto Ricans: A Socioeconomic Profile and Implications for Counseling

Although a very small percentage of the Puerto Ricans in the United States have climbed out of poverty and into the so-called American mainstream, the vast majority of Puerto Ricans in the United States continue to live at or below the poverty line. Incredibly, 30.9% of Puerto Rican families find themselves below the poverty level (U.S. Bureau of the Census, 1990).

Another statistical reality that continues to have significant implications for counselors in schools and social service agencies is the percentage of female-headed families in the Puerto Rican community— 39.6% (U.S. Bureau of the Census, 1989). The following characterization, proposed by Reyes (1987), reflects the potential complexity of social, economic, and psychological distress brought about by specific external realities:

> . . . the prototype of the Puerto Rican of today in the United States is a woman of 25 who dropped out of school, is the head of a household, is unemployed and has two children to maintain and educate. This is so, in part, because the majority of Puerto Ricans are women (53.2%) and the median years of school completed by Puerto Ricans is 11.2. (p. 2)

But as Rodriguez (1989) noted, the real issue in all this is the question of *poverty*, not the issue of the increased number of female-headed households. She further suggested that this kind of statistical profile does not portend the breakdown of the Puerto Rican family, as so many interpreters of these data would have us believe. It is critical that counselors who work within the Puerto Rican community suspend their own beliefs about what they consider a "typical" family, as well as explore the sources of strength that keep these families together.

This represents only one aspect of the socioeconomic challenges that have a direct impact on the lives of Puerto Ricans. In one form or another and in various settings, these challenges will become the concerns of the counselor. The issue discussed in this section may seem far removed from the area of cultural beliefs, attitudes, and values of the Puerto Rican migrant. It is, by and large, a problem that is a direct result of (a) the social and economic structure that exists in the United States; (b) the history of political, economic, and military control exercised over the people and resources of the island since the United States invaded and annexed Puerto Rico; and (c) the problems that spring from the fact that the "Puerto Ricans are both the only colonial group to arrive en masse, and the first racially heterogeneous group to migrate to the

U.S. on a large scale" (Rodriguez, 1989 p. xiv). All these conditions make for an environment guaranteed to create stress for the migrant who finds his or her way to an American metropolis. Counselors should be able to incorporate these kinds of observations into their work, and to set them into a broader societal framework.

Racial/Ethnic Identity and Racism: Implications for Counselors

It would be useful to look at a specific psychocultural issue that has been repeated in the literature, and in the practice of counselors working with Puerto Rican clients—**racial/ethnic identity and racism**. This issue will be explored and implications for counselors will be considered.

In one of the earliest community studies of Puerto Rican adaptation to life in an urban American setting, Padilla (1958) focused on the issue of racial and ethnic identity of the Puerto Rican in the United States. She noted that "both in Puerto Rico and in the United States social race is an important aspect of social life, but *race* is looked at, defined, and appraised in different ways in the two countries" (p. 69). This seemingly straightforward, yet complex, observation has been repeated a good many times in the literature since then, and has been linked to psychological stress in response to the chronic and persistent racism Puerto Ricans experience in the United States (Betances, 1971, 1972, 1973; Fitzpatrick, 1987; Longres, 1974; Martinez, 1986; Rodriguez, 1980, 1989).

If an individual is perceived to be phenotypically non-White in the United States, or if he or she is believed to be a member of an ethnic group—in this case Puerto Rican—that has been socially designated as non-White, regardless of within-group variability in phenotypes, all members of that group will then be considered socially non-White. And herein lies the psychological and social dilemma for many Puerto Ricans.

Puerto Ricans identify first culturally as Puerto Ricans, and then, secondarily, proceed to make racial distinctions from a variety of physical traits, such as skin color, hair texture, thickness of lips, and nose configuration. Any combination of one or more of these traits would place the individual, phenotypically that is, into one of several racially rooted categories, which, as indicated, are based on more than skin color: *blanco*, phenotypically White with a variety of Caucasian features; *trigueño*, brunette type, wheat color; *indio*, dark skin, straight black hair; *moreno*, dark skin with a variety of Negroid or Caucasian features; and, *negro*, equivalent to very dark skinned Black people in the United States (Rodriguez, 1989).

When forced to identify within the framework of the prevailing racial-social structure of the United States, many Puerto Ricans, particularly during the earliest stages of their migration, faced stress and confusion while trying to fit into the Black-White dichotomy offered by the American racial and social framework. If an individual's primary anchor of identity is cultural, and he or she is forced to identify as either White or Black, that person is essentially being deprived of a personal sense of identity (Rodriguez, 1989). This is especially confounding in families and in a population where racial phenotypes are quite varied. If I identify as Black, or am identified as Black in a family that contains significant racial variation, what does that do to my sense of connection and identification as a member of that family? How do I feel about my *lighter* brother or sister who may have benefited from this kind of perceptual distinction? On the other hand, what is the emotional price paid when the experience is one that Rodriguez (1989) calls "perceptual dissonance?" In this case, the individual sees himself or herself in one way, yet others see the individual quite differently. The experience, "particularly as it pertains to race, is clearly an unsettling process" (p. 76).

In an island where well into the latter part of the 19th century the merchants and landowners were primarily from Spain and other Western European countries, the "matter of color was also a matter of class" (Martinez, 1986, p. 39). According to Martinez, if "a non-white or racially mixed individual should rise in class status, then that person was accorded the deference of that class and the color disappeared" (p. 39). What he means is that racial identity, although not addressed directly, assumes less importance as measured against the individual's achievements as a university professor or an accomplished musician, lawyer, engineer, or successful public servant.

Today, after nearly 100 years of an American presence on the island, and more than 40 years since the beginning of the huge migrations to the mainland, the matter of racial identity and confusion persists in expressions of how Puerto Ricans see themselves and how they are racially perceived and designated by non-Puerto Ricans. For those who are involved in counseling Puerto Ricans, the issue of racial identity will be a repeated theme in the counseling process. Conflicts or uncertainty regarding racial intermarriage, incidents of racism and racial injustice, questions pertaining to racial/ethnic identity, and other related issues will continue to be raised in the counseling process as long as race and ethnicity continue to play a central role in the American social and political structure.

The following case illustrates the challenge in the counseling process of working with a client who specifically raises questions related to racial and ethnic identity.

The Case of Nydia

Nydia is a 30-year-old Puerto Rican woman, born in Puerto Rico, who at the age of 2 migrated along with her family to the United States. Nydia sought counseling shortly after her non-Latino fiancé made his first visit to meet her family. She came to me for counseling because she had heard that I was Puerto Rican and believed that I would be able to help her sort out the tension and fears that she was experiencing after her fiancé's visit.

Although her fiancé knew that Puerto Ricans were racially heterogeneous, he had no idea that this broad range of variability of racial phenotypes could also be seen within one nuclear family. He quickly identified some of the darker complected members in Nydia's family as "Black," and was quite taken aback by this observation. Up to that moment he had assumed (based on his American racial perception of race) that because Nydia was phenotypically "White" that all of her siblings would also be White. He asked her what she was—was she Black or was she White? As far as Nydia was concerned, she had always simply seen herself as a Puerto Rican who happened to be phenotypically White with darker and some lighter complected siblings and cousins. However, his subsequent persistent probing about Nydia's racial identity and pressing inquiries about her family's racial origins was sufficient to create a panic in her. Was he really telling her that this might be sufficient reason to call off their engagement? Nydia was concerned about her fiancé's preoccupation with her racial identity; and she was also uncertain about her own racio/ethnic identity at this point. Although she never denied her identity as a Puerto Rican, she had never really come to terms with the complexity of her own racial identity.

Intervention Strategy

My approach, after conducting a routine history, was to encourage Nydia to examine her ethnic identity as a Puerto Rican woman in the United States. What did it mean to her to have grown up as a Puerto Rican in New York? What was it like for her? I have found that a detailed, open exploration of the client's *ethnic self* or ethnic psycho-history will reveal a complex web of emotional experiences that ultimately allows the client an opportunity to examine more openly an aspect of the self that has heretofore remained vague, hidden, and undefined. This dynamic is quite common in American society. Although the American mythology espouses a so-called melting pot ideology, the real message we receive is that we must hide (or make little mention of) who we are ethnically. We are also asked to deny racial or cultural contradictions, especially when they are apparent or experienced as painful. Those who are unable to grasp the reality of racial and ethnic identity in American society have a tendency to create a kind of new personal mythology about who they are ethnically and racially.

As a society, we rarely challenge our ethnic perceptions of self and others, and the societal myths that belie the trail of tears that is a central part of America's racial and ethnic history. Instead, we manage to construct personal notions about who we are ethnically, and what other people think we are. Those who are members of the dominant society, particularly those who are considered White in this society, seem to have a greater tendency to accept an acculturated behavior pattern consistent with the core American society. On the other hand, I find that "people of color," (and Puerto Ricans regardless of phenotype are placed in this category), who are still socially and economically marginal in the society, are much more easily able to get in touch with this elusive ethnic self. And Nydia was no exception. She began to look carefully at her family's migration history, the existence of racism in American society, and how a multiplicity of social and economic realities had shaped a good deal of her life. Her need to drop out of school, and then to return to begin college again in her late 20s were events that she reexamined from a variety of perspectives. She reevaluated her own personal success in a blue-collar career in light of the choices she had, and the limited and imposed choices that were available to her family and to thousands of other Puerto Ricans who had come to the United States in order to survive. Looking at specific critical incidents in her life through the lens of her ethnic self gradually allowed Nydia to begin to come to terms with who she is ethnically and racially. Eventually, Nydia was able to present effectively some questions of her own, which sought to clarify her fiancé's racial belief system and some of his own preoccupations with race and racial identity.

The approach I use in cases like this, and in others where ethnicity or ethnic identity plays a role in shaping affect and cognition, is to explore the structural and functional aspects of race and ethnicity in American society, and the impact of these on the development of the individual. There is an attempt to connect these sociological and anthropological domains with the feelings, experiences, and meaning of these events in the life of the client. How has the client experienced these events, and what is the meaning of these events in the client's life? A blend of cognitive, phenomenological, existential, and didactic (sociological, anthropological, and historical discourse) strategies allows the therapist to link the many layers of experience and external events that would contribute to this kind of inner conflict.

The linkage between these domains is critical for movement in either the counseling process or in the educational process. There is no diagnosis, because there is no identifiable disorder or disease process going on. However, there is distress that grows out of the client's perception of self (ethnically and racially), and others' perception of the client. The phrase so often heard, "that's funny, you don't *look* Puerto Rican," tells worlds about the perception of the speaker. If the Puerto Rican accepts the phrase, one can also assume that there is confusion about the self in relation to others.

Martinez sees this racial identity confusion as a phenomenon that will continue to exist as long as Puerto Ricans "avoid or deny their reality in American society" (1986, p. 45). On the other hand, Rodriguez (1989) considers that the very ambiguity of racial and cultural identity can be viewed as a potential source of strength and as a healthy sign of adaptation, which perhaps will pose a direct "challenge to the U.S. bifurcation of race" (p. 77). She finds that many Puerto Ricans have been able to move back and forth between the White, Black, and Hispanic worlds. This, she suggests, "may be rooted in the ability to see oneself in a variety of ways" (p. 77). A new generation of Puerto Ricans may be emerging as truly tricultural, and perhaps bilingual or even trilingual. Is it a denial of a racial reality, or is it a forging of a new identity? Within the context of a rapidly changing racial and cultural America, this idea may begin to gain more meaning as racioethnic demographic balances shift in the 21st century.

Conclusion

Nydia's case raises a number of psychoculturally rooted issues that are frequently encountered when working with Puerto Rican clients. In order to serve the Puerto Rican client more effectively, the counselor must attend to a wide range of issues, which not only include racial identity, but also the importance of the continuity of language, implications of class, changing family patterns, and a societal structure that has shaped the migration and the life chances of Puerto Ricans in the United States and in Puerto Rico. In effect, the counselor must be fully prepared to explore issues that go well beyond the purview of the traditional counseling domain, and to use techniques and strategies that may challenge the current order of things.

Counselors can anticipate working with Puerto Rican clients who may express a wide range of degrees of acculturation, as well as those who have a clear sense of who they are ethnically and racially. Many may adapt to the mainland simply as an accommodation for the sake of survival, whereas others may reassert their identity in forms that may be outmoded and perhaps dysfunctional in a postindustrial world. Still others will fashion new ways of assuring their future, while holding on to what is valuable and enduring in their community of memory.

References

Betances, S. (1971). Puerto Rican youth: Race and the search for self. *The Rican,* *1*(1), 4–13.

Betances, S. (1972). The prejudice of having no prejudice in Puerto Rico, Part 1. *The Rican, 2,* 41–54.

Betances, S. (1973). The prejudice of having no prejudice in Puerto Rico, Part 2. *The Rican, 3,* 22–37.

Bonilla, F. (1989). La circulación migratoria en la década actual. *Boletín del Centro de Estudios Puertorriquños, 2*(6), 55–59.

Centro de Estudios Puertorriqueños. (1977). *Documents of the Puerto Rican migration: Hawaii, Cuba, Santo Domingo, and Equador.* New York: A publication of the Centro de Estudios Puertorriqueños, Research Foundation of The City University of New York.

Colon, J. (1982). *A Puerto Rican in New York and other sketches.* New York: International Publishers.

Fitzpatrick, J. P. (1987). *Puerto Ricans: The meaning of migration to the Mainland.* Englewood Cliffs, NJ: Prentice-Hall.

Iglesias, C. A. (1984). *Memoirs of Bernardo Vega: A contribution to the history of the Puerto Rican community in New York.* Translated by Juan Flores. New York: Monthly Review Press. Originally published in Spanish by Ediciones Hurácan Press as *Memorias de Bernardo Vega,* 1977.

Longres, J. F. (1974, February). Racism and its effects on Puerto Rican continentals. *Social Casework,* pp. 67–99.

Martinez, R. (1986). Puerto Ricans: White or non-white? *Explorations in Ethnic Studies: The Journal of the National Association for Ethnic Studies, 9*(2), 37–48.

Mohr, N. (1985). *Rituals of survival: A woman's portfolio.* Houston: Artes Publico.

Morales, J. (1986). *Puerto Rican poverty and migration: We just had to try elsewhere.* New York: Praeger.

Padilla, E. (1958). *Up from Puerto Rico.* New York: Columbia University Press.

Padilla, F. (1987). *Puerto Rican Chicago.* Notre Dame: University of Notre Dame Press.

Pantoja, A. (1989). Puerto Ricans in New York: A historical and community development perspective. *Boletín del Centro de Estudios Puertorriqueños, 2*(5), 20–31.

Reyes, L. O. (1987). *Demographics of Puerto Rican-Latino students in New York and the U.S.* New York: Aspira of New York.

Rivera, E. (1982). *Family installments: Memories of growing up Hispanic.* New York: Morrow.

Rivera, E. (1987). The Puerto Rican colony of Lorain, Ohio. *Boletín del Centro de Estudios Puertorriquños, 2*(1), 11–23.

Rodriguez, C. (1980). Puerto Ricans: Between black and white. In C. Rodriguez, V. Sanchez-Korrol, & O. Alers (Eds.), *The Puerto Rican struggle: Essays on survival in the U.S.* New York: Puerto Rican Migration Research Consortium.

Rodriguez, C. (1989). *Puerto Ricans born in the U.S.A.* Boston: Unwin Hyman.

Sanchez-Korrol, V. E. (1983). *From colonia to community: The history of Puerto Ricans in New York City, 1917–1948.* Westport, CT: Greenwood Press.

Silva, M. N., & Souza, B. C. (1982). The Puerto Ricans in Hawaii: On becoming Hawaii's people. *The Puerto Rican Journal, 1*(1), 29–39.

U.S. Bureau of the Census. (1990). *The Hispanic population in the United States: March 1989*. (Current Population Reports, Series P-20, No. 444, issued May, 1990). Washington, DC: U.S. Government Printing Office.

U.S. Bureau of the Census. (1989, July). *The Hispanic population in the United States: March 1988*. (Current Population Reports, Series P-20, No. 438, issued July, 1989). Washington, DC: U.S. Government Printing Office.

THE ARAB AMERICAN EXPERIENCE

Dynamic international social and political events make it mandatory that Americans gain a greater understanding of the centuries-old cultural traditions of the Arab-speaking world. Within the context of rapidly changing events taking place in that part of the world, Americans of Arab descent and their cultural traditions are gaining greater recognition in the United States. It is therefore incumbent upon professionals from every sector of American society to become more knowledgeable about important aspects of Arab American culture. As part of this, counseling professionals must develop an understanding of the cultural dynamics associated with Arab American mental health and development.

Arab Americans trace their cultural origins to the Middle East and northern Africa. They are a heterogeneous ethnic group differing in racial background and religious affiliation. The most significant dynamics of Arab American culture that need to be considered in counseling are religion and family unity. The traditions of both the Christian and Muslim religions influence basic attitudes, values, and behavior of Americans of Arab descent. Family unity is also a highly valued cultural dynamic among Arab Americans. The family is the primary source of emotional support and guidance for its members.

Chapter 15

COUNSELING ARAB AMERICANS

Morris L. Jackson

As a cultural group, Americans of Arab ancestry have received scant attention in the counseling literature. Counseling professionals have had little access to information that addresses the important cultural and developmental issues of this group. Significantly, the U.S. Bureau of the Census in 1990 granted Arab Americans the option to write in their cultural designation in the category "other" on census forms. This event truly signals the recognition of Arab Americans as a distinct cultural group in American society. History records that the first Arabic-speaking people came to American shores between 146 and 480 B.C. and were believed to be Phoenicians, people of the country known today as Lebanon (Boland, 1961). Currently, approximately 2.5 million people of Arab ancestry live in the United States (Zogby, Averderheide, & Mooney, 1984).

Like other ethnic minority groups in American society, Arab Americans face challenges to their overall development daily. These challenges take the form of discrimination, stereotyping, and general negative reactions to them as an ethnic group. During the course of their development, Arab Americans encounter a crisis of cultural identity common to many minority groups in the United States.

The purpose this chapter is to present information on some important dynamics of Arab culture. Such information is crucial if counseling professionals are to be prepared for effective work with members of the Arab American population both now and in the future.

Diversity of Arab Americans

Writers and researchers have traced the history and explored the diversity of Arab Americans in the United States (Naff, 1988; Hooglund, 1985, 1987; Orfalea, 1988). Generally, Americans of Arab ancestry are perceived to be a homogeneous group. It is important to recognize, however, that these people originally came from approximately 20 different countries in the Middle East and northern Africa. They are a heterogeneous group who differ in terms of race, religion, and political ideology.

The arrival of people of Arab ancestry in America occurred during three distinct time periods (Orfalea, 1988). The first of these was from 1878 to 1925. Census data indicate that in 1910 there were approximately 100,000 Arab Americans in the United States. The majority of Arabs arriving in this country during this period came primarily from Greater Syria, which today is the territory that includes Lebanon, Jordan, Israel and the Occupied Territories (formerly known as Palestine), Iraq, and Syria. These first Arab immigrants were of the Christian faith and were laborers, factory workers, and peddlers. They lived primarily in urban areas. The majority were poor and uneducated and sought refuge and contentment in the building of close-knit communities.

The second major period of Arab immigration to the United States occurred shortly after the Second World War. The people in this group differed sharply from the earlier immigrants in that they were primarily Muslim and better educated. Orfalea (1988) indicated that this was the beginning of the brain drain from Egypt, Iraq, Jordan, Syria, and North African countries. This period also was marked by the surge in Palestinian refugees and exiles who felt that they were without a country. Other countries represented in this wave, but with smaller numbers of immigrants, were Lebanon and Yemen. This second wave of immigrants often found themselves alienated from their Arab peers and American counterparts because of their Muslim religion and its accompanying culture.

The third period of Arab immigration has been occurring since 1966. This influx of people, approximately 250,000 individuals, is primarily the result of an easing of immigration regulations. This third group of people shares much in common with members of the second immigrant group. Mostly Muslim, with the largest ethnic group being Palestinian, these people are primarily professionals or technical workers.

It is essential, in order to obtain a comprehensive understanding of and perspective on this cultural group, to appreciate that Arab Americans migrated to the United States from a variety of countries in the Middle East. They have been living in the United States for over a century and represent a diverse cultural group with a growing impact in this country.

Arab American Culture

The most significant aspects of Arab American culture that must be considered in a counseling context are religion and family. Counselors intent on providing effective intervention to this cultural group must give considerable attention to understanding the importance of these two aspects in Arab American life.

Religion

Religion is a major vehicle by which Arab culture is transferred. Most Arab Americans are either Christians or Muslims. Those Americans of Arab ancestry who practice Christianity have found it somewhat easier to assimilate into the American cultural mainstream than have their Muslim counterparts. Nydell (1987) outlined some basic Arab values and religious attitudes commonly found among Arab speaking peoples:

1. A person's dignity, honor, and reputation are of paramount importance.
2. Loyalty to one's family takes precedence over personal needs.
3. It is important to behave at all times in a manner that reflects well on others.
4. Everyone believes in one God and acknowledges his power.
5. Humans cannot control all events; some things depend on God.
6. Piety is one of the most admirable characteristics in a person.

Family

The Arab American family has evolved over time. During the early years of Arab immigration to the United States, many Arab families were not greatly affected by Western values. Newly arrived families cultivated and reinforced values derived from their Arab tradition and heritage. However, as assimilation and acculturation began to occur, many Arab American families were faced with a choice. On the one hand, there was a strong desire to maintain traditional Arab family values. On the other hand, there was an awareness of the need to adopt the values of American culture.

Most Arab Americans belong to an extended family system, in which members experience loyalty, security, emotional support, and financial assistance (Nydell, 1987). Immediate family members and extended relatives share a closeness that is evident in a high degree of family unity. For example, despite differences they may have with each other, family members will collude with and support one another against an outsider whom they perceive as interfering with family unity. A traditional Arabic expression illustrates this family unity: "It is me and my brother against my cousin; but it is me and my cousin against the outsider."

In many Arab American families men generally are viewed as the head of the household. Older men in the extended family demand the most respect. Grown sons are responsible for their parents and, in the absence of their father, are responsible for their unmarried sisters. This is not to suggest that Arab American women do not play a significant role in family dynamics. Although women may typically adopt a submissive role in public, in the privacy of their homes they may exert a considerable amount of influence, even to the extent of adamantly disagreeing with their husbands on important family matters.

Children are raised in a manner that ensures that they will respect their parents. In Arabic culture, good children show respect for their parents, as well as for all adults, particularly older adults. Recently, however, many Arab American children have been rejecting their cultural traditions. Parents now have to spend more time and effort to exert control and instill traditional discipline in their children. Peer pressure in schools, for example, has begun to compete with parental influence.

Any discipline that would seek to understand the dynamics of Arab American development must take into account the experiences that shape that development. Counseling strategies and techniques for Americans of Arab ancestry, therefore, must be predicated on an understanding of Arab cultural dynamics, such as religion and family unity, and their important role in fostering attitudes, behaviors, and values.

Racial-Religious-Ethnic Identification

In the United States, skin color is a primary means of social identification and distinction. Americans of Arab ancestry, however, may trace their origins to countries that do not make skin color distinctions among people. The following classifications, based on racial, religious, and ethnic factors may be appropriate for identifying Arab Americans: White Christian, White Muslim, Black Christian, and Black Muslim. These four groups are examined here to assist counseling professionals in understanding the influence of race and religion in Arab American culture.

White Christian Arab Americans arrived in this country from Egypt, Iraq, Jordan, Lebanon, Palestine (currently recognized as Israel and the Occupied Territories), and Syria. Members of this racial-religious-ethnic group, despite cultural differences, have found it easier to assimilate into American society. This is primarily because of their racial and religious similarities with the majority American cultural group.

White Muslim Arab Americans are represented in the American population from all the Arab-speaking countries except Eriteria, Ethiopia, Somalia, and Sudan. This group has been subjected to various forms of discrimination and prejudice, primarily because their religious traditions differ significantly from those commonly found in the United States.

Black Christian Arab Americans are a relatively small group of people that may grow in the future. They are from Egypt and parts of northern Africa. Their experience in the United States parallels that of African Americans, who are often confronted with discrimination and prejudice because of the color of their skin.

Black Muslim Arab Americans may be divided into two groups. One group includes individuals whose mother tongue is Arabic or who were born in an Arabic country. The second group is composed of African Americans who were originally Christians, but who have adopted the Muslim faith. American society, however, often does not distinguish between these two groups. Black Muslim Arab Americans have two disadvantages in American society—they are Black **and** Muslim. This generally means that this group has been the least accepted of the four.

If counseling is to be effective with a client of Arab ancestry, it might be necessary to first identify the client's racial-religious-ethnic background. In so doing, a counselor might discover how a client's attitudes, values, and behaviors have been shaped by the experience associated with a particular identification.

Arab American Mental Health: The Counselor's Challenge

In American culture, seeking the services of a counseling professional for assistance with problem resolution is a common practice for many groups. However, this is generally not the case with Arab Americans. The first line of psychological defense for Arab Americans is a conference or consultation with a family member about a problem. A man provides guidance for another man, whereas a woman is counseled by another woman. Cross-sex counseling is uncommon. Young men seek guidance from older men and young women are advised by older women. When the nature of a problem is too sensitive to discuss with an immediate family member, a person will look to a more distant relative. If a family member is unavailable, an Arab American might then talk with a trusted friend.

Generally speaking, Arab Americans do not share personal problems with strangers. A professional counselor would be considered a stranger, outside the Arab American support system. If none of the previously mentioned counseling sources are available, the Arab American, as a last resort, may decide to seek the services a professional counselor.

Barriers to Successful Counseling With Arab Americans

Racial and ethnic barriers that have been discussed as problematic in the cross-cultural counseling relationship with culturally different clients (Vontress, 1981) seem to be applicable to Arab American clients. Of particular significance is how culture, religion, language, and rapport affect the counseling relationship. As a rule, Arab Americans do not disclose personal and family matters. Arab-speaking people feel more comfortable discussing academic and vocational matters. Some Arab American clients may be reluctant to engage in self-disclosure during the counseling process because of their inability to express themselves in English. They experience considerable frustration when they are unable to express themselves fully in English. It is important for them to communicate to the counselor exactly what they feel about problems. Those unable to do so may feel verbally handicapped.

As mentioned earlier, the traditional counseling process is an activity foreign to Arab culture, and therefore may be strange to many Arab Americans. Counselors interested in assisting their clients to self-disclose need to determine the degree of acculturation and assimilation of their client. Failure to make this determination could cause culture-specific barriers, such as language and religion, to be erected between counselor and client.

The most significant factor impeding a possible counseling relationship with Americans of Arab ancestry is historical hostility. This hostility has been fostered and developed through a continual barrage of negative publicity about and stereotyping of Arabs in American society. This negative stereotyping has been reported in the form of jokes, television programming, cartoons, comic strips, and movies (Michalak, 1983). Negative feelings resulting from this hostility, often undisplayed on the part of the Arab American client, is a matter to which counselors need to be sensitive.

Intervention Techniques and Strategies

Professional counselors working with Arab Americans must consider new ways to maximize their chances of therapeutic success with this population. In the counseling literature, rapport has been discussed as a significant factor in the establishment of a positive therapeutic counselor-client relationship. The building of rapport is generally focused on during initial counselor-client interactions. A sensitive counselor committed to bridging cultural differences with Americans of Arab ancestry should consider the following four suggestions to facilitate the development of rapport in the helping relationship.

The first suggestion is for counselors to develop knowledge and understanding of the religion and culture of Arab Americans. This is important so that intelligent differentiations can be made between Christian and Muslim Arab Americans. Counselors should read books and articles and attempt to converse informally with Arab Americans to increase their understanding of Arab religious and cultural differences. In general, Arab Americans are pleased and excited over opportunities to share information about their culture and religion.

The second suggestion is for counselors, if necessary, to learn six basic Arabic expressions that will enhance their rapport and possibly bridge cultural barriers. These are: **Assalamu Alakum** ("Peace be unto you"), **Mahaba** ("Hello"), **Kafe Hallick** ("How are you"), **In Sha Allah** ("If God is willing"), **Ma Sha Allah** ("This is what God wished"), and **Mas Alama** ("Goodbye").

The following are examples of how these expressions can be used in the counseling setting. The expression "Assalamu Alakum" is a formal greeting. The response is "Wa Lakum Salam," which means "And peace be unto you." This verbal exchange may be followed by a more informal statement such as "Mahaba," which prompts the response "Kafe Hallick." These three expressions may be used in the beginning of the counseling session. Another significant expression is "In Sha Allah." For example, it should be used in the following way. Should an Arab American client request that a counselor solve his or her problem, the counselor would preface a response with the preceding Arabic expression and, then, provide a normal counselor response. An example is:

> **Client:** It was suggested that I come to see you because you are an excellent counselor. I was told you could solve my problem.

> **Counselor:** In Sha Allah, I will do my best to help you with your problem.

It is common practice for counselors to offer their clients reassuring and reinforcing statements to help them achieve a better state of well-being. For example, the Arabic expression "Ma Sha Allah" has particular relevance for counselors assisting Arab American clients in changing unproductive behavior. One way counselors may help clients is to give positive statements followed by the Arabic expression, or the Arabic expression may precede the counselor's response. The example below illustrates this point:

> **Counselor:** You seem to be feeling much better today than you did the last session, Ma Sha Allah.

Counselor: Ma Sha Allah, I am pleased to hear that your studies are going well.

Munoz (1982) suggested that the faces of clients express positive signs when clients are greeted in their native tongue. The use of a few key Arabic expressions in counseling sessions, when appropriate, may have more meaning than the same ideas expressed in English, because it conveys the counselor's attempt to understand and respect Arab culture.

The third suggestion is for counselors to be mindful that Arabic-speaking people, as a rule, are not accustomed to, or comfortable with, expressing feelings about personal matters outside the context of the family. Professional counselors interested in maximizing their effectiveness may want to consider adopting a multimodal or eclectic approach to counseling this population.

The fourth suggestion is for counselors to establish relationships with the Arab American clients prior to actually starting the counseling process. Establishing such a relationship is called **prerapport.** The significant point is for counselors to converse and interact with clients from the four Arab American populations in settings outside the traditional counseling office. Consequently, when an Arab American client comes to begin counseling, the amount of time spent on building rapport and trust may be significantly reduced.

Beyond rapport building, there are some other strategies that counselors should consider in their work with Arab Americans. The importance of religion and the family system to Arab Americans cannot be overstated. Counselors familiar with aspects of the Christian and Muslim religions would be welcomed by Arab American clients to initiate a discussion about religion. The Holy Koran indicates that the closer one is to Allah, the easier it is to cope with psychic problems (Koran, 1983). All counselors need to be aware that Muslim Arab Americans view the Holy Koran and Sunna, which are the teachings and deeds of the Prophet Mohammad, as providing them with a way of life. These two documents regulate and govern the emotions of Muslim Arab Americans.

One method of intervention the counselor may use to introduce religion into the therapeutic process is to explain to the client in the first session that part of the technique used includes a holistic approach to the resolution of client concerns. This approach focuses not only on the mind and body, but on the spirit as well. This might provide the counselor with an opportunity to identify the religion of the client and its significance in the client's life.

Another method of intervention for maximizing success with Arab American clients is to involve family members in counseling sessions. It is recommended that counselors first meet with the client. The head of the family should be contacted next to discuss the nature of the client's concerns and to share possible solutions. Next, the counselor should meet with family members and the client to discuss the problem jointly.

Conclusion

In the emerging era of cultural diversity in American society, Arab Americans are stepping forward to proclaim their cultural heritage and traditions. These Americans of Arab ancestry are a flourishing cultural group whose diversity cannot be denied. They are represented by Arab-speaking people from throughout the Middle East and northern Africa. Like other immigrant groups before them, Arab Americans are assimilating and acculturating in varying degrees to American life-styles. In this process they experience problems related to their cultural identity. Arab Americans face the challenge of blending two unique and different worldviews into one homogeneous culture.

Counselors are urged to obtain a comprehensive understanding of the religion and family systems of Arab Americans because they are a significant aspect of their culture and are vital to their psychological well-being. Counselors concerned with bridging cultural barriers may need to rethink their techniques and strategies in order to work with this population effectively. Counselors can play a critical role in ensuring that Arab Americans are not an invisible cultural group.

References

Boland, C. M. (1961). *They all discovered America.* New York: Doubleday.

Holy Koran: Text, translation, and commentary, translated by A. Yusef. Maryland: Amana Corp. 1983.

Hooglund, E. J. (1985). *Taking root: Arab-American community studies.* Washington, DC: American-Arab Anti-Discrimination Committee Research Institute.

Hooglund, E. J. (1987). *Crossing the waters.* Washington, DC: Smithsonian Institution Press.

Michalak, L. (1983). *Cruel and unusual: Negative images of Arabs in American popular culture.* Washington, DC: American-Arab Anti-Discrimination Committee.

Munoz, R. F. (1982). The Spanish-speaking consumer and the community mental health center. In E. E. Jones & S. J. Korchin (Eds.), *Minority mental health.* New York: Praeger.

Naff, A. (1988). *The Arab-Americans.* New York: Chelsea House.

Nydell, M. (1987). *Understanding Arabs: A guide for westerners.* Yarmouth, ME: Intercultural Press.

Orfalea, G. (1988). *Before the flames: A quest for the history of Arab-Americans.* Austin, TX: University of Texas Press.

Vontress, C. E. (1981). Racial and ethnic barriers. In P. Pederson, W. J. Lonner, & J. G. Draguns (Eds.), *Counseling across culture*. Honolulu, HI: University of Hawaii Press.

Zogby, J., Averderheide, P., & Mooney, A. (1984). *Taking root bearing fruit: The Arab-American experience*. Washington, DC: American-Arab Anti-Discrimination Committee Research Institute.

PART III

CONCLUSION

Chapter 16

NEW APPROACHES TO DIVERSITY: IMPLICATIONS FOR MULTICULTURAL COUNSELOR TRAINING AND RESEARCH

Courtland C. Lee

The multicultural realities of American society call for counseling professionals who can effectively address the challenges of client diversity. Effective multicultural practice is one of the most significant challenges facing counseling and related human development professions. In order to meet this challenge, new directions are needed for the training of culturally skilled counselors at both the inservice and preservice levels. In addition, as models and methods related to the practice of multicultural counseling continue to evolve, they must be accompanied by empirical evidence of their validity.

The challenge of multicultural counseling practice, therefore, also implies charting new research directions. The purpose of this chapter is to examine some important implications of cultural diversity for future counselor training. Likewise, the chapter examines the implications of diversity for multicultural counseling research.

Training Implications

In order to engage effectively in multicultural academic, career, and personal-social practices, counselors must participate in an ongoing professional development process. The focus of this process should be the development and upgrading of skills to intervene effectively into the lives of clients from a variety of cultural backgrounds. The ultimate training goal is the emergence of a culturally skilled counselor who uses strategies and techniques that are consistent with the life experiences and cultural values of clients.

The concept of comprehensive multicultural counseling training has been addressed extensively in the literature (Casas, 1984; Casas, Ponterotto, & Gutierrez, 1986; Copeland, 1983; Parker, Valley, & Geary, 1986; Pedersen, 1988; Ponterotto & Casas, 1987; Sue et al., 1982). A major theme that has emerged from the literature is that in order to become culturally skilled as a counselor, one must become more fully aware of his or her own heritage as well as possible biases that may interfere with helping effectiveness, gain knowledge about the history and culture of diverse groups of people, and develop new skills. In conjunction with these notions, the Association for Multicultural Counseling and Development (AMCD), in 1986, developed a set of multicultural competencies to be used as guidelines for counselor education programs in the preparation of culturally skilled counselors. These competencies include: skills to establish rapport in individual and group counseling with culturally diverse persons; the ability to use various individual and group multicultural counseling techniques; the ability to plan, implement, and evaluate career development programs for culturally diverse persons; the ability to administer and interpret standardized tests that take culture or ethnicity into account in the assessment process; and the ability to implement various consultation models appropriate to culturally diverse individuals and groups.

In reviewing these competencies and the literature on multicultural counselor training within the context of the ideas on culture and culturally responsive counseling presented in this book, several points need to be underscored about training future counseling professionals. First, given the demographic realities of American society, a primary emphasis of such training should be on how to adapt the theories and techniques of traditional counseling to meet the needs of clients from ethnic or racial groups with non-European cultural origins.

Second, the major focus of future multicultural training must be skills development. How does one **actually** counsel someone from another culture? For example, what intervention strategies are truly effective with specific client populations from cultural groups with non-European backgrounds? What are some indigenous helping sources within a cultural group that have been used (in some instances for centuries) to deal with problem resolution and decision making? What cultural dynamics seem to affect optimal mental health and normal development among groups of people? How can these dynamics be exploited positively in a helping relationship? In sum, skills training should center around how to incorporate the cultural dynamics and naturally occurring support systems of diverse groups of people into counseling interventions.

Third, an important aspect of multicultural skills development should be an emphasis on experiencing cultural diversity **in vivo**. Through practicum or internship experiences, as well as "field trips" to diverse communities, counselors should have the opportunity to go out and experience cultural diversity and the dynamics associated with it first-hand. There is a limit to how much can be learned about cultural diversity from classes and workshops. Much more can be learned by actually going out and interacting with groups of people. Such experiences have the potential of raising levels of awareness, increasing knowledge, and providing important additions to skill repertoires.

Fourth, effective multicultural counseling skills can be developed and used only when counselors advance beyond a monolithic perspective about people. Therefore, training efforts must ensure that counselors progress beyond myths and stereotypes by helping them learn how to discern levels of acculturation and identity development among people.

It is obvious that in order to develop such skills, current multicultural counseling courses and training programs must be expanded. Additionally, counselor educators must ensure that issues of cultural diversity are effectively infused throughout the training curriculum. In addition to formal coursework at the preservice level, comprehensive ongoing professional development experiences related to multicultural counseling are needed for practicing professionals. Although such experiences provide the opportunity for self-exploration and the development of multicultural knowledge, the bulk of them should be devoted to the field-testing of culturally responsive intervention skills for academic, career, and personal-social development.

Research Implications

Research evidence must guide multicultural counseling practice. The primary goal of future research should be the empirical validation of the continuously evolving notions about multicultural counseling and human development. In the past several decades there have been extensive reviews of cross-cultural counseling research (Atkinson, 1983, 1985; Harrison, 1975; Sattler, 1970). From these reviews have emerged ideas that are important in establishing an agenda for future multicultural counseling research. First, new multicultural counseling process and outcome research must be conducted. Empirical evidence is needed to support ideas about the effectiveness of indigenous models of helping and culturally responsive counseling interventions in changing client attitudes, values, and behaviors. These investigations must provide an-

swers to fundamental questions such as: "Are culturally responsive helping models and methods more effective with American Indian, African
American, Asian American, Latino American, or Arab American clients
than traditional (i.e., White, European American) counseling interventions?" It is important that evaluation of culturally responsive method-
ologies be made an integral part of counseling service delivery in all
helping settings.

Second, research is also needed on culturally diverse notions of
normal human development. Specific investigations that assess mental
health outcomes by attempting to delineate the developmental processes
of person-environment interactions among culturally diverse people need
to be conducted. New studies need to investigate the coping styles and
mastery skills among diverse groups of people. An empirically validated
knowledge base concerning cultural variations on normal development
is crucial for proactive counseling interventions.

Third, empirical investigation should be initiated to produce inventories that assess significant developmental aspects of specific cultural
groups. A crucial aspect of this process must be studies that produce
validity and reliability information for instruments that assess personality
factors and behavioral dynamics. Although such instruments currently
exist (Cuellar, Harris, & Jasso, 1980; Parham & Helms, 1981), their
widespread usefulness is questionable due to limited empirical evidence.
Until such empirical data are provided, these instruments will remain
"experimental" in nature and of little practical use in providing valid
and reliable information to enhance counseling practice.

Fourth, research efforts should be structured to investigate intragroup differences among people. The majority of research evidence
concerning the dynamics of counseling people from diverse cultural
backgrounds has generally been gathered without consideration for differences in factors such as level of ethnic identity, level of acculturation,
or socioeconomic status. Such evidence lends credence to the concept
that cultural groups are monolithic entities with no within-group variability among people. Future counseling research efforts, therefore, should
investigate within-group differences among culturally diverse people.

Conclusion

As multicultural counseling continues to move from theory to practice, a dramatic shift in the focus of mental health intervention is needed.
Counseling services must be delivered in the belief that people from
diverse backgrounds are psychologically healthy, undergo normal developmental experiences, and have dynamics and resources indigenous

to their culture to deal with problem solving and decision making competently. Culturally responsive counseling practice, therefore, is predicated on exploiting these dynamics effectively and making use of indigenous sources of helping.

Counselor training and research efforts must coincide with the implementation of new innovations in practice. As the United States prepares to enter a new century, a new counseling professional must emerge— one who has a solid knowledge base with which to meet the challenges of counseling practice with culturally diverse client groups. The development and well-being of Americans from every cultural background demands no less.

References

Association for Multicultural Counseling and Development. (1986). *Multicultural skill competencies*. Alexandria, VA: Author.

Atkinson, D. R. (1983). Ethnic similarity in counseling psychology: A review of research. *The Counseling Psychologist, 11*, 79–92.

Atkinson, D. R. (1985). A meta-review of research on cross-cultural counseling and psychotherapy. *Journal of Multicultural Counseling and Development, 13*, 138–153.

Casas, J. M. (1984). Policy, training and research in counseling psychology: The racial/ethnic minority perspective. In S. Brown & R. Lent (Eds.), *Handbook of counseling psychology*. New York: Wiley.

Casas, J. M., Ponterotto, J. G., & Gutierrez, J. M. (1986). An ethical indictment of counseling research and training: The cross-cultural perspective. *Journal of Counseling and Development, 64*, 347–349.

Copeland, E. J. (1983). Cross-cultural counseling and psychotherapy: A historical perspective, implications for research and training. *Personnel and Guidance Journal, 61*, 10–15.

Cuellar, I., Harris, L. C., & Jasso, R. (1980). An acculturation rating scale for Mexican-American normal and clinical populations. *Hispanic Journal of Behavioral Sciences, 2*, 199–217.

Harrison, D. K. (1975). Race as a counselor-client variable in counseling and psychotherapy: A review of the research. *The Counseling Psychologist, 5*, 124–133.

Parham, T. A., & Helms, J. E. (1981). Influence of a Black student's racial identity attitudes on preference for counselor race. *Journal of Counseling Psychology, 28*, 250–257.

Parker, W. M., Valley, M. M., & Geary, C. A. (1986). Acquiring cultural knowledge for counselors in training: A multifaceted approach. *Counselor Education and Supervision, 26*, 61–71.

Pedersen, P. (1988). *A handbook for developing multicultural awareness*. Alexandria, VA: American Association for Counseling and Development.

Ponterotto, J. G., & Casas, J. M. (1987). In search of multicultural competence within counselor education. *Journal of Counseling and Development, 65,* 430–434.

Sattler, J. M. (1970). Racial "experimenter effects" in experimentation, testing, interviewing, and psychotherapy. *Psychological Bulletin, 73,* 137–160.

Sue, D. W., Bernier, J. E., Durran, A., Feinberg, L., Pedersen, P., Smith, E. J., & Vasquez-Nuttall, E. (1982). Position paper: Cross-cultural counseling competencies. *The Counseling Psychologist, 10,* 45–52.